JAMES CAMERON'S
TITANIC

JAMES CAMERON'S
TITANIC

FOREWORD BY **JAMES CAMERON**

PHOTOGRAPHY BY **DOUGLAS KIRKLAND**

UNIT PHOTOGRAPHY BY **MERIE W. WALLACE**

TEXT BY **ED W. MARSH**

PROJECT EDITOR **JAIN LEMOS**

BOOK DESIGN BY **JOEL AVIROM** AND **JASON SNYDER**

HarperPerennial

A Division of HarperCollinsPublishers

DESIGN ASSISTANT AND ART COORDINATOR: MEGHAN DAY HEALEY

FIRST EDITION
ISBN 0-00-649060-3 (paperback)
ISBN 0-06-757516-1 (hardcover)
98 99 00 01 / WZ17

A FOREWORD

After twelve trips into the abyssal depths of the North Atlantic I can honestly tell you that getting there is not half the fun. Imagine two Russian scientists and one Hollywood filmmaker crammed into a space smaller than your stereotypical clown car, free-falling for hours through two-and-a-half miles of blackness with the weight of the ocean tightening around the freezing metal crew sphere. There was plenty of time to reflect on the fact that we were completely dependent on the successful functioning of countless technological systems in order to reach and photograph the ultimate symbol of technological failure—*Titanic*.

Titanic still captures our imaginations after eighty-five years because her story is like a great novel that really happened. The story could not have been written better . . . the juxtaposition of rich and poor, the gender roles played out unto death (women first), the stoicism and nobility of a bygone age, the magnificence of the great ship matched in scale only by the folly of the men who drove her hell-bent through the darkness. And above all the lesson: that life is uncertain, the future unknowable . . . the unthinkable possible.

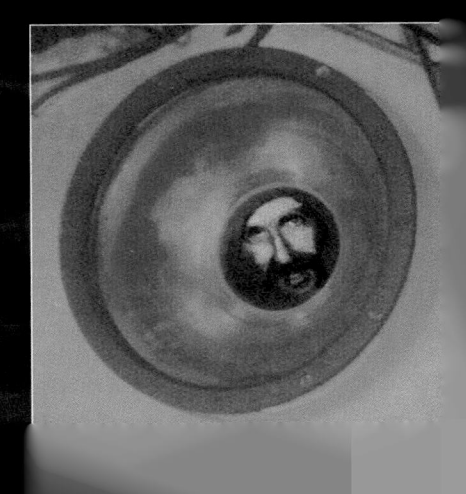

The tragedy has assumed an almost mythic quality in our collective imagination, but the passage of time has robbed it of its human face. Its status in our culture has become that of a morality tale, referred to more often as a metaphor in political cartoons than as an actual event. I set out to make a film that would bring the event to life, to humanize it; not a docudrama, but an experience in living history. I wanted to place the audience on the ship, in its final hours, to live out the tragic event in all its horribly fascinating glory.

The greatest challenge of writing a new film about such an oft-told subject is the very fact that the story is so well known. What to say that hasn't been said? The only territory I felt had been left unexplored in prior films was the territory of the heart. I wanted the audience to cry for *Titanic*. Which means to cry for the *people* on the ship, which really means to cry for any lost soul in their hour of untimely death. But the deaths of 1,500 innocents is too abstract for our hearts to grasp, although the mind can form the number easily.

Dive participants rehearse the day's work using a 1/33rd-scale model of the ship as she appears today, constructed for the mission by Lou Zutavern. "Every detail is important," explains Cameron. "If you plan a shot and suddenly find you cannot accomplish it because some of the wreck's rigging cables are threatening to tangle up the submersible you've just wasted a tremendous amount of resources." (Miniature replicas of these cables can be seen hanging off the port side of the model's bow.)

To fully experience the tragedy of *Titanic*, to be able to comprehend it in human terms, it seemed necessary to create an emotional lightning rod for the audience by giving them two main characters they care about and then taking those characters into hell.

Jack and Rose were born out of this need, and the story of TITANIC became their story. I realized then that my film must be, first and always, a love story.

And what could be more romantic, in the dark and heart-wrenching sense of the word, than *Titanic*, with its stories of men and women torn from each other en masse by a cruel twist of fate, of widows scanning the faces of the few male survivors for their husbands and lovers, of the terrible loss and grief of the morning after. . . of so many hearts broken.

The story of *Titanic* and her fate seemed a magnificent canvas on which to paint a love story, a canvas offering the full spectral range of human emotion. The greatest of loves can only be measured against the greatest of adversities, and the greatest of sacrifices thus defined. *Titanic* in all her terrible majesty provides this as does no other historical event.

Titanic's sinking is one of the better described events in history, thanks to both the American and English boards of inquiry, and to the decades of research done by Walter Lord and other fine historians like Don Lynch who followed his example. After six months of research I had compiled a highly detailed time line, which described the order of events on the ship in her last few hours, and the whereabouts and actions of the crew and passengers down to the minute. I made it a sacred goal of the production, a goal that came to be shared by everyone involved, to honor the facts without compromise.

I wanted to be able to say to an audience, without the slightest pang of guilt: This is real. This is what happened. Exactly like this. If you went back in a time machine and stood on the deck, this is what you would have seen. . . Second Officer Lightoller would be over there, at lifeboat number six, and Wallace Hartley would be leading the band in a lively waltz just there, a few yards away, by the port-forward first-class entrance, and Quartermaster Rowe would be firing the first distress rocket right about. . . now!

Slaloming between these immovable pylons of historical fact are Jack and Rose. I've woven their romance from the stern to the bow and through every interesting place and event in between, allowing us to experience the optimism and grandeur of the ship in a way that most of her passengers never did. They share the stage with such historic personalities as Captain Smith, Thomas Andrews and Molly Brown, who become all the more real and personable because of their interaction with the young lovers. Every seemingly innocent moment we spend with Jack and Rose is informed by the poignant truth that the ship and two-thirds of the people aboard her are doomed.

An epic love story, ironically, must be made up of tiny, intimate moments that seem natural and familiar, while becoming part of the fabric of an epic by juxtaposition to events that are beyond human scale. One gives power to the other.

My most daunting task on TITANIC was not, as might be expected, the creation of the great spectacle. It was the fashioning of the intimate moments, both during the writing and subsequently working with Kate Winslet and Leonardo DiCaprio. The three of us knew, to our ongoing terror, that the fate of our *Titanic* lay in our ability to steer her properly past the icebergs of bombast, and to create a living heart for the film out of gestures, glances, tentative smiles, halting awkward sentences . . . the vocabulary of nascent love.

But if we, the audience, are able to fall in love with Jack and Rose as they fall in love with each other, then we move from watching them, to looking over their shoulders, to seeing through their eyes as they live out one of the most horrific nights of the twentieth century. And then the film comes full circle, from being a film about *Titanic*, to being a love story that happens merely to be set on *Titanic*, back to being about the

With twelve missions lasting between ten and twelve hours at the wreck site (plus another six hours there and back), James Cameron spent more time on the *Titanic* than the ship's original passengers. "No," he corrects when presented with this fact, "more time than the *survivors*."

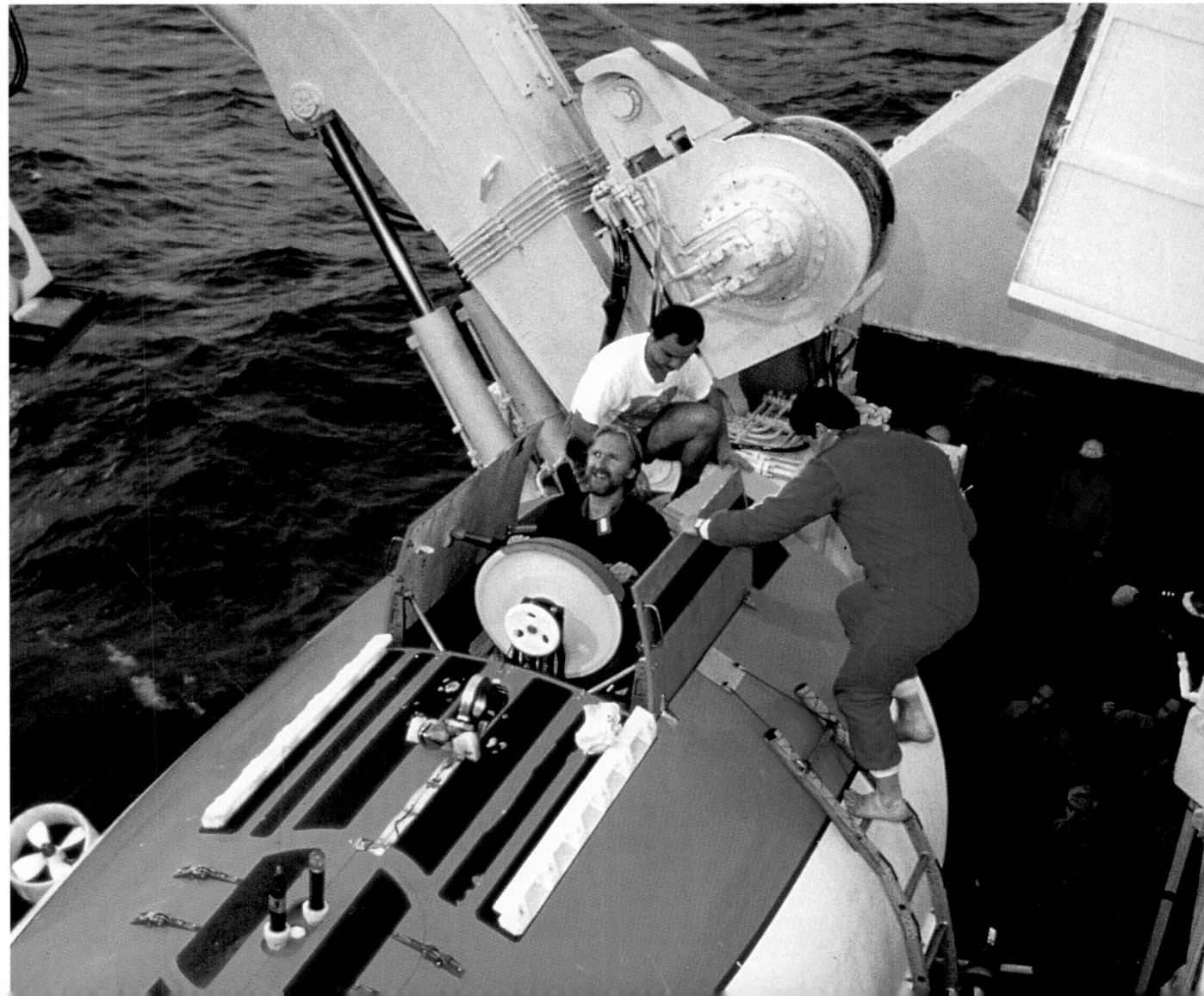

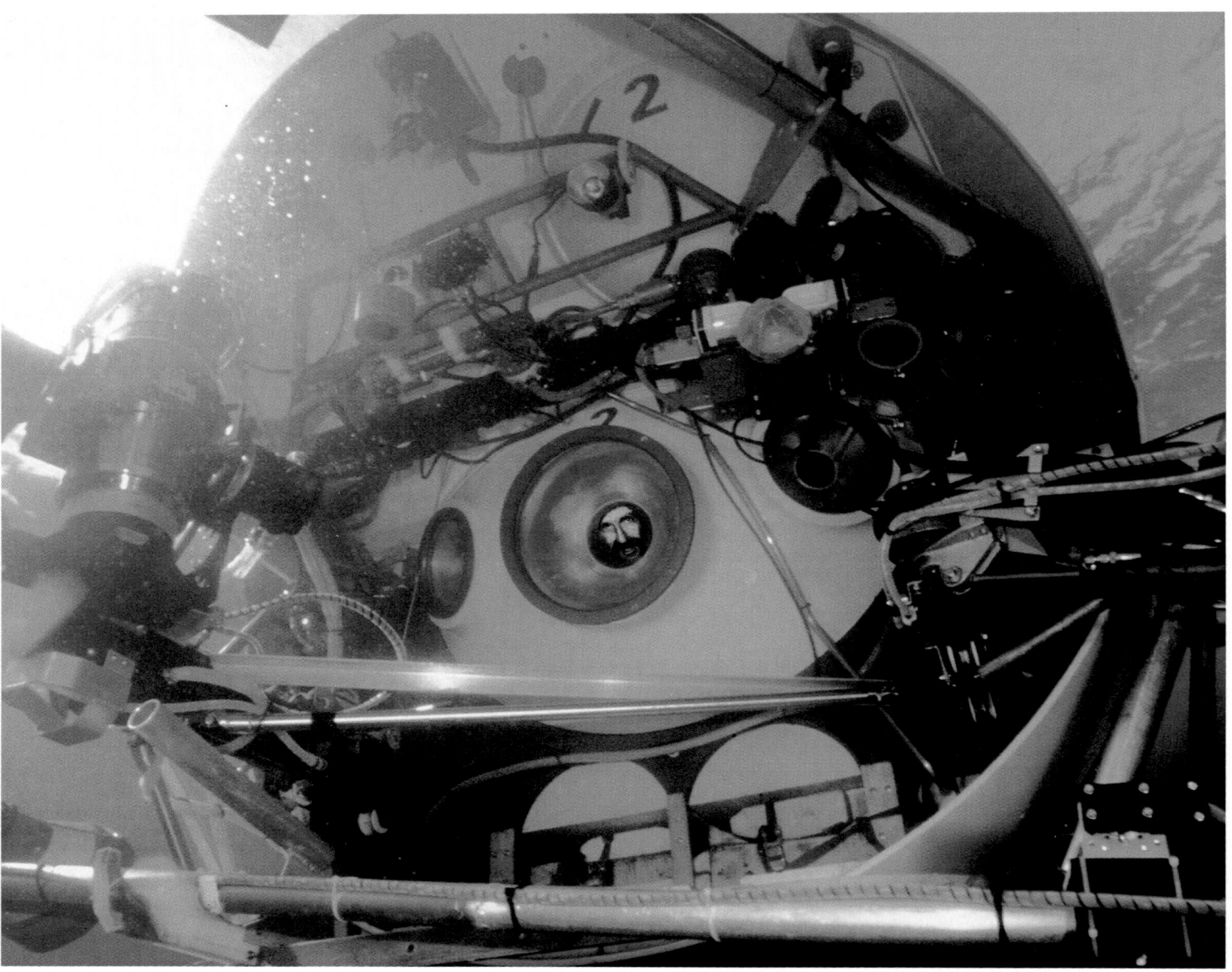

emotional truth of *Titanic* after all. By feeling the fear, the loss, the heartbreak of Jack and Rose, we finally can feel for the 1,500.

The last ingredient I chose to incorporate, in my search for ways to make history alive and palpable, was a present-day wraparound story, with ancient Rose as the storyteller. I thought this would connect the event to our time, and through the doorway of her memory invest it with an added layer of poignancy. This storytelling device also allowed the cinematic comparison of the wreck as she lies now in the abyssal depths, and the ship in her glory . . . from eternal night to sunlight and back again.

At some point it occurred to me, like a jolt . . . the *Titanic* is not a myth. Not only did it exist . . . it still exists. She sits now on the seabed, two-and-a-half miles below where she hit the iceberg all those years ago. And if you are enterprising enough, you can go there and see it.

And film it.

From the moment I had this thought, I knew not only that I must make this film, but that in making it I had to film the real ship . . . somehow.

Plexiglass circles seven inches thick serve as portholes for the seven-foot-in-diameter crew sphere of *Mir 1*. Exposed to more than 6,600 pounds of pressure per square inch, the danger of implosion is very real.

It took a couple of years to set up, but finally we assembled a "Deep Dive" expedition comprising the following components: one Russian research ship, *Akademik Mstislav Keldysh*, the largest vessel of its kind in the world; two submersibles, *Mir 1* and *Mir 2*, two of only five manned vehicles worldwide that can go to the depths of the *Titanic* wreck; one remote operated vehicle (ROV) named *Snoop Dog*, built for the film but functional at *Titanic*'s depth; and one specially designed motion picture camera and pressure housing, the first ever to function outside a submersible at deep ocean depths, and complete with a pan-tilt device for natural camera moves. Add to this a brace of powerful underwater lights, and a fiercely dedicated crew of Russian, American and Canadian engineers, film technicians, marine scientists and hard-core seafarers, and you have the world's first Hollywood deep-diving expedition.

Each dive was planned like a lunar mission, with hours spent simulating the movement of the subs with miniatures and video systems, with charts and diagrams and shot lists issued to each sub team before each dive. Invariably it all went wrong when we got down to the wreck. The pilot looks out a tiny viewport, and has very restricted visibility as he maneuvers his eighteen-ton vehicle around the wreck in strong, unpredictable currents and utter blackness. Add to this one lunatic director who wants the two subs to move as close to each other as possible while flying around a jagged metal mountain draped with hazardous steel cables, and you have a recipe for excitement.

The dives for me consisted of two and half hours of boredom, falling through blackness, followed by ten to twelve hours of intense, unbroken concentration as we positioned the two subs, the array of lights and the camera simultaneously, in freezing, swirling blackness, with crews that spoke little English, in our attempts to photograph *Titanic* as she had never been filmed before.

This trancelike focus and goal-oriented sense of purpose delayed my emotional reaction to the wreck until the second dive. Then suddenly it hit me. I was on the deck of *Titanic*. Time disappeared. Over there was the davit from which lifeboat number one was launched, carrying Lucille and Sir Cosmo Duff Gordon to safety. Later it was used to lower Collapsible C, but not before Bruce Ismay stepped into it, and stepped into history and infamy as the architect of *Titanic*'s fate who sat safely in a lifeboat while 1,500 people screamed on the plunging ship. I could visualize Captain Smith saying good-bye to his men just before the water poured like a wave over the bridge rail. I could see First Officer Murdoch, stricken with the knowledge that his failed efforts to turn the ship in time would consign over a thousand people to freezing death, and yet performing heroically to launch his boats as the final minutes sped by.

When I returned to *Keldysh* after that dive, I was overwhelmed by emotion. I had known the event so intimately from my research, and now I had been on the deck of the ship itself, and it just flooded over me. I wept for the innocents who died there. That night I realized that my project, my film, was doomed to failure if it could not convey the emotion of that night rather than the fact of it.

On the last of our twelve dives we piloted our ROV, our Hollywood-movie prop robot, *Snoop Dog*, inside the wreck. Where scientists had previously not dared risk their multimillion-dollar robots exploring inside

On April 24, 1912, the *Virginian-Pilot* ran this account of how the wealthy families of Astor and Guggenheim briefly explored what it would take to recover the bodies of their loved ones. The project was quickly declared impossible for the technology of the day.

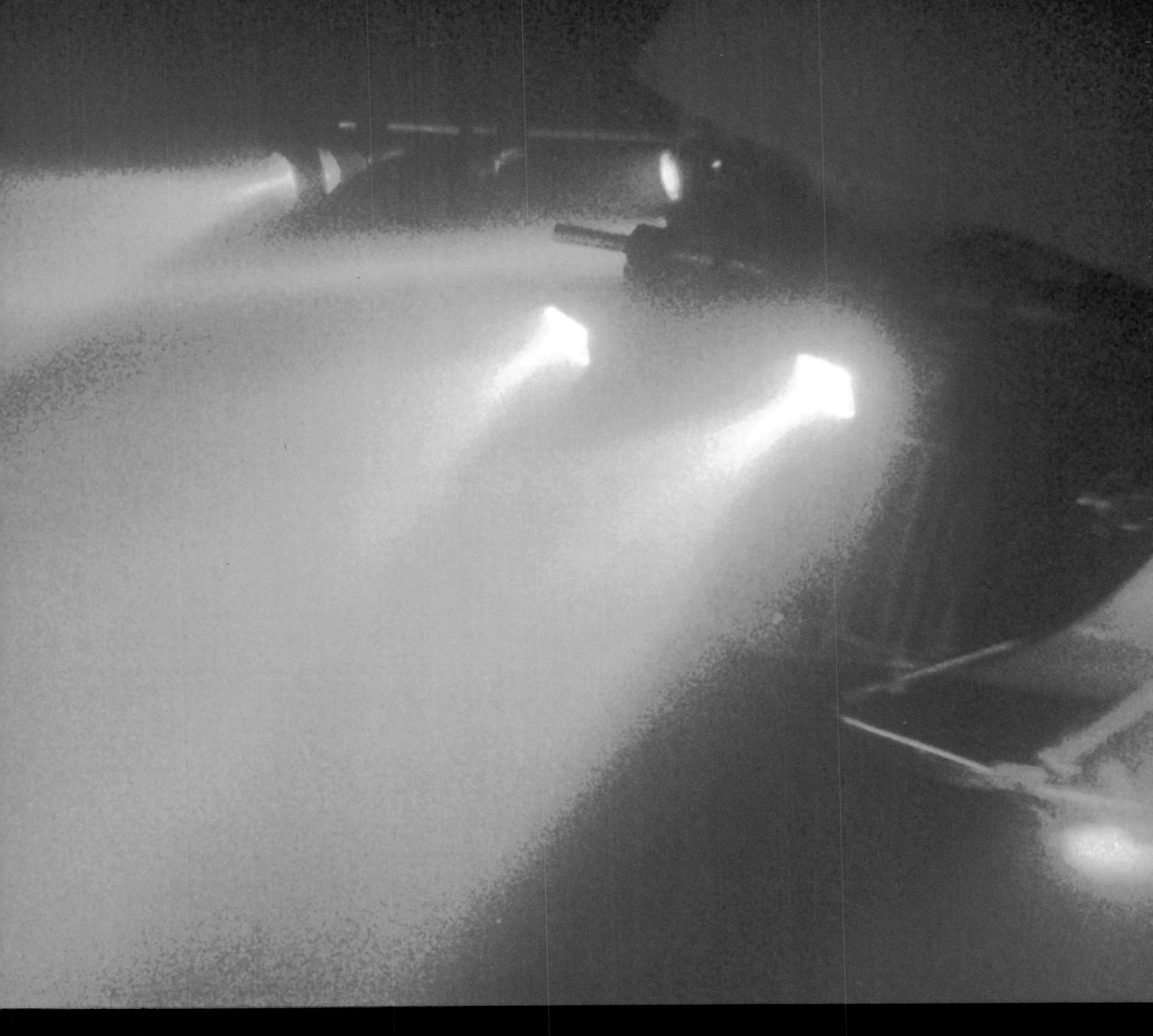

Out of the darkness, like a ghostly apparition, the bow of a ship appears. Its knife-edge prow is coming straight at us, seeming to plow the bottom sediment like ocean waves. It towers above the seafloor, standing just as it landed eighty-four years ago. [From the screenplay.] *Mir 1* rises over the bow of the great ship. Limited visibility and strong currents were a constant threat to the 1995 late-summer expedition. "The first dive was a nightmare," says Cameron. "We didn't see the ship until we were fifteen feet from it." Cameron adds, "Initially, I had totally superimposed my vision on to the ship and made the mistake of not letting *Titanic* talk to me. I was like the astronauts who experienced the moon as a series of checklists and mission protocols. So, at a certain point I abandoned 'the plan' and allowed the emotional part of my mind to engage with the ship. It made all the difference in the world."

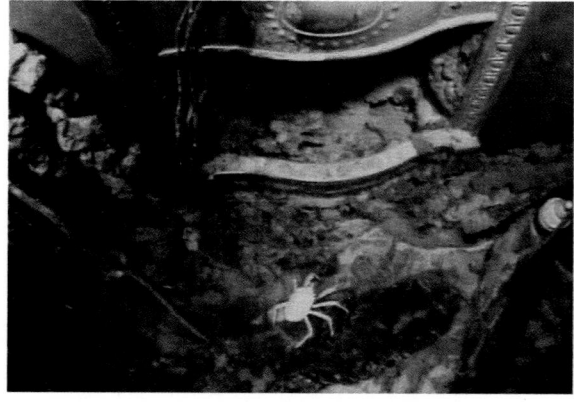

Titanic, we plunged ahead, perhaps foolishly. But *Snoop Dog* was performing so well I couldn't resist, despite my better judgment. I was seduced by the tantalizing shadows inside doorways and down the Grand Staircase.

Proceeding with extreme caution so as not to foul our vehicle or its umbilical cable, we explored spaces not seen by human eyes since 1912. The video images coming back into the *Mir* sub exceeded my wildest expectations. The ghost of her former elegance still resides in the bowels of the once resplendent ship. Since the wreck's discovery in 1985 it had been thought that wood-boring mollusks had devoured the ship's ornate finery, but we saw hand-carved oak columns and wall paneling gliding across our screens in a remarkable state of preservation. The white paint of the Reception Area and the adjacent Dining Saloon still glinted in the deeper recesses of the elegant carved patterns.

On B-deck, aft of the stairwell, we were able to reach the starboard "millionaire suite," which was booked by J. P. Morgan, the richest man in America (he cancelled his booking at the last minute). Inside the suite are the remains of furniture, wall sconces and the once beautiful fireplace. Its brass firebox gleamed in the lights of our ROV like it was brand new, while a pallid and alien Galathea crab crawled slowly over the hearth.

On D-deck, one of the swinging vestibule doors still hangs from its hinges, complete with its ornate bronze screen. Through this door Molly Brown and John Jacob Astor would have passed as they boarded from the tender ship *Nomadic* at Cherbourg. When old Rose stares at the video screen and imagines herself stepping through the entry doors into *Titanic*, the ghostly doors are real, just as they sit now down in eternal blackness.

Integrated into the fabric of the film, these video images possess an undeniable emotional power because of the fact that they are real, focusing our minds like a lens through the ravages of time. Everything else we subsequently created for the film had to live up to that level of reality. A rigorous philosophy of absolute correctness permeated every department, from Set Design and Construction,

Past, present and re-creation: Cal and Rose's sitting room fireplace (top) was an amalgam of many historical resources. "No known photographs exist for the port millionaire suite," explains Cameron. "All we know is that the rooms were of a different style than on the starboard side for which a photograph does exist and which clearly shows the brass hearth." [It is seen here in this rare archival print (second from top) and as it appears today in this video image from the ROV's camera (second from bottom).] This allowed Cameron the historical flexibility to base the style of his re-created millionaire suite on one of the parlor suites from the *Olympic* (bottom) while still incorporating his footage from the actual wreck into the motion picture. Audiences will actually see a total of three fireplaces: the pristine 1912 re-creation, its decayed, modern-day twin (built to be shot in a tank) and the actual fireplace on the *Titanic*.

through Decorating, Props, Wardrobe, Hairdressing and Visual Effects. In addition to how things looked, every nuance of human behavior had to be examined. How people moved, how they spoke, their etiquette, how the ship's crew would have performed its routine and emergency duties . . . all these things had to be known before a single scene could be staged.

There are responsibilities associated with bringing a historical subject to the screen, even though my primary goal as a filmmaker is to entertain. Research, and more research, ongoing and never-ending, was the key to complete accuracy. But from my own research I discovered that *Titanic*'s history is a form of consensus hallucination. It's really no surprise, for example, that crew members describe things differently than do passengers, or that first-class accounts do not match those from third-class. Consciously or not, each survivor has reasons for remembering events a certain way. Second Officer Lightoller, who clearly whitewashed many aspects of the sinking in his testimony, stated emphatically that the ship did not break up. Since he was the senior surviving officer his testimony was given greater weight than the large number of survivors who gave lucid accounts of the ship breaking in half. So Lightoller's testimony became history, part of the consensus hallucination, and all subsequent accounts, including the otherwise excellent A NIGHT TO REMEMBER, show the ship sliding gracefully under the surface in one piece.

But the wreck speaks for itself, its two halves lying almost a half mile apart on the sea floor. So not only is history a responsibility, it is also a challenge . . . the challenge of sorting out fact from misinformation, misperception and downright lying.

Where the facts are clear we have been absolutely rigorous in restaging events. Where they are unclear, I have made my own choices, a few of which may be controversial to students of *Titanic* history. Though I may not always have made a traditional interpretation, I can assure the reader and the viewer that these are conscious and well-informed decisions and not casual Hollywood mistakes.

And if it sometimes seems improbably spectacular and dramatic . . . it was.

I am writing this as I near the end of the odyssey of production. We are putting in the final music and sound effects, and there is light at the end of the tunnel after three obsessed years. I have no idea how the film will be received critically or commercially, but I know that my team and I have given our hearts to it, and tried to pass on the baton of telling *Titanic*'s story with respect, with dedication, with humility and with love.

Welcome to the ship of dreams. You'll find life belts on top of the wardrobe, just in case.

Using firsthand observation, Cameron discusses the terrain around the bow of Visual Historian Ken Marschall's *Titanic* illustration. Marschall's paintings and research materials were a tremendous help to every department.

New technology meets the old as the long neck of
an Akela crane and the gyro-stabilizing sphere of a
Wescam rig (mounted beneath the crane basket)
both take aim at the technological marvel of 1912.

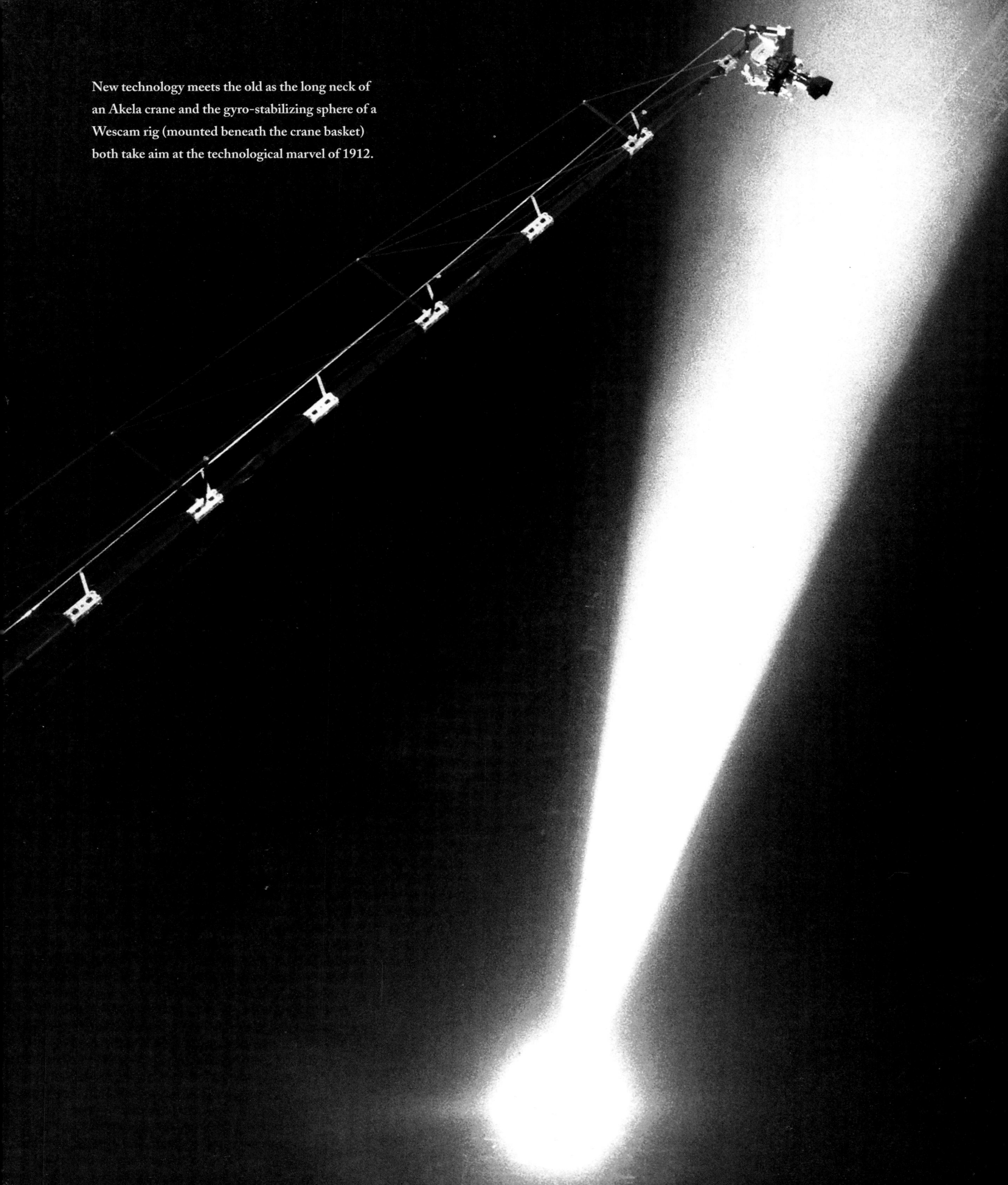

PROLOGUE

It was a time of constant wonderment—arguably the conclusion of the classic Renaissance, as da Vinci's plans for a flying machine became reality first in the workshops of the Wright Brothers and then in skies all over the world. The horrors of the American Civil War had been packed away for almost fifty years, making room for the optimism of a new generation—the first to come of age in the shiny new century. There was even the illusion of a stable (albeit impoverished) Europe. And the future? More of the same. Bigger. Faster. Better. What could possibly stop the engines of progress or the captains of industry at their controls?

Such is the mood of 1912 as Cameron re-creates the era for his cameras. Opulence and optimism are the watchwords as every department from Construction to Wardrobe participates in what can best be considered a practical exercise in time travel. At the same time, however, Cameron spins his tale from the informed perspective of the present and gives voice to the unseen force that will ultimately lead to the era's downfall . . . arrogance.

It is for this reason that the *Titanic* will endure as one of the most potent symbols of the twentieth century, more so, perhaps, than either World War or the atomic bomb. For the ship was not destroyed by an iceberg alone. . . it was also destroyed by a state of mind.

101-year-old Rose Calvert (Gloria Stuart) opens a window into her past with artifacts recovered from the wreck.

You see this little old lady and her Pomeranian staring out the window of what could be this Greyhound bus," explains James Cameron, "and then you pull out to see she's actually in this gigantic helicopter thundering across the Atlantic Ocean bringing her to this ship." It is July 1996, and Cameron has returned to Halifax, Nova Scotia, to film the modern-day story that takes place aboard the *Akademik Mstislav Keldysh* and sets his tale in motion. For Jim, it is a chance to reunite with the scientists and crew who made the 1995 Deep Dive Expedition so successful. Unlike the Deep Dive, however, the ship will be going nowhere—or almost nowhere—and millions of dollars in cutting-edge deep-sea technology will be reduced to the status of functioning props. The ship has gone Hollywood.

Dr. Anatoly Sagalevitch, the scientist and submersible pilot responsible for the *Mir* program, seems to take this in stride. "I prefer always the real," he declares in his trademark laconic style. Cameron would agree, and casts several members of the Russian crew in the film as fictional versions of themselves, including both Anatoly and Russia's premier submersible pilot, Genya Chernyaev.

The *Akademik Mstislav Keldysh* is one of the largest marine research vessels ever constructed. "There's something that's just so. . . Russian about her. It's like state sculpture," observes Cameron. Here, *Mir 1* is detached from the powerful hydraulic crane.

"It was a true cultural exchange," recalls First Assistant Director Josh McLaglen, "not just between Russians and Americans, but between filmmakers and scientists. They usually launch and recover their submersibles maybe once or twice a day—we were asking them to do it twenty or thirty times to get our shots done. In one marathon day we had a 400-foot Canadian Coast Guard vessel, two helicopters, both submersibles and assorted support boats all working on and around the *Keldysh*."

The story begins with treasure hunter Brock Lovett (Bill Paxton) having chartered the Russian research vessel for a clandestine mission to plunder *Titanic*'s interior with specially designed remote operated vehicles (ROVs) in search of the Heart of the Ocean, a rare thirty-million-dollar blue diamond thought lost with the ship. The mission is not without controversy. "He's a modern-day pirate," says Paxton without hesitation. "He's totally immersed himself in the physical details of the tragedy but has never connected to the human side. *Titanic*'s history is just a road map to the spoils as far as he's concerned." The ocean doesn't give up her secrets easily, however, and Brock's efforts are met with mounting frustration and deadlines. "Then this 101-year-old woman contacts him and asks, 'Have you found the Heart of the Ocean yet?' Everybody who knows about the diamond is either dead or on the expedition, so you can imagine how Brock wants to hear what she has to say."

When production started in Halifax, there were eight known *Titanic* survivors. The much-beloved Eva Hart, one of the most vocal survivors and a strong opponent of recent salvage operations, had passed away in February. Of those remaining, most were either too young to remember what had happened or too affected by age to talk about it coherently. Neither option would work as a role model for Old Rose, who Cameron describes in his script as having eyes *just as bright and alive as those of a young girl.* He found those eyes in eighty-six-year-old Gloria Stuart, an actress from the 1930s who gave up movies for a second career as an artist and mother. In addition to several Shirley Temple films, she credits herself as, "the highly visible woman opposite Claude Rains in THE INVISIBLE MAN." Only two years old at the time of the sinking, Gloria would have to undergo lengthy makeup

ABOVE: Brock Lovett (Bill Paxton) inside the mock-up crew sphere of *Mir 1*. Was the actor disappointed in not visiting the wreck for real? "No, not really. I promised my wife I'd stop doing crazy stuff like that. Eighteen hours in here would be pretty brutal."

RIGHT: Anatoly Mikaelavich (Anatoly Sagalevitch) watches Lewis Bodine (Lewis Abernathy) operate the controls for the ROV *Snoop Dog* (nicknamed *Snoop*). Dr. Sagalevitch created the *Mir*s and the deep-sea research program that depends on them. "Anatoly had to be in the film," says Cameron. "He's the real deal."

OPPOSITE: The support boat *Koresh* (Russian for "friend") tows *Mir 1* back to the *Keldysh*. Crew member Leonid "Lonya" Volchek stands by to attach the umbilical. How hard is it to ride the *Mir*? "No problem," says Lonya. And when the seas are rough? "A *little* problem."

sessions with Greg Cannom to add the missing years and become Old Rose. "It wasn't a happy moment, I must say, to see every wrinkle and liver spot I thought I didn't have multiplied several times."

"We don't know Rose's hidden agenda but we can bet she didn't fly out here to drop the diamond in Brock's lap," says Cameron. "She's mischievous and playful about it, but it's clear she's focusing in on something very private." Despite cold ocean nights, Gloria, wearing nothing but a nightgown and red toenail polish, kept pace with a director notorious for long hours and complex multicamera setups. "Where the script describes Rose as *looking impossibly fragile amongst all the high-tech gear,*" adds Cameron, "it could just as easily be referring to Gloria. She was a trooper."

But now the toys have been put away. While images of the wreck glow softly from a bank of TV screens, Cameron prepares to film Old Rose telling a story she has kept secret for eighty-four years. "Don't let Brock rush you," directs Cameron. "The images on the monitors will eventually trigger a connection. You'll see a davit that reminds you of all the husbands who did not get into lifeboats. You'll see a corridor that reminds you of the crying child who died there. And when you finally gather yourself and start to speak, you expect everyone to listen."

Rose is about to lead everyone on a journey through time, deep into the expanses of the human heart. . .

"The script is a dynamic document. Once I have the bones of a good scene in the can, I like to play with it and see what else it can yield," explains Cameron. Script Supervisor Shelley Crawford keeps abreast of the changes.

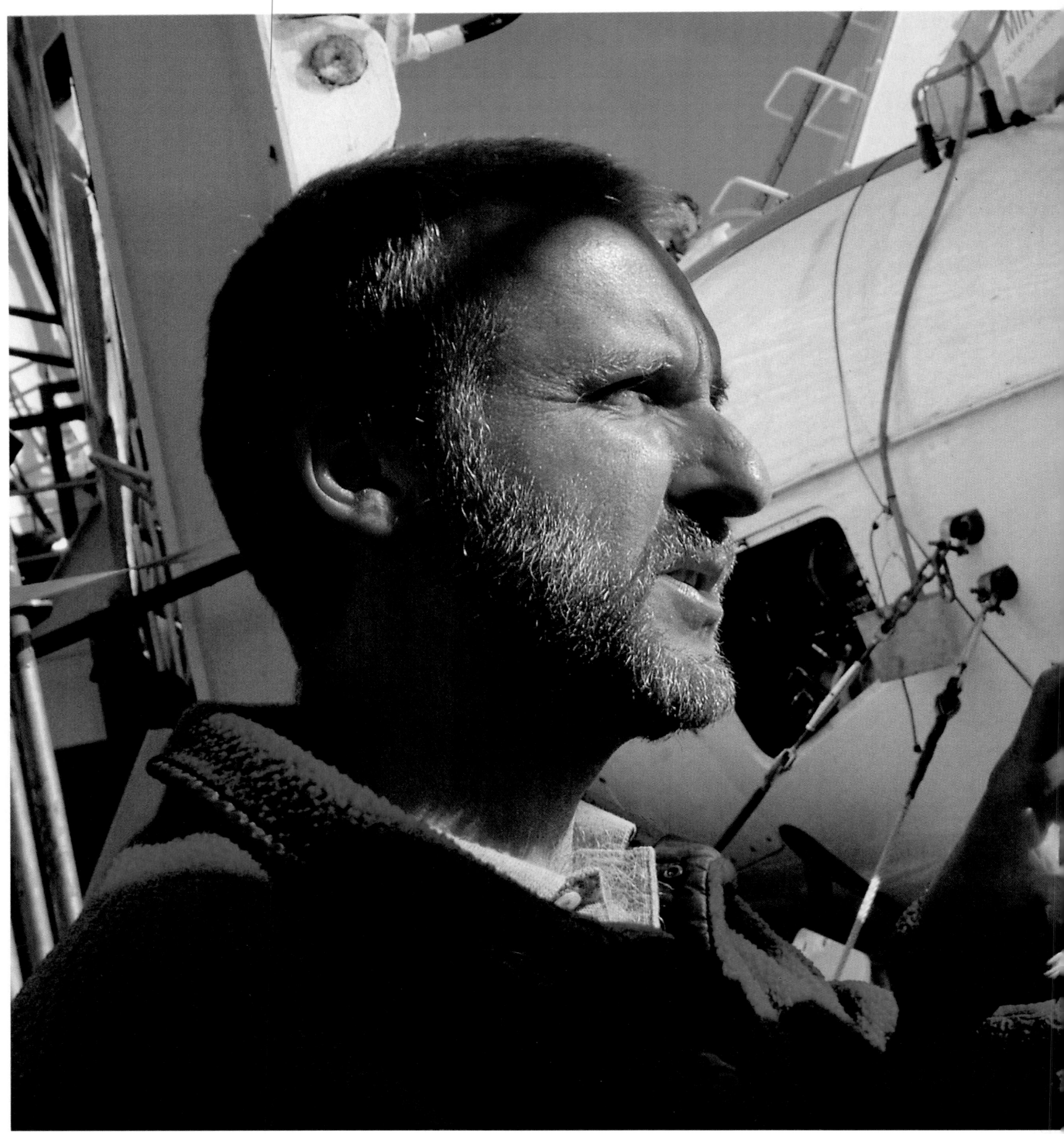

The promise of an unopened safe. Cameron shares a story: "On every dive, we saw a perfectly square safe-sized object on the sonar. We never had time to investigate it." Strictly on a photographic expedition, Cameron collected no artifacts from the wreck site.

A plaster caryatid from the walls
of the first-class Dining Saloon.

THREE MILLION RIVETS

"This movie is as close as you can get to being in a time machine and going back to the ship," says Cameron. It is a bold statement to make when one considers that, in its day, *Titanic* was not only the largest moving object ever made but also the most opulent and well-appointed. Of the achievement, *Titanic*'s Master Shipbuilder Thomas Andrews reportedly said, "It takes three million rivets and a lot of sweat to make a fine ship," words that the production's many carpenters, plasterers, painters, set dressers and model makers came to live by. "This project started with an expedition to the real *Titanic*," explains the director. "Everything else had to rise to that level of dedication. Everyone who joined the project subsequent to that expedition was shown the footage we brought back, and I looked each of them in the eye and asked, 'Are you ready for this challenge? Are you ready to be part of a movie that will not compromise? Are you ready to build the *Titanic?*'"

The filmmakers had organized the show into four distinct phases of production, the first three being the 1995 Deep Dive; a three-day shoot inside submerged, re-created interiors of the wreck as Brock's ROV looks for the Heart of the Ocean; and the modern-day portion of the story involving Brock and Old Rose on board the *Keldysh*. But by far the most logistically daunting phase

Nicknamed the "100-day studio," Fox Studios Baja began construction on May 31, 1996, the same day that *Titanic*'s hull was launched into Belfast Harbor at Harland and Wolff's shipyard eighty-five years previously. Key to the project was the seventeen-million-gallon oceanfront tank in which the near full-size exterior ship set was erected, providing almost 270 degrees of uninterrupted ocean view.

would be the final one, which required replicating the 1912 ship and then sinking it believably and in a manner true to history (see computer illustration on page 152). The events surrounding the tragedy both helped and confounded the filmmakers. It was a new moon the night of the disaster; had there been any moonlight at all the iceberg would have been easier to spot as the waves lapping at its base would have shimmered visibly against the dark sea. In terms of cinematography. This left Director of Photography Russell Carpenter with the challenge of creating a soft, nonshadowy illumination, which could not be mistaken for moonlight, once the lights on the ship went out for the last time. Any portion of the ship built at full scale would require a unique, positionable soft lighting system of equal scale. On the plus side, the size of the ship made the sinking a slow process—one that was not perceived by her passengers for some time, allowing the filmmakers to build large sections of the ship at "preset" angles. Unlike previous *Titanic* movies, however, Cameron wanted to spend a great deal of time exploring the ship during the four-and-a-half days before the collision and would require the ability to shoot the ship in the daytime traveling at full speed. "Initially we felt that we needed to be out on the ocean for our daytime sailing sequences to convey the power and exuberance the passengers must have felt," says Producer Jon Landau, "but ocean-based shooting solutions had several drawbacks. For example, one early proposal involved

ABOVE: The *Titanic*'s hull nears completion in the early spring of 1911. More than fourteen thousand laborers contributed to her creation.

BELOW: Model Shop Co-Foreman Gene Rizzardi assembles a commercial kit of the *Titanic* for use as a study model during the research and design phase.

RIGHT: Original designs from Harland and Wolff (thought lost since World War II) allowed the filmmakers to re-create the ship with unprecedented accuracy and detail. Photographs of a twenty-five-foot study model flank the blueprint.

S.S. "TITANIC" No. 401
RIGGING PLAN
1/16"=1'-0"

LEFT: The leviathan begins to take shape. "The ship is, in fact, full scale," explains Production Designer Peter Lamont, "but we've eliminated some of the redundant sections on the superstructure and forward well deck to allow our ship to fit the tank. We had to shrink the funnels and lifeboats ten percent in order to compensate for this reduction."

ABOVE: Construction Coordinator Les Collins. "I don't think we could have squeezed another construction crane in there if we tried. There were days when we were laying and welding a major piece of steel every four minutes."

BELOW: Construction workers appear dwarfed by the sixty-five-foot funnel.

LEFT: Lamont stands above the framework that will soon house the elegant Grand Staircase and first-class Dining Saloon. These sets will eventually be destroyed when massive hydraulics lower them into five million gallons of seawater. Lamont is resigned to the loss. "It's what they were designed to do."

BELOW: Mexico City's Estudios Churubusco Azteca served as the birthplace for many of the film's sets. The first-class Dining Saloon took shape several weeks before being disassembled and shipped hundreds of miles to Rosarito after the new soundstages had been completed.

TOP: Preparations continue. Mounted on a 600-foot run of railroad track, the 162-foot tower crane was modified to function as a combined construction, lighting and camera platform.

ABOVE: "Raise the *Titanic!*" During construction, Almas International provided lifting power to raise the six-million-pound set fifty feet into the air before its hull siding could be attached. Later, Almas and M. Industrial Mechanical, Inc. would tilt the set six degrees, lowering the bow and raising the stern.

LEFT: An international team of Mexican and British artisans created thousands of plaster pieces to grace the ship's lavish interior: here, a section of plaster surrounding the dome skylight over the Grand Staircase.

TOP, CENTER, BOTTOM: While the full-size ship came together in Mexico, several smaller incarnations began to take shape in Los Angeles. Digital Domain's 1/20th-scale model of the pristine ship is over forty-five feet long. Model makers dress the interior spaces with furniture and curtains, as they are visible when the windows are lit at night. Seeing the model in "dry dock," one is struck by how small the propellers look in relation to the ship as a whole. Cameron contends that when the engine room executed the "all back full" order just prior to the fateful collision, the center propeller made the ship's rudder less effective than it could have been, preventing *Titanic* from turning in time to avoid the collision. "It probably only had to turn another ten or fifteen feet to clear the iceberg entirely," explains the director.

RIGHT: Model Shop Co-Foreman Gene Rizzardi consults blueprints while model makers install millions of tiny brass nails as rivets on the ship's hull. Digital Domain's model stage is one of the hangars in which Howard Hughes built sections of his *Spruce Goose*—another famous vessel whose maiden voyage was also her last.

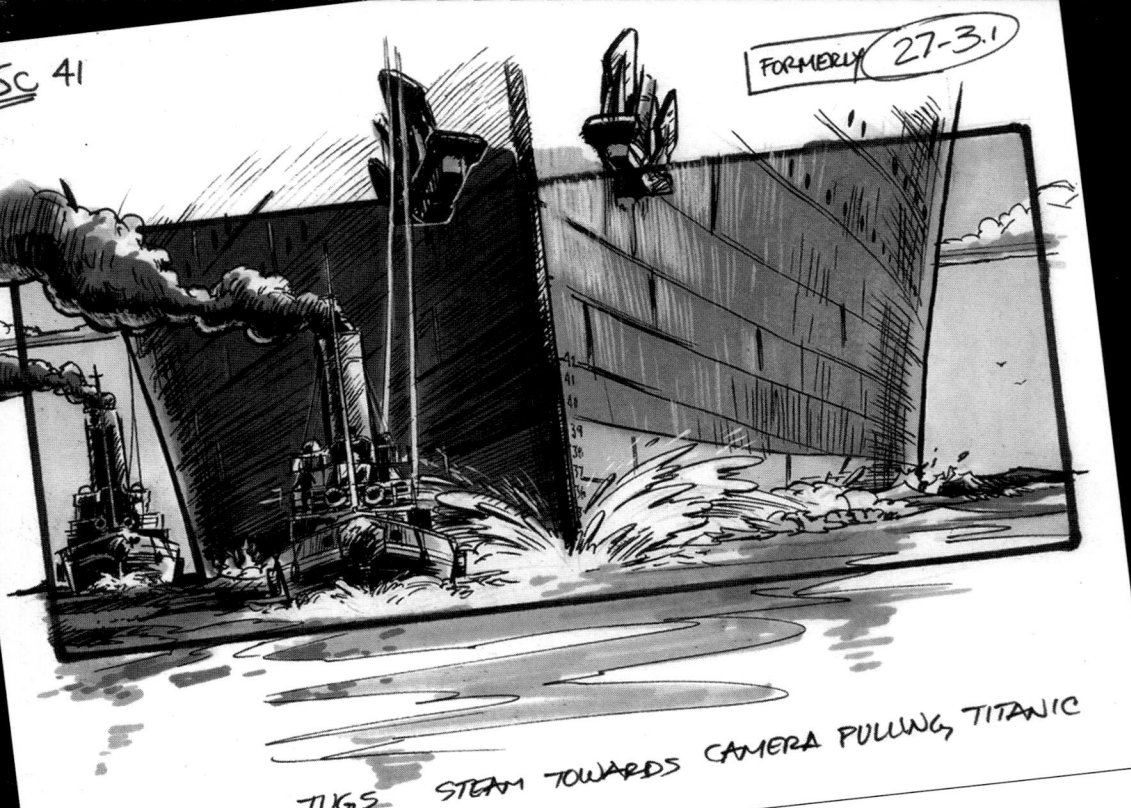

SC 41

FORMERLY 27-3.1

TUGS STEAM TOWARDS CAMERA PULLING TITANIC

117 CONT.

TITANIC AGAINST POST-SUNSET SKY WITH THE NOMADIC

FORMER # 31-1

Storyboards help delineate what is shot "real" from what will require visual effects. "As part of the storyboarding process, Cameron uses large-scale study models and a lipstick video camera to previsualize the shots," explains Producer Jon Landau (see photograph on page 26). "He even has lenses that approximate the primes we use in production."

MILL POND SHOT : "I DON'T THINK I'VE EVER SEEN SUCH FLAT CALM..."

REVISED 5-1-96

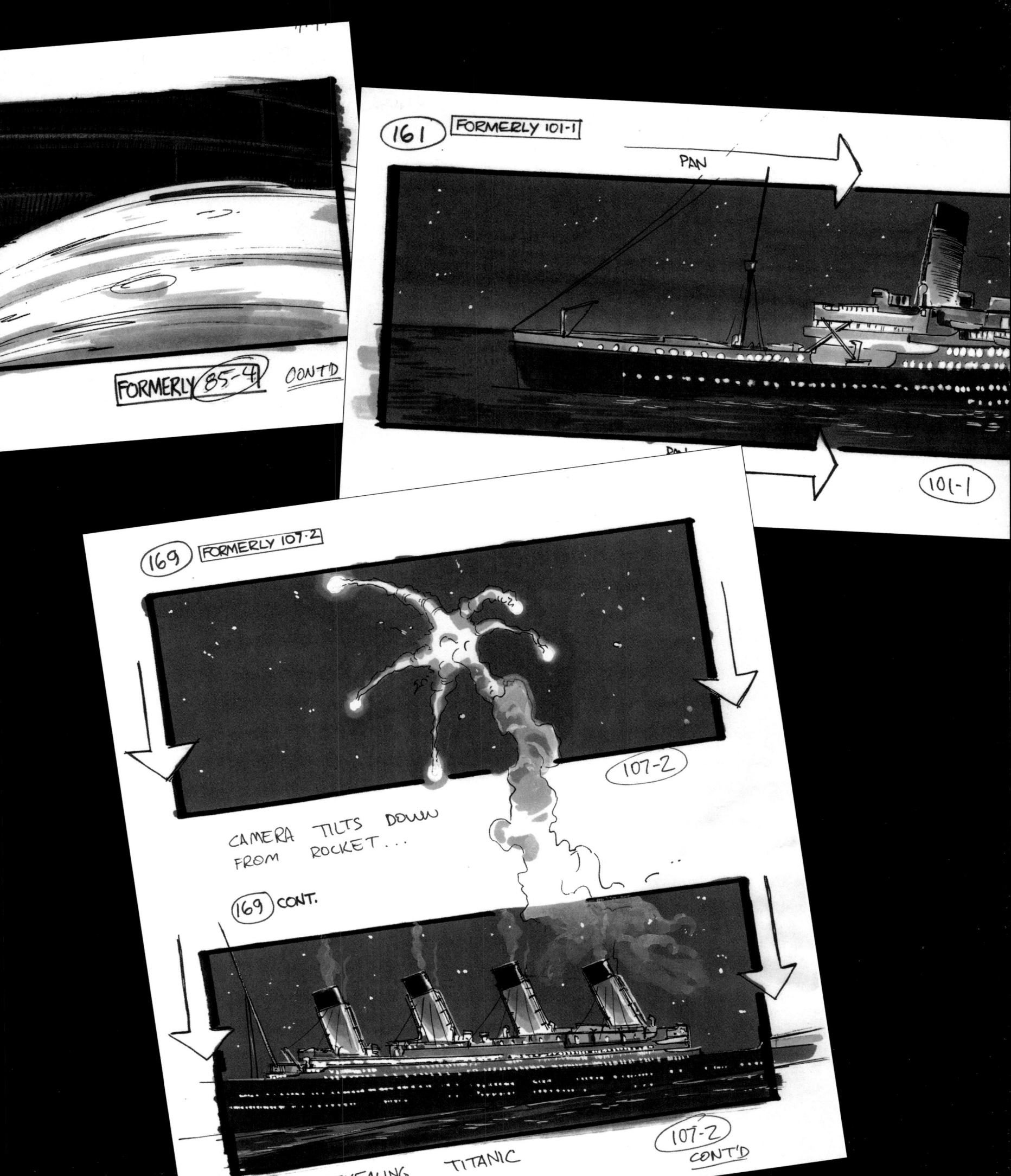

FORMERLY 85-4 CONT'D

161 FORMERLY 101-1

PAN

101-1

169 FORMERLY 107-2

107-2

CAMERA TILTS DOWN FROM ROCKET...

169 CONT.

107-2 CONT'D

REVEALING TITANIC

mounting three hundred feet of *Titanic*'s decks on a cargo ship and photographing her at sea. We could then remove a number of containers to 'sink' our set in increments, but too many of the shots would have required whole sections of the ship to be added digitally. Lighting was also a problem and there was still no easy way to sink the ship completely under the water or to raise her stern into the air after she breaks in two. For the shots Jim needed to tell his story—which has our two main characters moving all over the *Titanic*— the simplest, most cost-effective solution was to build a substantial portion of the ship's exterior and sink it in a tank built to our strict specifications. Every other decision fell into place based on this choice."

For the daytime scenes the tank would need to be properly situated along a coastline with an unbroken view of the ocean to create the illusion of an infinite horizon. The night scenes would require a tower crane to position lights at a height relative to the ship's boat deck, forty-five feet above the surface of the water when level, higher at the stern when sinking. The ship itself essentially would become a two-decked platform (A-deck and the boat deck with a facade of riveted steel hull plating descending to the water line) that could then be angled over time by changing the heights of its steel support structure. For the final stages of the disaster, the ship would be separated into two pieces, the front half sinking in forty feet of water using powerful hydraulics (see page 138) while the aftmost section of the ship would be relocated onto a special tilting plat-

Cameron researches lighting scenarios for the full-sized ship using a twenty-five-foot study model. To the right of Cameron: Gaffer John Buckley, Key Grip Lloyd Moriarty and Director of Photography Russell Carpenter.

form built at the edge of the tank (see page 130). While these two extremes would require some "digital set extension" and other effects work, Jon Landau estimates that almost a thousand effects shots were eliminated because of the ability to shoot on the full-sized ship. "We realized that our hydraulics could sink the interior sets as well, which meant a second platform and a second tank needed to be built, this time inside a sound-stage." One soundstage quickly became four because it proved to be less expensive to build a comprehensive facility tailored to production's needs than it was to relocate every time there was a group of interior scenes to be shot. "If we were on the ship at night and it got too foggy or windy we could quickly move to one of the soundstages and keep working," says Landau. "Building the studio gave us that level of flexibility."

Twentieth Century Fox acquired forty acres of waterfront property south of Rosarito in Baja California, Mexico, and began to construct the first full-service motion picture studio seen on the West Coast in thirty years. Blasting started in early June of 1996 to clear away tons of volcanic rock for the two main tanks—the seventeen-million-gallon tank, which would become home to the exterior ship set, and the five-million-gallon enclosed tank, which would house her lavish interiors. Two more nonflooding sound-stages, a wet/dry soundstage and a support infrastructure equivalent to a small town

Visual Effects Director of Photography Eric Nash stands beneath the 1/20th-scale wreck model. Suspending the model from the ceiling gives the motion-control artists better access to their work, using less cumbersome and complicated rigs.

OPPOSITE: The Grand Staircase landing as viewed from A-deck on *Titanic*'s sister ship, *Olympic*.

OPPOSITE INSET: Workers install the first landing of the Grand Staircase. "The Mexico City construction crews are arranged into small groups, kind of like sports teams," says Art Director Martin Laing, "and each group has a portrait or statue of the Madonna that they maintain at the studio. It's interesting because Harland and Wolff supposedly didn't allow Catholics to work in their shipyard at all in 1912."

ABOVE RIGHT: Detail from a re-created carving. "The woodwork of the original ship was all done by hand. Each side of each newel post on the Grand Staircase, for instance, had a different motif carved onto it," explains Senior Art Director Charles Lee.

RIGHT: Adjustments are made to the "hero" piece of debris, a large carved oak wall panel on which Jack and Rose find temporary refuge. Lee modeled the piece loosely after a fragment recovered from the wreck, which is now on display in the Maritime Museum of the Atlantic in Halifax, Nova Scotia.

completed the facility. But with construction beginning at the end of May 1996, the filmmakers were left with less than four months before shooting would begin. As Cameron told the crowd at the ground-breaking ceremony, "There's nothing quite so terrifying or exhilarating as a deadline."

Three-and-a-half million pounds of steel, thirty thousand rivets, fifteen thousand sheets of plywood, and several tons of paint are just a few of the statistics Construction Coordinator Les Collins produces from memory. Some of that steel belongs to the girders that hold the ship forty-five feet above water level (and ninety feet over the deepest part of the tank), hoisted there by powerful hydraulic jacks that inched the set skyward over a period of days by lifting the entire support structure off the ground, welding new girders and supports to the bottom and then repeating the process. (Later, the jacking process would be reversed to lower the set at the bow and raise it higher at the stern, bringing the ship to an angle of six degrees.) For the ship itself, the production enlisted a crew of welders and shipwrights who normally construct submarines to work under Production Designer Peter Lamont and Special Effects Coordinator Tommy Fisher to achieve the twin goals of realism and structural integrity. "This one set alone is the equivalent of building a seventy-story skyscraper on its side," says Collins. "And if you include the interior sets designed by Peter Lamont and

OPPOSITE: For Master Shipbuilder Thomas Andrews, *Titanic* was a work-in-progress. The architect spent much of the voyage in his stateroom working on improvements to the ship which, presumably, would also have been applied to the *Britannic,* the last of the three sisters.

ABOVE: Artist Tom Lay's set design concept for Thomas Andrews's stateroom.

RIGHT: Molly Brown's elegantly appointed stateroom. Had she ventured a peek out the window after the collision, she would have seen third-class passengers kicking ice fragments around on the forward well deck.

BELOW: Lay's set design concept for Molly Brown's stateroom.

OPPOSITE: A first-class corridor on B-deck. A closer look reveals the join between the set and a forced-perspective miniature extending the length of the hallway deep into the distance.

ABOVE: The Grand Staircase landing on D-deck, opening out on to the first-class Reception Area. Constructed over a five-million-gallon tank of seawater and capable of being lowered into it at a rate of almost one foot every second, the water waiting in the stairwell leading to E-deck hints at the shape of things to come.

RIGHT: This archive photo of the *Olympic* serves as a testament to the art department's many accomplishments. Touring the set, Visual Historian Ken Marschall even declared the wicker furniture to be "spot on."

BOTTOM: Cameron's ROV revealed this video image of a D-deck Reception Area column as it appears today (note the matching inlaid leaf pattern).

LEFT: *Honour and Glory Crowning Time*. This richly detailed oak carving from the top of the Grand Staircase was re-created under the supervision of Master Sculptor Dave Coldham. When the *Olympic* was scrapped in 1935, many of her elaborate carvings found new life as interiors for the White Swan Hotel in England. The owners graciously allowed the filmmakers to measure and photograph much of the woodwork. *Olympic*'s carving (above) resides at the Ulster Folk and Transport Museum in Northern Ireland.

OPPOSITE: "I can assure you that our first-class Dining Room chairs are just as stiff and uncomfortable as the originals," jokes Set Dresser Michael Ford, who was responsible for creating exact replicas of the furniture and countless other items unique to the ship. Other set dressing pictured includes hundreds of suitcases, teacups, first-class ashtrays (note the White Star emblem), lamps and mailbags.

ABOVE: Wardrobe Supervisor Adolfo Ramirez sizes a derby for an extra. The bowler hat was the epitome of style in 1912. It would be several years before Chaplin would adopt the hat as a comical symbol of the working stiff, long after the hat had fallen out of favor. Over five hundred derbies were collected from the United States and England.

RIGHT: Rose's Art Deco hand mirror features prominently in both the 1912 and modern-day scenes. Photographs reveal some of the design choices considered

Charles Lee and constructed by Tony Graysmark's teams, we've furnished that skyscraper as well."

"Re-creating the ship wouldn't have been possible without the unprecedented cooperation of her original builders," says Cameron, referring to Harland and Wolff, the respected ship-building firm in Belfast, Ireland, which opened its private archive to the production. "I think they realized that this was the first time someone was going to dedicate the resources necessary to re-create the ship faithfully in every detail and as a consequence they were great to us. We saw plans and photographs that haven't been looked at in decades. They even shared blueprints that were thought to have been lost."

"The blueprints were incredibly detailed as to how the ship was constructed, right down to individual rivet diagrams for the hull," says Lamont, "but when it came to the design of the ship's interiors, sadly, there was very little reference at all." More than anyone, Lamont assumed the role of Master Shipbuilder Thomas Andrews in building the ship. Every day he bicycled around the site and walked the sets, quietly poring over blueprints and drawings. With seventeen James Bond movies and three Academy Award nominations to his credit, Lamont was ready to retire when Cameron called. Re-creating the legendary steamer proved an irresistible challenge. Joined by Senior Art Director Charles Lee, Lamont assembled an art department that spanned many countries, all dedicated to a task that was a mix of reverse engineering, traditional set design and archaeology. "We traced artifacts. A hotel in England has woodwork from the first-class lounge of *Titanic*'s sister ship, *Olympic*. There was a deck chair recovered in Canada. . . ." Pieces came together like fragments of ancient pottery with photographs of the twin sister ships serving as glue.

Designs were not approved until Lamont and Cameron were satisfied that the sets were as close to the real ship as possible.

The devotion to accuracy continued as Set Dresser Michael Ford commissioned thousands of pieces of china, crystal and silver cutlery—the paraphernalia associated with an Edwardian formal dinner rivaled the implements of a surgeon—and imprinted them with White Star's emblem and pattern. The cavernous prop building was soon choked

with hundreds of first-class Dining Room chairs, deck chairs, light fixtures, mailbags, suitcases, carpeting and other fine furniture and props, all re-created in exquisite detail by the finest artisans in Mexico City, London and Rome. The combined effect was overwhelming. "Opulence was an important story point," explains Executive Producer Rae Sanchini. "Mark Twain coined the phrase 'the Gilded Age' as a critique of the excess he saw around him, and the elaborate first-class interiors of *Titanic* were created at the very peak of this trend toward ostentation. Also, for our Rose character to emerge from this crystal and silk daydream into something more tangible the contrast had to exist visually." Surprisingly, the production's decision to re-create the ship of dreams in all of its splendor came as somewhat of a bargain. "Since the newness of

critical story point and so many of our props and set dressings would

'sinking' the ship, rental was out of the question,"

-era stock we could have rented

d ways to manufacture mass

na and life belts to table lamps,

d specifications we were able to

mpliments Leonardo DiCaprio of

andering artist who wins tickets

tail and realism that everyone

to top it as far as the *Titanic* is

cameras, but if ever there was a

this film."

aments a ruined evening gown:

derfully ornate dress for the first

n the front and

ostume shop—a

earch of buried

wner to stuff the

es, delivering it

ilm. While le Vey

of ornate beading

wing it with a rich-

s no small task,

e opulence of

TOP: Head Beader Paule Drissi refines the detail on one of Kate Winslet's many dresses. Drissi, who restored scores of 1912 evening gowns for the production says, "It's a privilege. We've seen them in books, but now we have them in our hands. There's a soul in every dress."

CENTER: Molly Brown (Kathy Bates), the Countess of Rothes (Rochelle Rose) and Ruth DeWitt Bukater (Frances Fisher) "take the air" on the A-deck promenade dressed in period finery.

BOTTOM: White Star's Managing Director, J. Bruce Ismay, was notorious for his attention to creature comforts—such as these elegant hangers that would have graced all the closets in first class. Such amenities prompted naval historian Kit Bonner to refer to the *Olympic* class of ships as "luxury hotels with engines."

first class. "It was an explosion of excess," observes Costume Designer Deborah Scott. "What it says about the period that produced these detailed works of art—and the lives of the people who spent hundreds of hours sewing them—is incredible. And when you realize that there were sometimes five or six complete changes of clothes each day it becomes even more staggering." Scott engineered a symphony of looks, taking advantage of the fashion revolution in progress at that time. The Victorian hourglass ideal was giving way to a cleaner, straighter, girlish silhouette, a look Scott utilized for Young Rose, while her mother, Ruth, would be dressed in accordance with the old school. Colors were another consideration. "The photo research is all black and white and when we started collecting the old gowns it was like, 'My god, this is bright purple.' After discussing it with Jim we decided on a bold approach to Rose's colors, especially because she's the centerpiece of this world." When asked how Cameron's dedication to realism affects the wardrobe department, Scott shares a story. "We filled a whole wall of the office with photographs of *Titanic*'s passengers, and we'd look at them very analytically: 'So Jock Hume was wearing that, and Lady Duff Gordon might have been wearing that.' And while I was standing there, with all these faces staring back at me, I suddenly thought, 'We're not looking at research here. We're looking at the real people who were on that ship, who lived that moment.' It was eerie. It becomes more than just making a movie—you want to live up to history."

ABOVE: Costume Designer Deborah Scott shows Cameron the fabrics she's incorporating into Rose's Sunday evening outfit. "This is the dress Rose swims in," says Scott. "Jim wanted it diaphanous and fragile."

RIGHT: First Assistant Designer David le Vey refines one of his many concept sketches.

"In the story, Rose has just been on a shopping spree in Paris, so her fashions had to be really up-to-the-minute," explains Deborah Scott. David le Vey adds, "It was an unprecedented chance to re-create the opulence of an era that would never be seen again." Before World War I the wealthy spent more of their money on clothes than during any other period in history.

Rose
KIMONO

Rose
DINING SALOON

Rose
BOARDING OUTFIT

Molly Brown
FIRST-CLASS RECEPTION

Ruth
DINING SALOON

"Menswear of the time was accessory hell," says Scott. "A lot of shirts buttoned up the back, for starters. Then you had collar buttons, tie pins, cufflinks, watch chains, gloves, hats and walking sticks. Billy Zane's character, Cal, is probably the most fashion conscious of the bunch." Zane declared his character is more than a "fashion horse." He's a "fashion Clydesdale."

Jack
BASIC OUTFIT

Captain Smith
FORMAL UNIFORM

Cal
BOARDING OUTFIT

Thomas Andrews
DAY SUIT

Cal
DINING SALOON

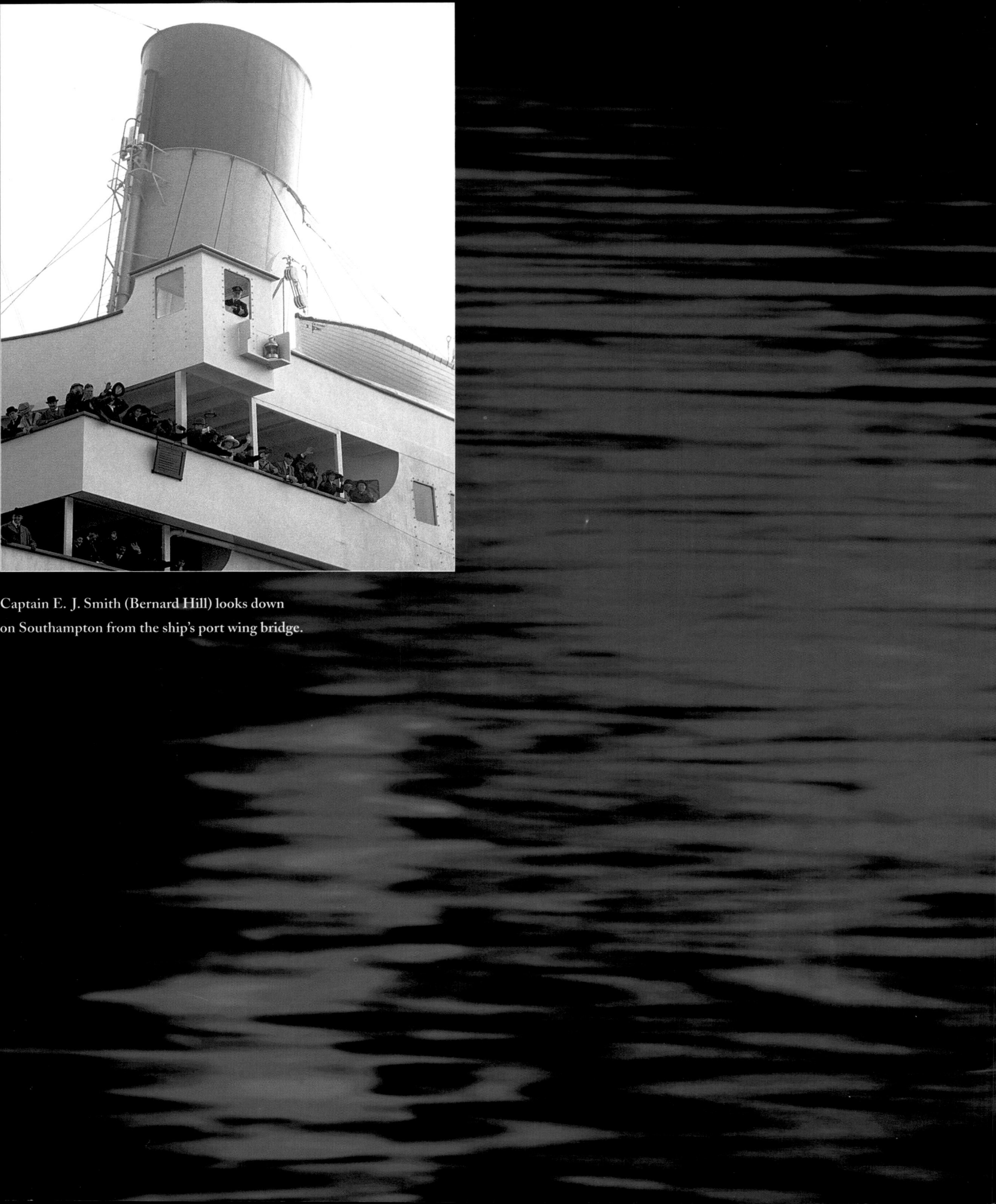

Captain E. J. Smith (Bernard Hill) looks down
on Southampton from the ship's port wing bridge.

A

GLORIOUS REVEAL *as the gleaming white superstructure of* Titanic *rises mountainously beyond the rail, and above that the buff-colored funnels stand against the sky like the pillars of a great temple. Crewmen move across the deck, dwarfed by the awesome scale of the steamer.* [From the screenplay.]

"I'll never forget the moment I first walked onto Southampton dock," smiles Jon Landau. "The ship was up and the sense of accomplishment was tremendous. We had not only built the *Titanic*. We had built a studio."

It is sailing day, and White Star's dock swarms with activity. With most of the passengers already onboard, the pier is still choked with onlookers, luggage and last-minute provisions arriving in amounts that defy comprehension: two tons of Oxford marmalade; fifty tons of fresh fish, meat and poultry; twenty thousand bottles of beer and stout. The last batch of immigrants undergo health inspections, scrutinized for lice and other maladies. Stepping from a gleaming white Renault, Caledon Hockley's wedding party arrives just before sailing. Cal (Billy Zane) has taken advantage of last-minute arrangements to provide fiancée Rose DeWitt Bukater (Kate Winslet) and her

The Renault stops and the liveried driver scurries to open the door for a young woman dressed in a stunning white and purple outfit, with an enormous feathered hat. She is seventeen years old and beautiful, regal of bearing, with piercing eyes. [From the screenplay.] "It's very clever the way Jim is directing how the audience will see young Rose for the first time," says Kate Winslet. "I'm wearing this huge hat and my head is tilted down and then I look up at the ship and say, 'It doesn't look any bigger than the *Mauretania.'* I love it. Everyone is so excited about the ship and my character completely snubs it."

mother, Ruth, with the finest accommodations White Star Line has to offer—the millionaire suite on B-deck, replete with its own private promenade deck. Cal is the richest man on the ship—at least until J. J. Astor boards at Cherbourg—and the expense of the gift is not lost on Rose any more than it will be lost on the social elite whom Cal strives to impress. "The challenge of the great ships was to provide an experience equivalent to one of Europe's first-class hotels," observes Zane. "It's incredible to think how these exquisite examples of art and architecture were compressed into little metal balls and cast adrift on the ocean. Passengers weren't even supposed to realize they were at sea."

Spirits are high for cast and crew alike. As filmmakers they have heard stories about what it was like to film GONE WITH THE WIND or DR. ZHIVAGO—classics remembered for their casts of thousands—but very few projects in recent history have truly aspired to that tradition. "Deborah Scott has done an incredible job because even the extras in the deep background are dressed to the nines," says Frances Fisher. "Every single woman has a corset on and nothing has been left to chance. Every department is doing their best and it really shows." Frances plays Ruth DeWitt Bukater, an established matriarch of Philadelphia society unaccustomed to the hustle and bustle of a busy pier. The lively sights, sounds and smells of horses and vintage cars pushing their way past the awestruck crowds complete the illusion.

LEFT: **Caledon Hockley (Billy Zane) tips an unsuspecting porter (the wealthy never traveled light).**

BELOW: **Hockley's wedding party makes its way along the pier. Cal's future mother-in-law, Ruth DeWitt Bukater, and fiancée, Rose, are trailed by Rose's maidservant Trudy Bolt (Amy Gaipa).**

White Star Line's Southampton Pier comes to life for sailing day (April 10, 1912), as nearly one thousand extras, twenty-five horses, and a dozen vintage automobiles vie for position in the shadow of the newly completed ship exterior, the largest set in motion picture history.

For all the exuberance around her, however, Rose seems almost bored. "I hope that when the audience meets Rose they'll actually think she's rather spoiled," shares Kate Winslet. "Then we'll come to know why she's so mysterious around Cal, because boarding the ship is very much like she's walking to her execution, really." Rose is drowning before the *Titanic* even sets sail, flailing against the restrictions of gender and class washing over her. "She's a very spirited girl and she has a lot to give," explains the young actress. "She wants to explore the whole world but she knows that it's never going to happen because she's engaged to Cal and she's being pressured into his limited world of what's proper and what's acceptable. Initially, she probably did fall in love with him and was very flattered by his affections and attention. Nobody forced her into the engage-

The Cyclopaedia of Social Usage

Manners and Customs of the Twentieth Century

By

Helen L. Roberts

CHAPTER EIGHTEEN

TRAVELERS BY LAND AND WATER

THE wanderer to foreign lands, when taking leave of friends and relations on the steamer's deck, should accompany these amiable ones to the head of the gangway leading to the dock, as last good-bys are uttered. It is only polite to express warm thanks for the compliment that the exertion of "seeing-off" implies.

At the sailing of a ship

There is a degree of tact to be shown by the "seeing-off" friends that is sometimes recklessly ignored. They should not, for instance, hang about the ship's deck till the last moment, causing deep anxiety to the already nervous traveler; and they should not exaggerate and prolong to a wearisome extent the business of speeding a seafarer on his way.

In a case where friends and relatives gather on deck to see a voyager off, the friends should make farewells and take their departure before the relatives do so. Wanting in delicacy, indeed, is the mere acquaintance who stands by while devoted members of a family exchange tender and sometimes tearful farewells.

There is no rule that may be cited to decide whether it is better to take in one's hand, or to send from a shop, flowers, fruit, books, or bonbons intended as a solace

441

ment. It was only later that she realized he's rather a pompous piece of work." Her mother is not helping matters. Deep in debt after the death of her husband, Ruth is encouraging Rose to marry for money as a means of saving them both. "The wedding being planned around her is like a death trap."

As the entourage approaches the gangway Cameron calls out for Kate to turn to her left—no, her "flopped left." While there is no visible reason to the uninitiated, everything Cameron is shooting at Southampton Pier has been created flopped, or mirror-image reversed. "Oh, don't even talk to me about flopping," groans Winslet. "I haven't been able to get my head around it at all. It made me laugh when I saw sailors with 'ENIL RATS ETIHW' written across their hats."

"We built the ship's riveted steel hull all the way down to the waterline on only one side of the ship as a cost-saving measure," Cameron explains. "We chose starboard primarily because months of collected weather data indicated a pre-

The social elite devised rules of behavior for every imaginable situation. This period etiquette manual discusses the dos and don'ts of an ocean crossing.

RIGHT AND BELOW: Since the riveted hull was only completed down the starboard side of the ship, sequences of the film featuring the port side had to be shot "flopped." This required that everything be doubled in reverse, from lettering on signs to wardrobe with buttons on the opposite side. One performer joked, "I wasn't dyslexic before I started this show. I am now."

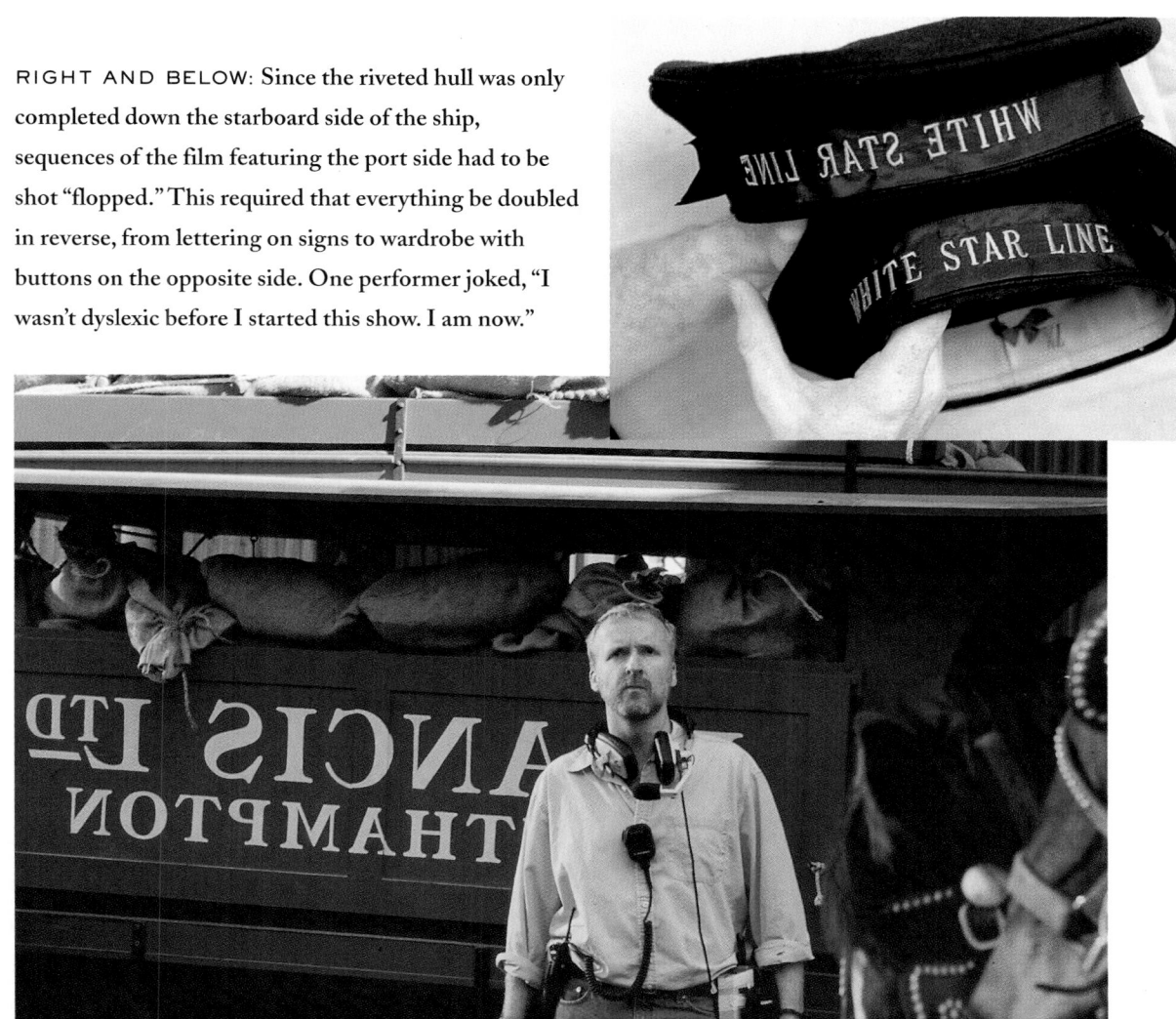

vailing north to south wind that would blow our funnel smoke aft and help the ship look like it's moving forward. However, when the ship sailed from Southampton, it was docked with its port side to the pier. So, since we were making most of our props and costumes anyway, we decided to go for historical accuracy by flopping the scene to its correct orientation in post-production. There were some real instances of pretzel logic, though, when we had to match some of the later scenes, which we shot *both* ways. 'Is it right? Then it's wrong. It's wrong? Good!'"

In one of many public houses nestled in and around the docks, a barkeep points to the *Titanic*'s pending departure. At least one group of stokers (grabbing a last-minute pint) failed to watch the time and missed their ship. Cameron himself operates the camera for this handheld shot. Many shots in the film were taken by Cameron.

Jack is American, a lanky drifter with his hair a little long for the standards of the times. He is also unshaven, and his clothes are rumpled from sleeping in them. He is an artist, and has adopted the bohemian style of the art scene in Paris. He is also very self-possessed and sure-footed for twenty, having lived on his own since fifteen. [From the screenplay.] Four hopeful travelers have bet their dreams on one honest hand of five-card draw. "Moment of truth," says Jack Dawson (Leonardo DiCaprio, opposite). "Someone's life is about to change." Fabrizio de Rossi (Danny Nucci, above left) counts heavily on his friend's luck.

ABOVE: William Carter's Renault touring car is loaded into the Number 2 cargo hatch. "I made that car's interior an important location in the script," says Cameron, who tried to reach the car on the wreck by sending his ROV down through the very same hatch. Collapsed supports and other debris ultimately blocked the attempt. Nevertheless, several historic documents (including Carter's insurance claim for the vehicle) provided enough information for the Renault to be re-created faithfully in every detail, down to the crystal flower vases in the passenger compartment.

LEFT: Back to basics. Cameron operates a vintage motion picture camera. Documentary director Ed Marsh actually shot hand-cranked footage, employing as many period techniques as he could re-create. "They used to keep time on the hand crank by humming a familiar tune. 'Turkey in the Straw' yields a pretty consistent sixteen frames per second."

As onlookers wave their farewells, *Titanic* is about to receive two more passengers.

The ship glows with the warm, creamy light of late afternoon. Jack and Fabrizio stand right at the bow gripping the curved railing so familiar from images of the wreck. Jack leans over, looking down fifty feet to where the prow cuts the surface like a knife, sending up two glassy sheets of water. [From the screenplay.]

Detail from the bow of re-created lifeboat number six. The legend in the circle indicates that the boat is thirty feet long and capable of carrying sixty-four people. It was launched less than half full.

UNSINKABLE

The year 1912 must have felt like a tremendous mixture of both enormous optimism and a certain amount of nail-biting," says Jonathan Hyde, who plays White Star Line's managing director, J. Bruce Ismay. "When developments become too rapid, people begin to get breathless and anxious."

Competition was stiff between the trans-Atlantic commercial lines. The Cunard Line enjoyed a large British subsidy while White Star was bankrolled by owner J. P. Morgan. Both lines vied for mail contracts and the lucrative immigrant trade. While Cunard had focused on speed—their record-holding *Mauretania* had a top speed of almost twenty-seven knots—White Star had focused on size. *Titanic* had a gross tonnage in excess of forty-six thousand tons, fifteen thousand more than Cunard's largest vessel. Twenty-four boilers fed *Titanic*'s twin, four-story-tall reciprocating

engines. A third engine, a steam turbine, allowed for a combined speed in excess of twenty-two knots, or approximately twenty-five miles per hour. The boast of being unsinkable stemmed from the ship's sixteen watertight compartments and twelve watertight doors (see computer illustration on page 152). If flooding were to occur, the watertight doors could be shut automatically or

After her last stop in Queenstown, Captain Smith orders the ship to sea. "Let's stretch her legs." In exploring potential effects shots, Cameron encouraged Digital Domain to pretend they actually had the ship at their disposal. "Imagine we're making a commercial for White Star Lines," he explained, "and we need beautiful shots sweeping around the ship from a helicopter out between Long Beach and Catalina Island."

"The Millionaire's Captain" poses on the wing bridge with his officers (left to right): Sixth Officer Moody (Edward Fletcher), Second Officer Lightoller (Jonathan Phillips), Third Officer Pitman (Kevin De la Noy), Captain Smith (Bernard Hill), Fourth Officer Boxhall (Simon Crane), First Officer Murdoch (Ewan Stewart), and Fifth Officer Lowe (Ioan Gruffudd). Not pictured: Chief Officer Wilde (Mark Lindsay Chapman).

from the bridge, isolating the affected compartments from the rest of the ship. Any two of these compartments or the first four compartments could be breached and the ship would stay afloat indefinitely, a design consideration that placed the greatest emphasis on the danger of a front end collision—hardly a surprise in the days before radar and sonar. And while many find it hard to believe, the *Titanic* actually had more lifeboats than was required by law, even though there were not enough lifeboats for everyone on board. "The British Board of Trade regulations were developed in the late 1800s when few vessels displaced more than ten thousand tons and you could reasonably calculate passenger capacity using tonnage alone," explains *Titanic* Historian Don Lynch. "No one could have anticipated ships of the *Titanic*'s magnitude. They were complying with a law that no longer made any sense."

In a column on page 44 of a notebook of specifications for the *Olympic* kept by Thomas Andrews, Master Shipbuilder of the *Titanic* (portrayed in the film by Victor Garber), a mental exercise in alternate history is briefly played out. In a column showing the total number of lifeboats the number sixty-eight leaps off the page while only twenty lifeboats (including the four "collapsibles") were installed on each ship. Closer examination reveals that this page was added to the notebook after the tragedy, when the Board of Trade revised its regulations to require a lifeboat seat for everyone on board. Historians paint Andrews in a favorable light, however, claiming that the pressure to keep the number of lifeboats to a minimum came from a higher authority and that Andrews had lobbied for more. Given the shipbuilder's reputation as a perfectionist, the theory rings true. "He was obsessed with the ship and was constantly taking notes about things that could be corrected or improved, no matter how big or how small," explains Garber. "He was apparently taken to task in social situations quite often because he was always preoccupied with something or other."

Cameron found a kindred spirit in the historical Andrews: "As an engineer he never would have believed his own publicity, so to speak. The ship was made of iron. Of course she could sink if the conditions were right. Imagine what it must have felt like, standing in the foyer of the Grand Staircase—architecturally the most beautiful place on the ship—a ship that *he had designed*—knowing that in an hour or so all of it was going to be at the bottom of the Atlantic. Can you imagine the responsibility he must have felt?"

"If you came on board before the disaster you would sense an apparent air of complacency, but that's because everybody knew what they were doing," argues Bernard Hill in defense of his character, Captain E. J. Smith. "There's no reason to go around shouting and issuing orders and being noisy. The bridge of a ship was a quiet and serene place." By and large, the character of Smith has been lionized by history, though there are still families in Southampton who would paint a very different portrait (loss of life was greatest to this community). "He was called the 'millionaire's captain,' because he was obviously very good with the upper class even though he was not a member of that class himself. People would make the journey on his ship specifically because of him," says Hill. The actor enjoyed being called "El Capitan" by members of the Mexican crew. "He ran a very good ship, you know. There's that famous quote of his: 'When anyone asks me how I can best describe my experience in nearly forty years at sea, I merely say, uneventful,' which, considering what happened, has an amazing resonance."

ABOVE: Harland and Wolff's Master Shipbuilder Thomas Andrews (Victor Garber). His surviving design notebook for the *Olympic* reveals a man obsessed with both the mechanics and aesthetics of shipbuilding.

LEFT: The production's re-creation of the ship incorporated davits provided by the same company that manufactured them for the real *Titanic*. Andrews supposedly chose the Welin quadrant davits because there was to be a second row of lifeboats adjacent to the ones already hooked into the mechanisms and this particular model of davit could be used to launch the additional boats. White Star's management, however, decided that the boat deck would look too "cluttered."

Seven officers served under Smith, all of them considered masters of their trade, and it fell to Naval Historian Kit Bonner to acquaint the actors with the traditions, mannerisms and protocols associated with bridge operations. "There was a strict hierarchy from seaman to quartermaster and on up the ranks of the officers, and there wasn't a member of Smith's team who didn't want command of his own ship one day. They were the cream of the merchant marine and as such they were incredibly reserved. They rarely spoke, especially in public." How did the actors fare? "Bernard is probably the best Captain Smith I've ever seen. He really has that air of authority," says Bonner. "As for as the others, they're doing it exactly as it would have been done, I feel. The other night when they were filming the scene where the iceberg hits the ship, I wanted off the set."

"I think Ismay is more or less directly blamed for the reckless speed at which the ship was traveling," says Jonathan Hyde. He is referring to a moment from history that Cameron has re-created faithfully. On Saturday, April 13, passenger Elizabeth Lines was having coffee. Next to her, Ismay was talking loudly to Captain Smith about beating *Olympic*'s record and arriving in New York on Tuesday night instead of Wednesday morning. Smith

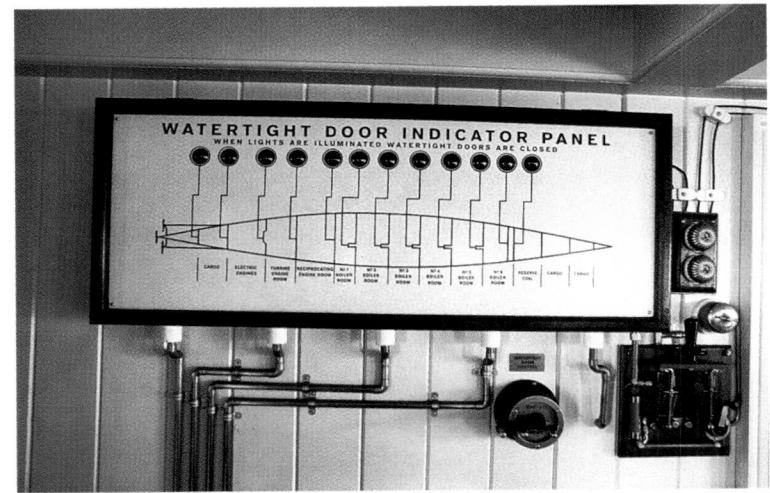

TOP AND LEFT: "Practically unsinkable." *The Shipbuilder* touted *Titanic*'s system of watertight doors as the latest innovation in ocean safety. A simple switch could close the doors either from the bridge or at the bulkheads. As a last resort, a system of floats would close them automatically when flooding occurred.

ABOVE: "Bridge operations were taken very seriously," says Naval Historian Kit Bonner. "They said that the only place quieter than the bridge of a White Star Liner was the morgue." "That's certainly true now," observes Cameron. All that remains of the ship's wheelhouse at the bottom of the ocean is a fragment of this telemotor mechanism.

Cameron blocks scenes in the wireless room with Jack Phillips (Gregory Cooke) and Harold Bride (Craig Kelly). With the wireless still in its infancy, Marconi operators spent most of their time sending and relaying private traffic for paying customers. Ship to ship messages—including ice warnings—were relayed to the bridge almost as a professional courtesy and rarely with any sense of urgency. In his published account, Second Officer Lightoller writes that it was just such a delay that "proved fatal and was the main contributary cause to the loss of that magnificent ship and hundreds of lives."

"Everyone is eager to point the finger at someone else," says Naval Historian Kit Bonner. "But in reality no one person can be blamed. The collision with the iceberg was the culmination of several minor mishaps and 'if only's.'"

was only nodding in apparent agreement. Ismay had no official sway over the captain. In fact, White Star made its top officers sign a pledge with that implicit agreement. Smith, however, seemed to acquiesce to the managing director. "Ismay was always saying, 'Of course I'm just a passenger,' but it was slightly dishonest to twist the captain's arm that way," admits Hyde. "Whether he did it blatantly or subtly, it was coercion. Later Smith gave Ismay an ice warning, and he showed it to one of the passengers as if to say, 'What a lot of poppycock.' You know, 'Fat chance we'll be sunk by a piece of ice.' Perhaps Captain Smith was giving Ismay a subtle reminder that he was at least partly responsible for their speed at the time. One could say Ismay was a little bit arrogant."

"Digital Domain is incorporating traditional model photography with some of the latest digital skills available," offers Producer Jon Landau. "We can shoot our ¹⁄₂₀th-scale *Titanic* on a motion-control stage and add the water and smoke digitally. Then we can add computer-generated passengers and crew walking the decks using motion capture as the realistic basis for their movement and adding appropriate 1912 wardrobe via texture maps. For one shot, we'll start with a wide view of the whole ship and move in close on the bridge, transitioning seamlessly from a computer-generated Captain Smith to Bernard Hill as he delivers his lines. Audiences have never seen this before." In this shot, you can just make out a CGI Captain Smith adjusting his hat on the starboard wing bridge. Visual Effects Supervisor Rob Legato asked other effects professionals to identify which people in this shot were real and which ones were computer generated; no one guessed that they were all, in fact, computer generated.

One of three elevators that carried passengers between the decks.

O*h, they loaded up the boats so very far from shore*
but the rich refused to associate with the poor.
So they put the poor below,
where they were the first to go.
It was sad when the great ship went down.

—FOLK SONG

"The *Titanic* was a symbol of structured society," remarks Bernard Hill. "Everyone knew where they belonged, up and down the social classes or up and down the decks, if you like. And when the ship sank, people realized that a certain amount of exploitation had been going on." The *Titanic* tragedy—one of the first international news stories to spread via wireless—captivated the world with individual tales of

heroism involving the richest and most influential personalities of the day. Beyond the headlines, however, the disproportionate number of second- and third-class passengers who perished became fuel for a growing class war.

"We're holding just short of Marxist dogma," jokes Cameron. In the tight confines of the aptly named "third-class labyrinth" the director is staging his own class war: Third-class passengers surge forward against a locked metal

The social center of steerage life. It is stark by comparison to the opulence of first class, but is a loud, boisterous place. There are mothers with babies, kids running between the benches yelling in several languages and being scolded in several more. There are men playing chess, girls doing needlepoint and reading dime novels. [From the screenplay.] White Star Lines prided itself on providing **excellent steerage accommodations.** Simple but comfortable. **"When you think about it, the immigrants were probably living in better conditions aboard the ship than they had left at home,"** observes Cameron.

gate while stewards beat them back with the butt of a fire ax. "The truth of the matter is that a third-class male on the *Titanic* stood a one-in-ten chance of surviving whereas a first-class female stood a nine-in-ten chance. I've emphasized those odds so the audience will understand exactly what kind of sacrifice Rose makes when she chooses to be with Jack."

On a ship physically designed to prevent them from ever meeting, third-class passenger Jack and first-class passenger Rose have fallen in love. "I think the story is that much more compelling because of the approaching disaster," says Cameron. "You witness these two people coming together in complete defiance of their world. They don't know that in the space of a few days everything they see around them will be gone."

It was this cross-class love story that attracted Leo DiCaprio to the project despite some early reservations. "I didn't really think of this film as something I would do until I realized I was discriminating against it purely because of its scale. For all the epic size of this production, at its heart it's a great love story," says the actor. "Another big reason I

Jack passes the time drawing pictures with young Cora Cartmell (Alexandrea Owens).

ABOVE: Fabrizio wins the attention of beautiful Norwegian immigrant Helga Dahl (Camilla Overbye Roos).

LEFT AND OPPOSITE: Director of Photography Russell Carpenter (upper inset) says, "I was very happy with the third-class General Room scenes. The light was supposedly motivated by the sun streaming in through these large cargo hatches, and it ended up creating these glowing pools of brilliance." The film marks the third collaboration between Carpenter and Cameron. "Jim's constantly moving camera is a challenge for any cinematographer. It's a very dynamic frame that can go from wide shot to close-up in seconds. Oftentimes I'm right behind camera with a fill light so I can finesse the close shots." A-Camera Operator James Muro (lower inset) operates with Steadicam.

took the role was Kate. She's got a lot of integrity and as an actress she's extremely talented."

"I was afraid Leo wasn't going to like me," confesses Winslet. "I thought he was going to have this image of me as this starchy Brit who recites Shakespeare left and right and absolutely insists on drinking tea in the afternoon. When I first met him I realized I was going to have to let him know that I had my funky side as well. We're very close now. He's got lots of my secrets, and I've got heaps of his." The way the two characters meet (Jack saves Rose from throwing herself off the stern) begins an intimate relationship beyond the restrictions of class. "Jack's the first person, the first man certainly, who has ever come into Rose's life and said, 'How do you feel?' and shown interest in her desires and her dreams," says Winslet. "They share so many of the same passions for life, which he's already attained, and to which she's aspiring."

"Jack opens her eyes to the world outside her gilded cage," says Executive Producer Rae Sanchini, "and Jim needed a young actress who could play these very emotional beats and affect this almost total transformation of character over the four-and-a-half-day journey. I think everyone involved with the film feels that Kate's performance has been absolutely stunning. The audience will

ABOVE: Rose self-consciously enters the third-class General Room looking for Jack.

RIGHT: "Next, it'll be brandies in the Smoking Room." Rose sums up the arrogance of her class: "They retreat in a cloud of smoke and congratulate each other on being masters of the universe." Cal enjoys a moment of repose with Colonel Archibald Gracie (Bernard Fox, middle) and Sir Cosmo Duff Gordon (Martin Jarvis, right).

OPPOSITE: Caledon Hockley in the doorway leading to his private promenade deck. "I love this period in history," says Zane. "If I'd lived then I would have tried to make it as a silent film actor."

RIGHT: Rehearsals for a delicate scene in Rose's bedroom. "You have to play the scene in light of what just happened," says Cameron. "You just tried to throw yourself off the ship and Cal is trying to cheer you up the only way he knows how. And when you see the jewelry box it's like, 'Oh, please. The last thing I need is another jewel from Cal.' It speaks right to the heart of what's wrong in the relationship." "Diamonds are forever," adds Winslet. "If it was ever possible to call the wedding off before that moment, then the diamond seals her fate."

OPPOSITE: Cal woos Rose: "There is nothing I couldn't give you." In his script, Cameron explains that today the Heart of the Ocean would be worth more than the Hope Diamond.

understand all of the choices Rose has made up to this point and how meeting Jack Dawson and the love affair that ensues could change her life completely."

"Jack had to be someone you never forget," explains Cameron. "Their connection on an emotional level is what transforms Rose from this sort of Edwardian first-class geisha who is dying on the inside into this spirited young woman on the cusp of a new life. And Leonardo DiCaprio just possesses this natural energy and purity of spirit as an actor, which makes that transformation seem possible."

"Leo's character doesn't exist as far as my character is concerned, at least not at first," observes Billy Zane. Except for servants, the lower classes were pretty much invisible to the super-rich denizens of Hockley's class. "It's embarrassing for Cal to even acknowledge him."

"Billy Zane was the perfect juxtaposition to Leo as the third segment of the love triangle," says Sanchini. "His character is sort of the poster boy for Edwardian excess, and yet you have to believe Rose loved him at one point for the story to work. Billy was able to capture all of those facets in a performance that balances powerful charm with great arrogance."

OPPOSITE: **Cal and Rose's millionaire suite. (Top) Cal's bedroom, (bottom) the private promenade. Rose's bedroom (page 82) and the ornate sitting room (page 115) complete the elaborate suite.**

RIGHT: **The Palm Court Café (seen here in this archive photo and in re-creation) was actually two identical rooms, one on each side of the ship, which could be entered through sliding doors at the aft end of the A-deck promenade or through large revolving doors leading from the first-class Smoking Room. According to Historian Don Lynch, the café was also used as a playroom by the first-class children.**

RIGHT: This magnificent twenty-one-light candelabrum (shown real and in re-creation) rested on the newel post at the base of the Grand Staircase, welcoming diners into the reception area on D-deck.

BELOW AND BOTTOM: The first-class Dining Saloon. Hundreds of stewards, stewardesses, waiters and cooks helped prepare and serve over six thousand meals aboard ship each day. This archival photo from the *Olympic* (below) reveals a slightly different carpet design and no table lamps. To this day it is not known whether or not the lamps manufactured for *Titanic* were ever installed.

SATURDAY, APRIL 13, 1912

To thank him for saving Rose (and to provide some unusual entertainment), Cal has invited Jack to dinner, the most formal and important ritual of the upper class. As the ship's string quintet wafts melodies into the air, more than three hundred men and women descend the Grand Staircase and stroll into the expanse of the first-class Dining Saloon. Even the detailed plaster ceiling is in place, fully enclosing cast and crew inside the jewel-encrusted belly of the leviathan. "Shooting 'real for real' is apparently a trademark of Mr. Cameron's, but the Dining Saloon was an absolute miracle," exclaims Jonathan Hyde. "It was first class in every respect. All compliments belong to the art department, but—as I'm playing the ship's managing director—I must admit to feeling extremely proud for the old line."

Many of the passengers taking their places at the tables belong to the "Core Extras Group," an ensemble of one hundred and fifty background performers who have populated the rooms, decks and corridors of both first and third class since day one of the production. "It's an enclosed ecosystem,"

OPPOSITE: *Jack steps in and his breath is taken away by the splendor spread out before him. Overhead is the enormous glass dome, with a crystal chandelier at its center. Sweeping down six stories is the first-class Grand Staircase, the epitome of the opulent naval architecture of the time.* [From the screenplay.] At night, both the dome and the windows of the first-class Dining Saloon were lit from behind, bathing everything in a warm, soft light.

explains Josh McLaglen, who deserves credit for the concept along with Jon Landau. "We didn't want to bring in fresh, uninitiated extras every two or three weeks because over the course of the entire production we'd end up showing more people than could possibly have been aboard the ship, not to mention refitting expensive period wardrobe for each new person and grounding them with enough historical background to know how they are supposed to behave. Also, the Core provided an emotional face for the two thousand plus individuals on board, and Cameron found ways to feature many of them prominently so that recognizing them again as the ship goes down will strike a powerful chord in the audience."

"I can honestly say that the Core extras cared as much about this project as I do," exclaims Cameron. "I've never seen a group so into their work that they could correct me and Josh about their actions and blocking for a scene we may have started in October and then continued in March. They never once flinched while we strapped them into the railings of the sinking ship or soaked them for hours on end in the tanks, and their command of the period's mannerisms was unequaled."

How to walk, sit, eat, meet and not speak until spoken to in perfect Edwardian style was the responsibility of Etiquette Coach and Choreographer Lynne Hockney, who even taught the Core that there was a proper way to laugh. "It was the 'Gilded Age,' a time of the grand hostess, lavish parties and tireless pleasure seeking, and each social class was scrambling to reach the one above it. This made proper behavior terribly important," observes Hockney. Her "basic training" was a three-hour course. She also produced a video called *Titanic Etiquette: A Time Traveler's Guide*, which was repeated on a loop in the wardrobe building. Was such in-depth training really necessary for all one hundred and fifty of the background performers? For the illusion Cameron is striving to create, the answer is yes. "The body language of today is so different from back then," explains Hockney. "Just look at the

First-class opulence. Passengers descend the Grand Staircase in all of their finery. Historian Ken Marschall was enthralled. "It's like watching a picture from the *Illustrated London News* come to life."

A kiss for the lady. "I saw that in a nickelodeon once, and I've always wanted to do it," whispers Jack with a smile.

clothes. Those women had long corsets and the men had high wing collars. The clothes encouraged a certain way of moving, which goes a long way toward establishing the period. You cannot slouch in a corset, for example; you perch. Without proper training, however, these elegant first-class dinner guests would end up looking stiff and unnatural, tripping on the ladies' long dress trains and sitting with their elbows on the table. *Scandalous.*" Of course, such training was not limited to first class. High society rested firmly on the backs of its servants, who were forced to adhere to their own code of behavior: ladies' maids, valets, wine servants and secretaries. Hockney's printed guidelines filled twenty pages: food in from the left and taken from the right; drinks poured from the right and never more than two-thirds full unless it's wine (half full); when and how to bob a curtsy and how subservient to be. As her reputation grew, Hockney

Cameron weaves his fictional characters into the tapestry of history: Madeleine Astor (Charlotte Chatton) eyes Jack, saying "It's a pity we're both spoken for" (above). Rochelle Rose portrays the Countess of Rothes (above right), while Sir Cosmo Duff Gordon charms Ruth (right). Swiss classical string quintet I Salonisti lent their musical talent for the much-beloved band, with Jonathan Evans Jones joining them as lead violinist Wallace Hartley (below).

Thomas Andrews

Ruth DeWitt Bukater

Captain E. J. Smith

Jack Dawson

Rose DeWitt Bukater

Caledon Hockley

Countess of Rothes

Molly Brown

J. J. Astor

ABOVE AND RIGHT: Captain E. J. Smith seats a guest at his table in the luxurious first-class Dining Saloon. In a subtle touch of authenticity, BMK-Stoddard of England, the company that supplied carpeting for the real *Titanic*, has re-created the weave for this eighteen-thousand-square-foot reproduction.

"The dinner party scene went on forever and a day," remembers Winslet. "It was very glamorous with the three-thousand-course meal, Russell's glorious lighting and the hair and makeup people running in and out between takes making everyone look fantastic, but it was all upper class and stiff as well. I was much more comfortable shooting the steerage party."

returned to her hotel room one night to find a box of chocolates from the hotel staff with a note addressed to "Miss Etiquette" asking for private lessons. "I was very flattered."

As Cameron blocks the dinner party scene he explains to the actors how his first shot will function as a sort of "who's who" of the *Titanic*'s first-class passenger list. Seated around the elegant spread are such historical personalities as Sir Cosmo and Lady Duff Gordon (Martin Jarvis and Rosalind Aires), Archibald Gracie (Bernard Fox), the Countess of Rothes (Rochelle Rose), Benjamin Guggenheim (Michael Ensign), J. Bruce Ismay, Thomas Andrews and, of course, Molly Brown (Kathy Bates). "Jim has marvelously taken our two principal characters and woven them throughout the historical highlights of the journey in a meaningful way," explains Landau. "Molly Brown is vital to our story in that she becomes an ally in Jack's attempts to win Rose—she loans him a tuxedo—and yet the interaction does not change what we know to have actually happened."

"The scene begins with Ruth going out of her way to trash Jack's reputation by letting everyone know he's from third class," explains Cameron to the assembled cast.

Cameron discusses the action with Winslet. "This whole scene has to play in looks. You're communicating with Jack on a level that nobody else even senses."

Edwardian Etiquette Coach Lynne Hockney gives a crash course to these waiters. In prepping the cast, Hockney outlined the seven to ten courses one would have eaten that night, ending with these dessert creations. "Dining was a social occasion that could last several hours," she explains. "Imagine what a relief it must have been to eat at home."

"Cal's brought this monkey up from steerage for the amusement of one and all; and Jack, without any artifice or prethought, ends up turning the tables by just being himself."

"That's Jack's scene," recalls DiCaprio proudly. "It's not really about when he talks about how he grew up or where he's been as much as it's about the fact that Jack is able to sit in front of all these people who are completely detached from everything he represents and, without fear, just lay it all out. 'This is what I am. Accept me for that or not.'" With thirteen performers at the table, however—each with dialogue and private asides to fellow diners all requiring close-ups, two shots, over-the-shoulder shots, etc.—capturing the complex scene on film takes the better part of two days. Tedium sets in. The caviar quickly loses its appeal. At one point Leo motions to the sea of forks in his elaborate place setting and asks Kathy Bates, "Which one of these do I use to lobotomize myself?"

"The cast did an excellent job of keeping the moment fresh," says Cameron, "but it was a long scene. I think we were all grateful to get out of that stuffy room and go party down in steerage."

While the ship's first-class music is both majestic and beautiful, the foot-stomping, beer-swilling, spin-yer-gal jam session happening down in third class is just the right antidote for the pomp and circumstance of the last few days. Gaelic Storm, a Santa Monica–based pub band, was enlisted to play for the scene with Brian Walsh, their piper, also taking the role credited simply as "Irish Man."

"I like to think I'm playing Eugene Daly," shares the musician. "As *Titanic* was leaving Queenstown, Daly went up on deck and played 'Erin's Lament' on the aft well deck with his bagpipes as the Irish bid a tearful farewell to their homeland. Can you imagine the mix of sadness and hope those immigrants must have felt?"

Two days into the journey from Ireland, hope is winning out.

RIGHT: "The caviar was very high quality," says Jonathan Hyde. "I made an acting decision on the spot that Ismay was a big eater."

BELOW: Cal casts a wary eye toward his invited dinner guest.

Gaelic Storm brought the house down with their fast-paced traditional Irish dance music. "If they don't play the wrap party, I'm going to kill myself," complimented Russ Carpenter.

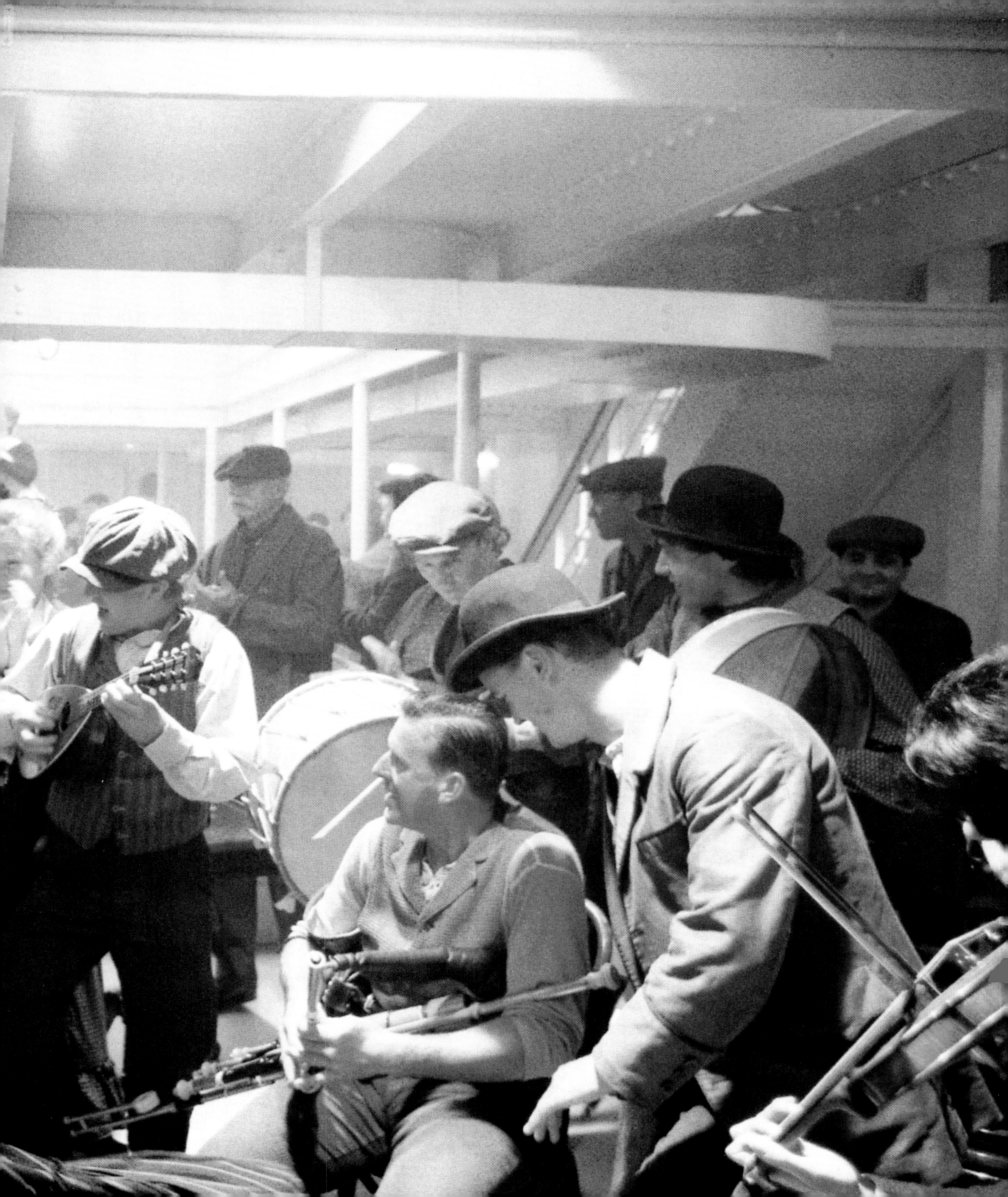

LEFT: Jack asks young Cora for permission to dance with Rose. "We'd never rehearsed it together until that day," explains Winslet. "Leo had been practicing hard. I was really proud of him for getting the footwork down."

ABOVE: Spicer Lovejoy (David Warner) keeps tabs on his employer's fiancée.

LEFT: "I grew up with that music!" says Winslet excitedly. "I really loved that scene because it was such a wonderful change after the first-class formality."

BOTTOM: Swedish immigrant Olause Gunderson (Anders Falk) performs the time-honored balancing act of transporting beer safely across the dance floor.

OPPOSITE: Bert Cartmell (stunt man Rocky Taylor) with daughter, Cora. Cora's doll is identical to the one seen at the beginning of the film as the ROV's lights drift slowly across the lifeless debris field (see page iv). "It creates a resonance with history," shares Cameron, who has planted several such ominous reminders throughout the film. "When Robert Ballard explored the wreck in 1986 his heart stopped when he found a doll's head just like this one. For a split second he thought it was a skull."

"You have to accept that it was a different time," observes DiCaprio. "Dancing was more than dancing. It was part of the communication between men and women, which was very different in 1912, especially between a first-class lady and someone like my character. But I think Jack kind of ignores all of that and it's why Rose is interested in him. He doesn't hesitate."

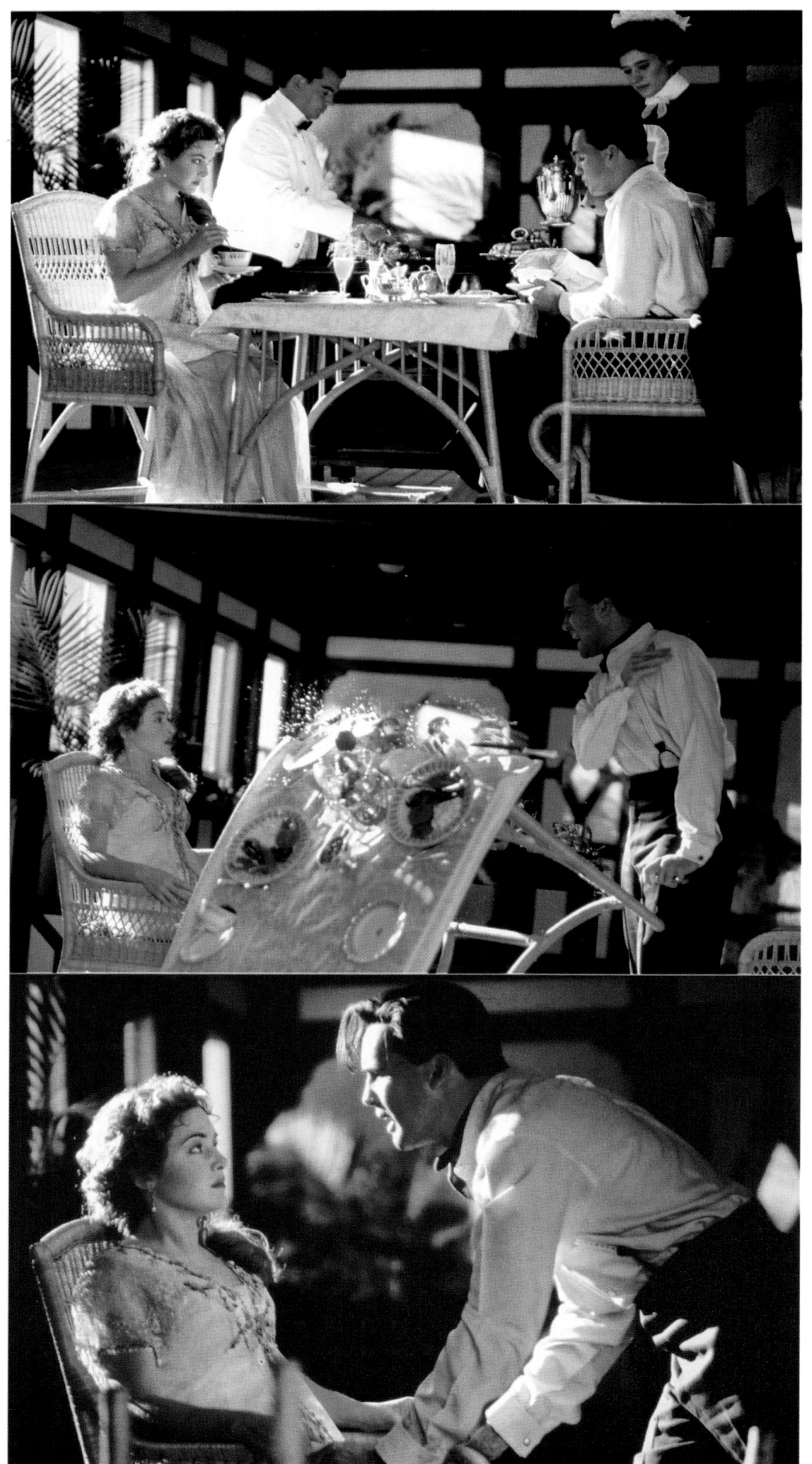

LEFT: In the controlling environment of the Edwardian upper class, Rose's "exertions belowdecks" bring immediate consequences. "Cal is obsessed with proper appearances," explains Cameron. "He never allows himself to lose control for very long, but when he does it's explosive." "Every decision Cal makes is with the intent to mine the approval of his social set," says Zane. "He could benefit from a loving relationship based on communication and respect but he's been brought up his whole life to believe such things are not important. He's the product of bad programming and we witness it short circuiting pretty violently. His heart is breaking just as he's realizing he has one."

OPPOSITE: Ruth laces up Rose's corset. "This match with Hockley is a good one," she implores, tightening both the laces and the confines of her daughter's gilded cage. The scene was originally written for Rose to lace Ruth's corset but Cameron and the actors quickly decided that the reverse situation would be more dramatically powerful.

ABOVE AND LEFT: Ruth enjoys afternoon tea with the Countess of Rothes and tries desperately to avoid the company of Molly Brown. Molly was a pariah to the upper class—the curse of "new money." It wasn't until after the disaster, when tales of her heroism spread, that she joined the circles to which she aspired. "Her character is a bit of a paradox because she admired the social hierarchy, but she didn't tolerate its snobbery," explains Cameron, who incorporated one of Brown's famous tall tales into Kathy Bates's performance. "That story about burning money in the stove? First of all it wasn't a 'fortune,' it was seventy-five dollars. Second, it was coins and not bills. There's a great line in her biography where she admits, 'I'm a bit of a confabulator.'"

Winslet and DiCaprio share a private moment on the Gymnasium set. The Gymnasium was located on the boat deck, just aft of the starboard first-class entrance. Since the wreck's discovery in 1985, its roof has caved in.

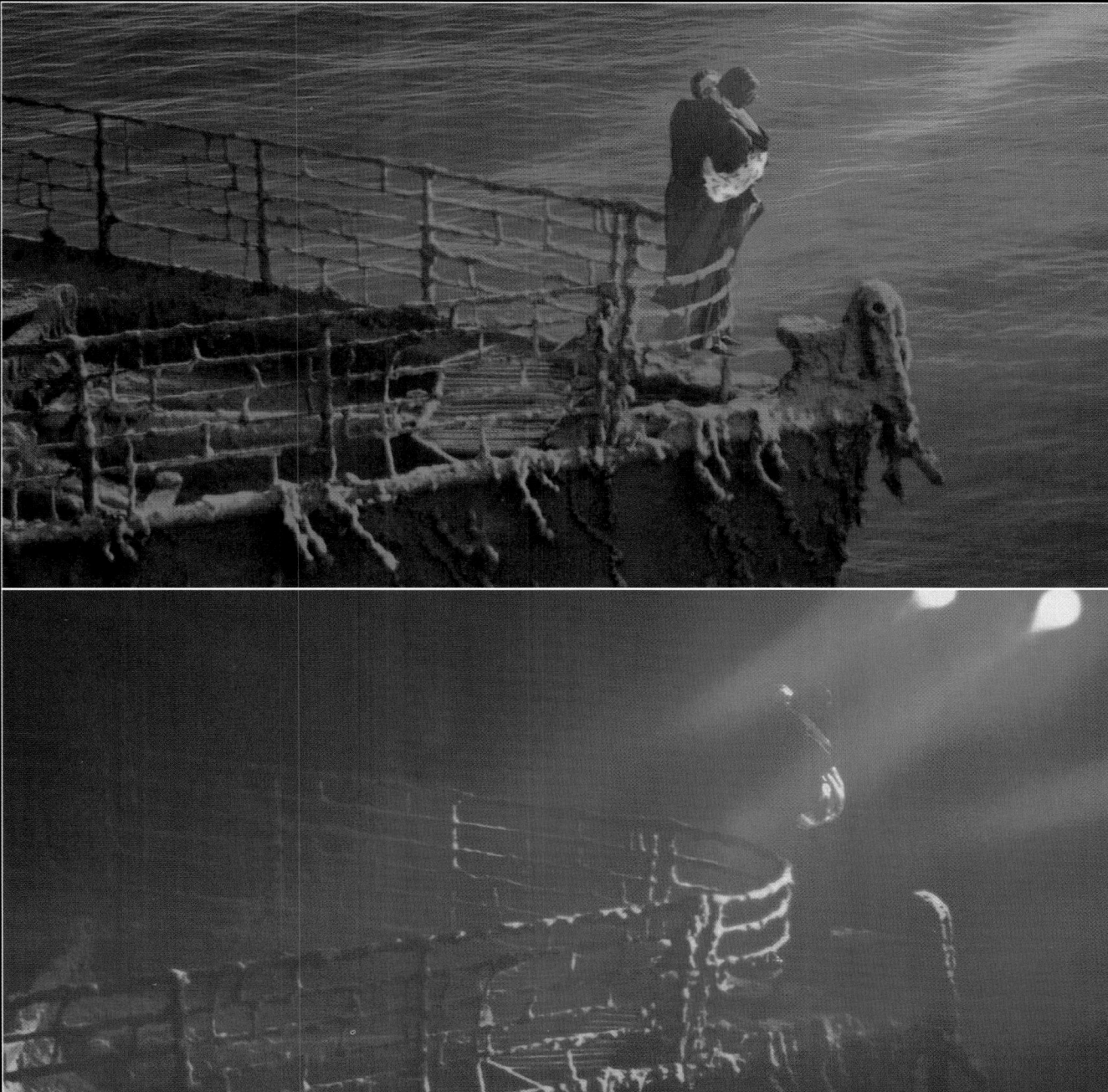

ROSE: *I'm flying!*

    . . . Jack tips his face forward into her blowing hair, letting the scent of her wash over him, until his cheek is against her ear.

    Rose turns her head until her lips are near his. She lowers her arms, turning farther, until she finds his mouth with hers. He wraps his arms around her from behind, and they kiss like this with her head turned and tilted back, surrendering to him, to the emotion, to the inevitable. They kiss, slowly and tremulously, and then with building passion.

    Jack and the ship seem to merge into one force of power and optimism, lifting her, buoying her forward on a magical journey, soaring onward into a night without fear. . . .

    As Jack and Rose embrace at the bow rail, they DISSOLVE SLOWLY AWAY, leaving the ruined bow of the WRECK . . . [From the screenplay.]

This elegant transition in time and memory (which ends with Old Rose watching the image of the wreck on a video monitor) combines many levels of story, character and emotion into one image and is the result of Cameron and Digital Domain's vision to extend the boundaries of visual effects in the service of storytelling.

Jack explores the opulent world of first class, waiting for Rose to emerge from her private suite. "I was naked in front of Leonardo DiCaprio on his first day of shooting," confides Winslet. "It almost always happens that some of the most important scenes get shot at the very beginning when you're still getting to know each other," adds DiCaprio. "Kate is great. She had no shame with it. She wanted to break the ice a little bit beforehand so she flashed me. I wasn't prepared for that so she had one up on me. It was pretty much comfortable after that."

Cameron's script describes Jack's sketch of Rose as *soulful, real, with expressive hands and eyes*. Cameron drew the sketch himself (along with all of Jack's drawings). Eighty-four years later, the discovery of this drawing—which clearly shows the Heart of the Ocean diamond—sets the events in motion and brings Old Rose venturing out to the North Atlantic.

After the ship strikes the iceberg," explains Cameron, "the passengers pass through all the stages of death: fear, denial, anger, depression and acceptance. The full spectrum of human behavior unfolds in two hours and forty minutes onboard ship. Weave into that a passionate story about these two kids who fall in love, and it takes on a whole other level of emotional impact."

Creating the romance was one challenge. Sinking the *Titanic* was quite another.

In the late spring of 1996, a twenty-five-foot study model of the ship and its surrounding tank environment was set up alongside a selection of miniature cameras and cranes. The construction logistics of angling the 775-foot set to its six-degree tilt were largely in place, but Cameron wanted to explore the best means of working on and around the full-sized set. "Our goal was to develop a versatile set of tools that could function wet or dry," explains Cameron. A tiny lipstick video camera allowed the crew to execute

shots and record them for future reference. Positionable barges of various heights seemed to work well for the brontosauruslike Akela cranes, and if the 162-foot tower crane (which had been primarily intended for lighting and construction) could be mounted on railroad tracks, then Cameron would have the

A cold interruption to a warm embrace. Digital Domain composited the iceberg into this ominous shot.

SEAMS OPEN BELOW THE WATER LINE, LETTING THE SEA POUR IN   132

REVISED 5·30·96
FORMERLY 89·4

The iceberg scrapes hard against the hull. Plates buckle or shatter. Rivets pop or shear off. Water streams in, flooding the first five compartments faster than pumps could ever clear them. *Titanic*'s fate is sealed. "The iceberg actually penetrated into the first six compartments," says Cameron, "but it's the first five that mattered. It's interesting, in that the way we show the iceberg penetrating the hull has since been confirmed by later expeditions to the wreck site."

THE BERG PUNCHES 4 FT. INTO HOLD № 1 134

RUPTURE MOVES ACROSS BULKHEADS

"B" CAMERA OF 132

REVISED 5·30·96

FORMERLY 89-13

April 15, 1912, 12:45 A.M. The first emergency distress rocket brings a hush over the crowd. Cast and crew returned from their holiday vacation to discover the set "sinking" six degrees at the bow. "It is very surreal to be driving down the coast and suddenly discover this wounded leviathan," observes Jonathan Hyde. "I wonder if anyone has phoned the Coast Guard saying, 'There's a rather expensive-looking ship over there and I think it's in trouble.'"

world's tallest camera dolly. "Why don't we mount the Wescam on that?" asked Cameron, instantly eliminating all but one helicopter shot from the production schedule.

Watching the crew work with the miniatures, one is struck by the image of children at play (at one point, Cameron even provides "cool" sinking sound effects). Unlike children, however, these professionals are charged with the task of making these shots work in the real world, where safety, schedules and budgets are real concerns. "The thing I appreciate about Jim," says Director of Photography Russell Carpenter, "is that his ideas are very adept technically, but at the same time they're so audacious you just know you're probably doing something for the first time." Carpenter credits all of the departments for rising to the challenge of sinking the ship, especially the electricians and grips, who attacked the assignment with zeal. "We had over three thousand lights working on the ship with enormous power requirements. Our gaffer, John Buckley, told me there's over seventy miles of cable out there. Whole sections of the interior look like Bell Telephone in the fifties. And Key Grip Lloyd Moriarty has been flying in bounce fills [large reflective surfaces used to diffuse light], using two-hundred-foot construction cranes. It's insane."

Now, watching the crew work with the giant ship, one is struck by the image of Lilliputians shooting an epic about Gulliver's favorite bathtub toy. "You're at the apex of a shot with insane production value, the likes of which hasn't been seen in almost half a century," says Billy Zane. "Behind us are almost five hundred extras trying to get into the lifeboats, Jim's swooping toward us in the tower crane basket, and David Warner and I are just standing at the edge of this mile of metal called a film set, smiling. I mean, how fortunate we are as actors to be standing at the spout of this leviathan."

TOP: *The boat lurches as the falls start to pay out through the pulley blocks. The women gasp. The boat descends, swaying and jerking, toward the water sixty feet below. The passengers are terrified.* [From the screenplay.] No cinematic trickery can compete with lowering real lifeboats from real davits. "Under the weight of a fully loaded boat you could see the tips of the davits flexing almost a foot," recalls Cameron. "I can understand why many people felt safer remaining on the ship."

ABOVE: Molly and Ruth react to the approaching death of the titan.

OPPOSITE: A gyro-stabilized Wescam mounted from the tower crane became the world's largest crane dolly. "We also had room for the Steadicam and a handheld rig," explains A-Camera Operator James Muro. "We'd fly first thing and wouldn't come down for six or eight hours, sometimes." This approach eliminated all but a handful of helicopter shots.

Much of the ship's lore stems from the tearful good-byes witnessed on the boat deck, and Cameron has layered several historic moments into this portion of his tale. "Accuracy is a big challenge for us," says the director. "Wherever possible we want to tell our story within an absolutely rigorous, historically accurate framework, complimenting history rather than distorting it." In one scene a father puts on a brave face as he places his daughters in a lifeboat. "*Hold your mummy's hand and be a good girl. Good-bye for a little while. Only for a little while.*" The audience does not need to know

that Cameron has taken these words from the accounts of survivors to appreciate their power. But for every story told, such as Molly Brown's bravery, there are the stories that have either passed into obscurity or were never brought to light in the first place. Many of these tales fall into a gray area bounded by fact on one side and varying combinations of information and conjecture on the other. Was the band's last musical number "Nearer My God to Thee" as commonly believed or was it "Songe d'Autumne," a popular waltz of the time? Survivors' accounts do not agree (though overwhelming support goes to the former, a personal favorite of Bandleader Wallace Hartley).

"In some instances it is impossible to separate human emotion from the truth," explains Cameron, who chose to photograph one of the ship's officers shooting himself shortly before the last lifeboat is launched. Despite considerable evidence (including an unpublished account from an officer and research by Historian Walter Lord for *The Night Lives On*), the details of the suicide remain unresolved. This is in part out of respect for the memory of a career seaman who stayed at his post and saved hundreds of lives. "I'm not sure you'd find that same sense of responsibility and total devotion to duty today," says the director. "This guy had half of his lifeboats launched before his counterpart on the port side had even launched one. That says something about character and heroism." Cameron's high opinion of the officer is echoed in a letter sent days after the sinking by a first-class passenger who claims to have witnessed his death: "The dear officer gave orders to row away from the sinking boat at least two hundred yards; he, afterwards, poor dear brave fellow, shot himself. We saw the whole thing."

The lifeboats are being lowered by a team of eighteen specially trained stunt people, who performed endless boat drills to familiarize themselves with the workings of the 1912-era Welin davits provided to the production by the original manufacturers. The process is not easy, and the heavy boats make their way to the water in a series of terrifying jerks, tipping first forward, then aft, until the teams on both "falls" can synchronize their ropes. "We have to treat this set as if it is a real ship because it's no less dangerous," explains Stunt Coordinator Simon Crane. "We've had to do our homework because this is not an action movie in the traditional sense. It cannot look 'stunty.' In 1912, you have to remember, there wasn't the same emphasis on physical fitness. A lot of people couldn't even swim and they'd

"Women and children only" was strictly enforced on the port side of the ship. This rule, along with misinformation about the lifeboats' maximum weight limits, led to several being launched half full.

certainly never jumped off a ten-story building, which is what it would have been like once the *Titanic* reached a certain angle." Soon, the lifeboats are gone. Passengers surge up the decks, heading for the stern. Hundreds of men and women make a jump for it, afraid the ship will suck them under if they don't get away. "We had twenty-six men and women jumping in every take from an average height of forty feet. The stunt itself wasn't difficult, but the scale in terms of numbers was massive."

"The discovery of the wreck in 1985 revealed a tremendous amount of information about the fate of the ship," explains Executive Producer Rae Sanchini. "She didn't just 'sink.' Even her final death throes lived up to her pretentious name. The ship's maiden voyage ended in a nightmare beyond comprehension as she ripped in two and her stern half rose into the sky before disappearing under the water." On the edge of the seventeen-million-gallon tank, the production has reconstructed the ship's aft-most section—the poop deck—and balanced it over a drop-off on a series of massive hinges and hydraulics. The whole mechanism can tilt from zero to ninety degrees in the space of a few seconds—a teeter-totter on the scale of Paul Bunyan.

ABOVE: "There were fourteen hundred people at the stern of the ship," calculates Cameron. "When it started to go vertical the pileup of bodies on the railings must have been horrific." Makeup artists prepare human-shaped stunt pads for the pending cataclysm.

LEFT: "I was prepared to shoot this sequence with blimps, if necessary," explains Cameron. The tilting poop deck went from level to tilted ninety degrees in a matter of seconds, taking the cast more than one hundred feet into the air and making it difficult for traditional camera platforms to keep up. The impressive reach of two Akela cranes and several construction cranes helped complete the sequence.

Jack and Rose struggle past Father Byles, who is holding on to one of the poop deck's giant capstans, reading scripture to his flock. Suddenly, his congregation starts to slide away from him as the angle becomes steeper and steeper. Soon hundreds of bodies are tumbling out of control down the deck, grasping at anything to break their fall. "We had a hundred stuntmen and -women tumbling down the deck for at least ten full takes," says Crane. "That's the equivalent of one person doing a *thousand* such falls. Meticulous planning was crucial."

Once again, study models enabled Cameron and Crane to discuss methodologies months in advance, observing how people might fall and pile up against the deck's various railings and equipment. The scene was somewhat surreal as the two men lifted handfuls of small figurines and dropped them onto the model—a miniature human pinball machine. The exercise also determined how other departments could help the stunt team's efforts: Cameron instructed the art department, for example, to "nerf" the entire set, creating soft foam rubber and break-away duplicates of the heavy capstans, bench supports and superstructure; Wardrobe provided high-traction shoes disguised as appropriate period footwear and the grips devised a way to tilt a gigantic false horizon in the opposite direction of the deck so that a thirty-five-degree angle could be cheated as steeper.

Once the tilting poop deck set became operational, Crane and his team prepared for the sequence by rehearsing at lesser degrees of tilt, videotaping their efforts and rig-

Cameron directs extras in the foreground of a shot that will be extended through the use of green screen, model photography and computer-generated passengers. "Remember, the stern was sticking almost three hundred feet out of the water at one point. Can you imagine shooting that 'real for real' with a thousand extras safety-harnessed onto the railings and with hundreds of stunt men performing free falls? Computers are increasing the visual scale of shots while keeping the physical scale within the realm of feasibility."

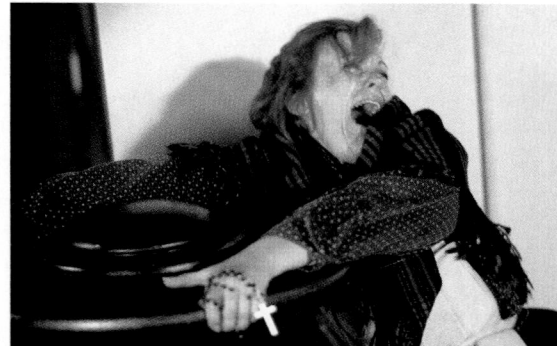

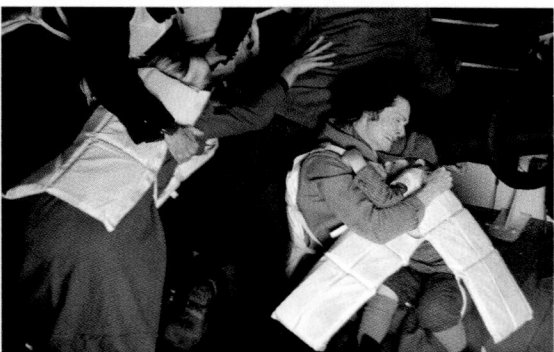

TOP AND CENTER: "Irish Woman" (Linda Kerns) clings to her faith while a steerage mother (Rebecca Klinger) comforts her child.

ABOVE: Stunt coordinator Simon Crane.

LEFT: Stunt people crash down the tilting poop deck.

orously separating what worked from what didn't before sharing the results with Cameron. As rehearsals progressed so did the degree of tilt. A series of marks next to the hydraulics charted the team's progress from ten to ninety degrees (a few degrees beyond ninety, one stuntman humorously added the mark labeled "no fear"). Concurrent with this testing, the stunt team also worked with the Core Extras, fitting them with safety harnesses and making sure they were comfortable working on the tilted set. No extra was allowed on the deck unharnessed if the angle was going to reach thirty degrees or greater. "Thirty degrees of tilt is a lot steeper than you'd imagine," says Crane. "I'd be on the radio asking the effects guys, 'Okay, is that thirty degrees yet? It sure feels like it.' And they'd come back and say, 'No, sorry. We've just hit twenty.'"

As the angle of the set increased, so did the mayhem. For when the deck reached ninety degrees the stunt team rigged several descender rigs on the back side of the poop deck, extending their cables through sheaves embedded in the deck planking. These machines—originally designed to help train paratroopers—allowed up to a dozen stunt people to lose grip of various railings and "fall to their deaths" in a controlled and safe manner, decelerating and stopping rapidly at a preset distance above the ground.

The hull splits down through nine decks to the keel. On the poop deck everyone screams as they feel themselves plummeting. The sound goes up like the roar of fans at a baseball stadium. . . . Jack and Rose struggle to hold on to the stern rail. They feel the ship seemingly RIGHT ITSELF. Some of those praying think it is salvation. "We're saved!" Jack looks at Rose and shakes his head grimly. Now the horrible mechanics play out. . . . [From the screenplay.]

LEFT: "When we flooded the Dining Saloon everything turned to chaos in less than fifteen seconds," recalls Russell Carpenter. "The teacups and china drifted about like little boats. The chairs formed islands in the currents. Resetting for take two was always a real bitch."

CENTER AND BOTTOM: French doors like the ones separating the Reception Area from the first-class Dining Saloon (re-created, center) still stand in the wreck, a haunting portal into a world of chaos and rust (bottom, from Cameron's ROV explorations of the wreck).

"Her whole world is sinking with the ship," observes DiCaprio. "Rose has to choose her old life or risk everything and follow her gut passion. Every decision she has to make is heightened by a thousand." Cameron's tale pits a first-class girl against the labyrinth of flooding rooms and corridors below decks as she searches for her lover. Stage 2 was designed with this very purpose in mind. Built over a five-million-gallon tank the stage utilizes a permanently installed steel lifting truss as its floor. This truss is attached via steel cables to a computerized lifting system called "the riser," which consists of eight cannon-sized hydraulic rams that, working together, can sustain over a million pounds of lift. The riser is the creation of Special Effects Coordinator Thomas L. Fisher, who has provided large-scale mechanical and pyrotechnic effects for Cameron's last two pictures, *Terminator 2: Judgment Day* and *True Lies*. A man of few words, Fisher is likely to scratch the back of his head for a moment in a manner reminiscent of a trusted garage mechanic before offering solutions to problems of a much grander scale. His gruff workingman's appearance makes him stand out all the more amid the Edwardian finery of the first-class Dining Saloon. "What we found," he explains, "is that six degrees of tilt is just enough when working on the interior sets, but that exaggerating it a little bit makes it look even better. The room is a hundred and eighty feet long and if you lower the whole set ten feet into the water at an angle of six degrees the water will only creep halfway up the room. What we were able to do in a couple of instances is fill the tank a little higher, 'bottom out' the set on one end of the riser and lift the other side up more than we'd planned." The sensation is very strange. With no visual clues to indicate the room has started to descend, it is a surprise to see water creeping through the French doors and over the elaborate carpet. A small tidal wave of tables and chairs floats forward as the ceiling and walls start to creak and pop from the strain. The illusion is total . . . and frightening.

While the production was busy shooting on soundstages, construction crews split the 775-foot set into two halves and lowered the front half down into the drained pit of the exterior tank (Stage 1) in preparation for the ship's final curtain call. Now, with the hydraulic rams repositioned at the north end of the tank to raise and lower the ship, the tank flooded to capacity and the cast and crew standing by, the massive *Titanic* exterior seems almost reluctant to repeat history. The ship is sinking far too slowly.

Special Effects Co-Coordinator Scott Fisher explains. "On paper, we always knew that the forward half of the ship was going to be the heaviest set we'd be moving with the riser, so we compensated by installing foam flotation inside the superstructure to keep its weight within safety tolerances. But what we've found in addition to that is that the set is behaving like a hydraulic shock absorber. The pit isn't much bigger than the ship itself and when we lower the set the water doesn't have anywhere to go."

Hip waders, wet suits, and dry suits became acceptable dress code in the flooded first-class interiors. "There were times when we looked like a misplaced group of time-traveling bass fisherman," laughs Cameron, who operates the camera assisted by Assistant Cameraman Kirk Bloom.

One solution presents itself immediately. Satisfied with his coverage showing the flooding on A-deck promenade, Cameron instructs the art department and construction crews to remove large sections of the set's inner walls and steel floor (which is helping to displace as much air as an eighty-foot yacht). The modifications, however, will take a minimum of twenty-four hours and the production is ready to shoot right now. Cameron begins smashing out the A-deck promenade windows in an attempt to increase the set's sinking speed by providing more openings for water to flow through. Having worked so hard to re-create the ship the destruction seems somehow sacrilegious, but Cameron doesn't mind. In fact, he's having fun. "There isn't an engineer in the world who can tell you exactly how this stuff will work because nobody has ever done this before. And when you're shooting nights and you know that God's ten-million-kilowatt light is speeding toward the horizon you either get creative or you give up. I don't give up." Cameron asks Fisher if they can "supercharge" the riser by first lowering the set until A-deck floods, then *lifting* the set with tons of trapped water above the waterline, and then slamming the combined mass back down, giving the whole descent a boost. "If it doesn't work, what do we have to lose?" asks Jim over the radio.

It works.

TOP: Rose races through the third-class labyrinth only to find another locked gate.

CENTER: "There were a few heroes among the stewards who helped third-class passengers find their way to the boat deck," explains Cameron, "but for every hero we know about it's likely there was another guy just 'doing his job' by quietly locking the gates and walking away. In fact, I've seen a handwritten report from one of the stewards that states unequivocally that gates were locked." Here, Tommy Ryan (Jason Barry) makes a plea for compassion: "For God's sake, man! There's women and children down here!"

BOTTOM: The front half of the ship is separated and lowered into the forty-foot pit in preparation for sinking her into the depths again and again via the "riser" hydraulic system. Every aspect of the set's construction was reverse-engineered with an eye toward this final configuration.

Millions of pounds of steel, wood and paint sink below the waves as the hydraulic riser lowers the set into the water. Visually, it is some of the most complex imagery of the show and much of the action can only be discussed before being shot. "The physical stresses were too great to sink the set unless we were rolling film. So you can look at it two ways: either we shot every rehearsal or we never rehearsed," says Cameron and smiles.

ABOVE: "Elegance submerged." The Grand Staircase was lowered at a rate of one foot every second. Ninety thousand gallons of water in overhead dump tanks added to the destruction, crashing through the domed skylight and ripping the staircase from its steel foundations.

RIGHT: Four of the eight hydraulic cylinders that give the riser its muscle.

"In all of these scenes we had to approach the work from an amphibious perspective," observes Russell Carpenter. "Jim gave up nothing in terms of dynamic camera moves just because a set was going underwater. This was especially true for the Grand Staircase because Cameron wanted to show the arrogance of the 'Gilded Age' transformed into visual carnage as the whole thing comes crashing down." Special flotation platforms were constructed. Underwater camera housings were suspended from overhead tracks. A hole was cut into the ceiling as an emergency escape route for James Muro and his Steadicam. Everyone carried an emergency canister of air.

No longer satisfied with a mere six degrees of tilt, Fisher's team cut Stage 2's steel truss in half, leaving the Dining Room behind so they could have better control working with just the Grand Staircase. "This allowed us to move the set faster at a greater degree of tilt," explains Fisher. "At twelve degrees the flooding looked really great." The final touch was the implosion of the elaborate dome skylight that crowns the six-story staircase. Eleven cameras roll as stunt people fight the rising water in a futile attempt to reach safety. On cue, massive cargo containers filled with seawater blow open, their contents crashing through the dome and plunging the set into chaos. Unexpectedly, the waterfall rips the massive staircase from its steel-reinforced foundations though no one is hurt. Cameron comments, "Our staircase broke free and floated to the surface. It's likely that this is exactly what happened during the actual sinking, which would explain why there isn't much of the staircase left in the wreck and why pieces were spotted floating on the surface the morning of the rescue. The matching physics serve as a form of 'proof of concept' in terms of our accuracy," says the director, smiling, "but I'm glad we didn't need a second take."

Cameron discusses the pending Grand Staircase dome implosion with Special Effects Supervisor Thomas L. Fisher. Fisher and his team designed the computerized hydraulics that allowed Cameron to repeatedly sink both the two-million-pound ship exterior and the cavernous interior sets.

ABOVE: The production re-created the millionaire suite and the first-class Reception Area as they appear within the wreck today. "Jim's ROV made it into both areas and the video left us speechless," says Art Director Bill Rhea. The sets were made to film the ROV's search for the Heart of the Ocean, and many felt eerie to be diving the wreck on SCUBA. If there are ghosts on *Titanic*, then this is surely how they move—floating through the corridors, no longer subject to the intense pressure or cold. What do they make of these strange creatures invading their elegant tomb?

LEFT: Producer Jon Landau.

RIGHT: Re-created relics form an impromptu *Titanic* exhibit. Tanned leather survives surprisingly well underwater, unlike most metals or wood. Robert Ballard originally reported that wood-boring organisms had devoured all traces of wood on the wreck, but Cameron's ROV ventured deeper and further into the wreck than ever before to discover the remains of *Titanic*'s ornate woodwork. "The D-deck Reception Area is phenomenal," says Cameron (see page 33). "These strange, glassine, rat-tailed fish swim in and out of the remains of these elegant hand-carved columns. My hypothesis as to why this one area is so well-preserved is that the white paint that decorated the woodwork in this part of the ship contained a high amount of lead and the organisms simply couldn't digest it. And after a few years the wood-eating creatures that penetrated the wreck died off from lack of new food sources."

CENTER AND BOTTOM: Cameron shoots the ROV *Snoop* as it enters Cal and Rose's sitting room for the first time.

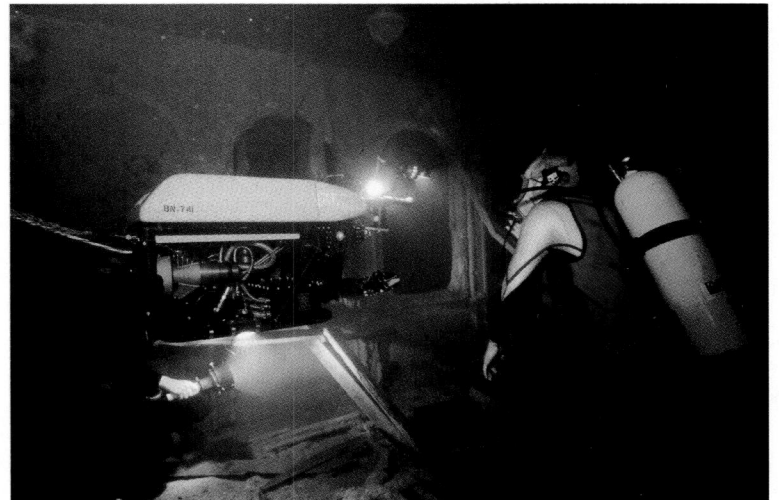

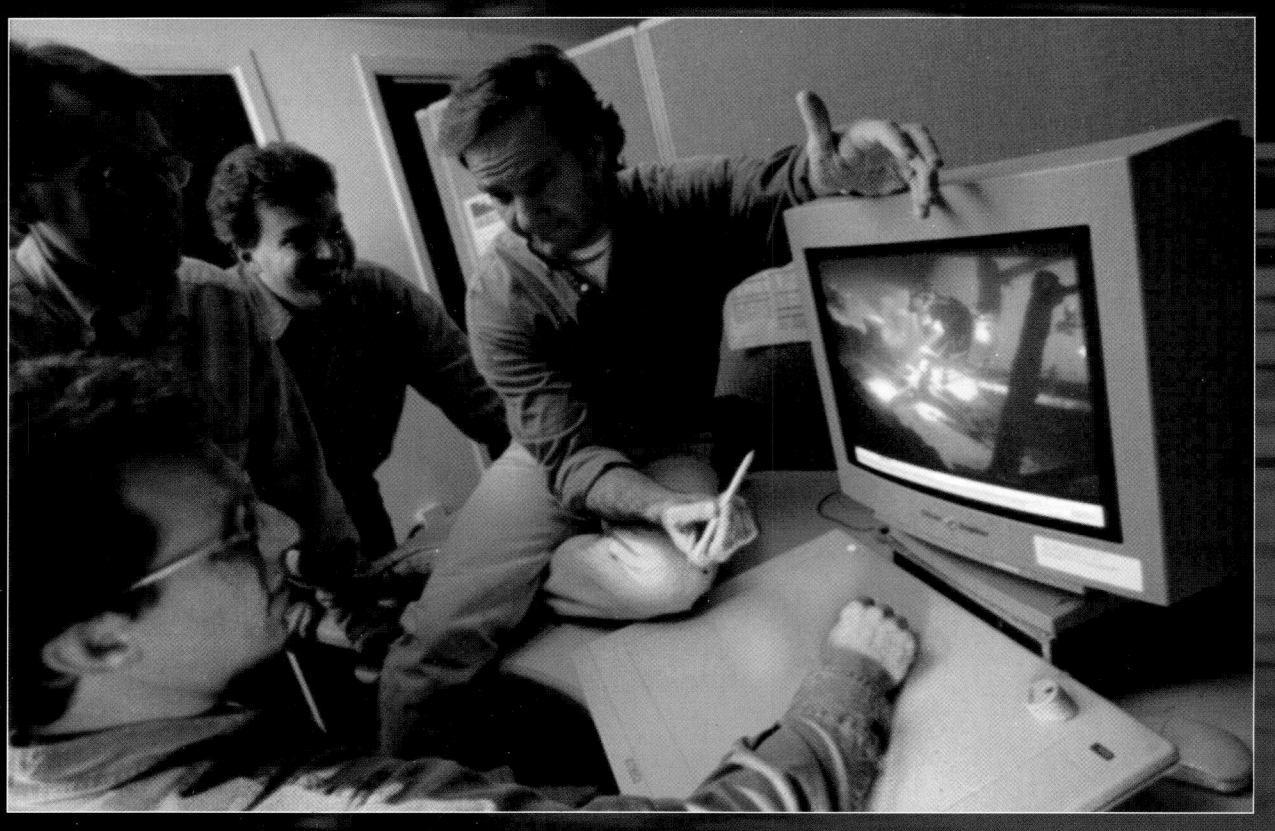

Visual Effects Supervisor Rob Legato leads a discussion with Michael Kanfer, Mark Forker and Mark Lasoff, analyzing footage from the 1995 Deep Dive. Digital Domain has built its reputation largely on effects that do not *look* like effects, including the hyperrealism of *Apollo 13* and *True Lies*. "Anyone can create beautiful images of things we've never seen before," observes Cameron, "but there are relatively few people who can hold the mirror up to reality."

"Cheat the size of the tugboats ten percent smaller," explains Cameron to the model makers, "Nobody will question the scale and it will make the ship look even more majestic as it leaves Southampton." The model shop at Digital Domain is starting to look like a miniature version of Harland and Wolff's shipyard, circa 1912. And yet, one cannot help but wonder. . . *models*?! Wasn't that the problem with the *Titanic* movies of the fifties as filmmakers cut from teary-eyed close-ups of the survivors to a wide shot of the lifeless miniature slipping gently beneath the waves amid dry-ice bubbles and little wind-up lifeboats?

"Digital technology is allowing us to approach model photography in a new way," explains Jon Landau. "The problem with water is that it simply doesn't scale down for work with miniatures. In the past the way around that  involved shooting everything in slow motion, which helped turn ripples into waves and gave the model a greater sense of mass, but the technique has never been terribly convincing." Cameron feels that the eye knows when it's being fooled even if it doesn't know why, and he strives hard to keep "unreality" from ever entering his frame. For *The Abyss*, he commissioned a surface miniature of such a vast scale that it required a Coast Guard license to film in the open ocean. The water looked real, but there was very little control over the photography. "What we're doing on this show," says Landau, "is placing our model of the pristine *Titanic* on a green-screen stage and shooting it with a motion-control camera. We can then computer generate (CG) our ocean into any sort of amazing helicopter shot we create, and the water will scale perfectly." Realistic digital water came, in part, from an unexpected source—the defense industry. "These scientists were trying to find a way to track and identify ships and submarines from satellites by analyzing the ocean's surface and the wake patterns these ships were generating. That's all they did for years—study the motion of water," explains Landau. "And what they developed is an algorithm that told them how the ocean behaved normally and how it behaved in the presence of these vessels." Adapting that algorithm into a "rendering" engine capable of responding to the nine-hundred-foot hull of the ship as it presses through the water was no simple task, and individual frames have taken several hours to render. The results, however, have been well worth the effort. The *Titanic* sails forward, her hull slicing through the cold, unforgiving Atlantic, her decks populated with passengers and crew. The technology of the future has opened a powerful window on to the past. "The water looks great," adds Landau, "but the real key to these model shots are all of the computer-generated people we're adding."

"The shot's almost there," says Visual Effects Supervisor Rob Legato proudly as he watches one of the early effects shots of the ship under way. "We show it to people involved in the effects industry and ask them to point out which of the

RIGHT: Eric Nash makes adjustments to a camera move over the wreck model.

BOTTOM: Legato on the motion-control stage with the forty-five-foot *Titanic* model. Legato had his face and the faces of his children "cyber-scanned" to join the library of digital people who will populate the decks. "I know, I know. I'm a horrible father to put my own kids on the ship I have to sink. I promise you they will survive."

OPPOSITE: "This is the beginning of the coolest sequence of the movie," says Legato, who has been charged with making the demise of the great ship live up to her name. The sixty-five-foot stern was constructed by Don Pennington, Inc., and is the only model to see extensive use in water. "The scale absolutely forces you to shoot like it's the real thing."

actors are CG, and they have trouble guessing. They say, 'Maybe those three.' Of course, everybody in the shot is CG, so we're very happy." Using motion capture technology to record a performer's unique movements is an established technique, as is re-creating an actor's face and physical form in the digital realm. (Cameron pioneered several techniques for *Terminator 2: Judgment Day* that have since become industry standards.) But using these tools in tandem to populate life-

less model shots with CG human beings (including principal actors) is a major advance in the process that has never been seen before. On a semi-darkened stage, performers wearing black tights and a series of round reference markers not unlike Ping-Pong balls perform various actions inside an all-seeing ring of infrared-sensitive cameras: walking up a ramp and waving good-bye; struggling up the boat deck of the rapidly sinking ship; children

In lifeboat number two, which is just off the stern, passengers gape as the giant bronze propellers rise out of the water like gods from the deep, filling frame behind them. [From the screenplay.] The lifeboat and its occupants were shot in a tank against green screen and digitally composited into a shot of the ⅛th-scale *Titanic*'s propellers.

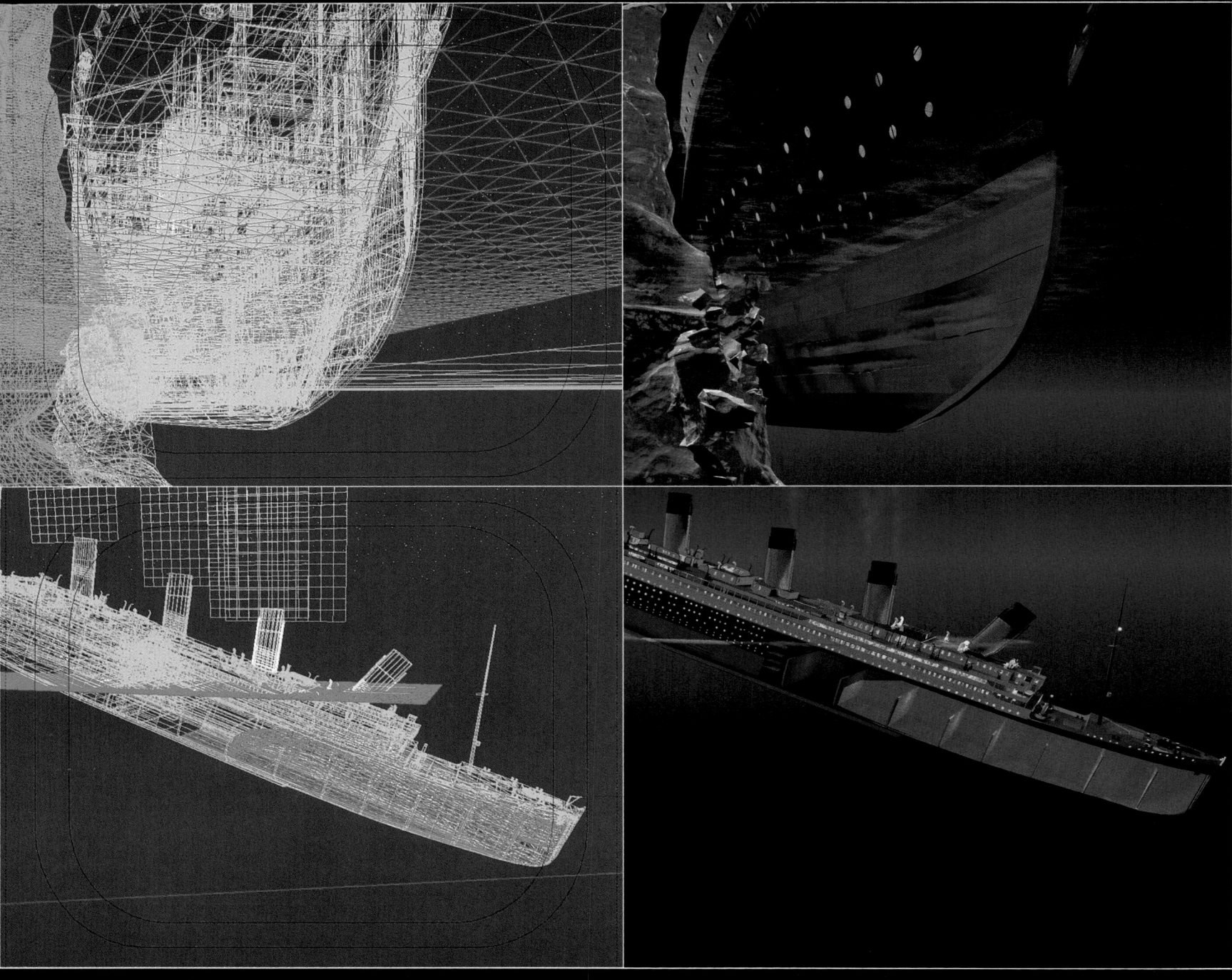

*Bodine starts a COMPUTER-ANIMATED GRAPHIC on the screen, which parallels his rapid-fire narration. "She hits the berg on the starboard side and it sort of bumps along. . . punching holes like a Morse code. . . *dit dit dit, *down the side. Now she's flooding in the forward compartments. . . and the water spills over the tops of the bulkheads, going aft. As her bow is going down, her stern is coming up. . . slow at first. . . and then faster and faster until it's lifting all that weight, maybe twenty or thirty thousand* tons. . . *out of the water and the hull can't deal. . . so* SKRTTT*!! It splits! Right down to the keel, which acts like a big hinge. Now the bow swings down and the stern falls back level. . . but the weight of the bow pulls the stern up vertical, and then the bow section detaches, heading for the bottom. The stern bobs like a cork, floods and goes under about 2:20 a.m. Two hours and forty minutes after the collision. . . . Pretty cool, huh?"* [From the screenplay.]

This simulation was created by Digital Domain's NY group on PC computers utilizing as much factual data about the sinking as possible. "I wanted to set up the forensics of the sinking in detail at the start of the movie because once we're experiencing it with Jack and Rose I didn't want to have to step back from the action," explains Cameron. "Nobody on the ship knew everything that was happening. We've only pieced it together over decades and a lot of it is just a well-connected series of educated guesses. I've often wished there was a black box recorder." Interestingly, Cameron's depiction was validated by a 1996 expedition to the wreck, which used ground-penetrating imaging techniques to peer below the silt and inspect the iceberg's damage to the hull. "Three long openings and three short openings; just like the Morse code analogy I put into the dialogue."

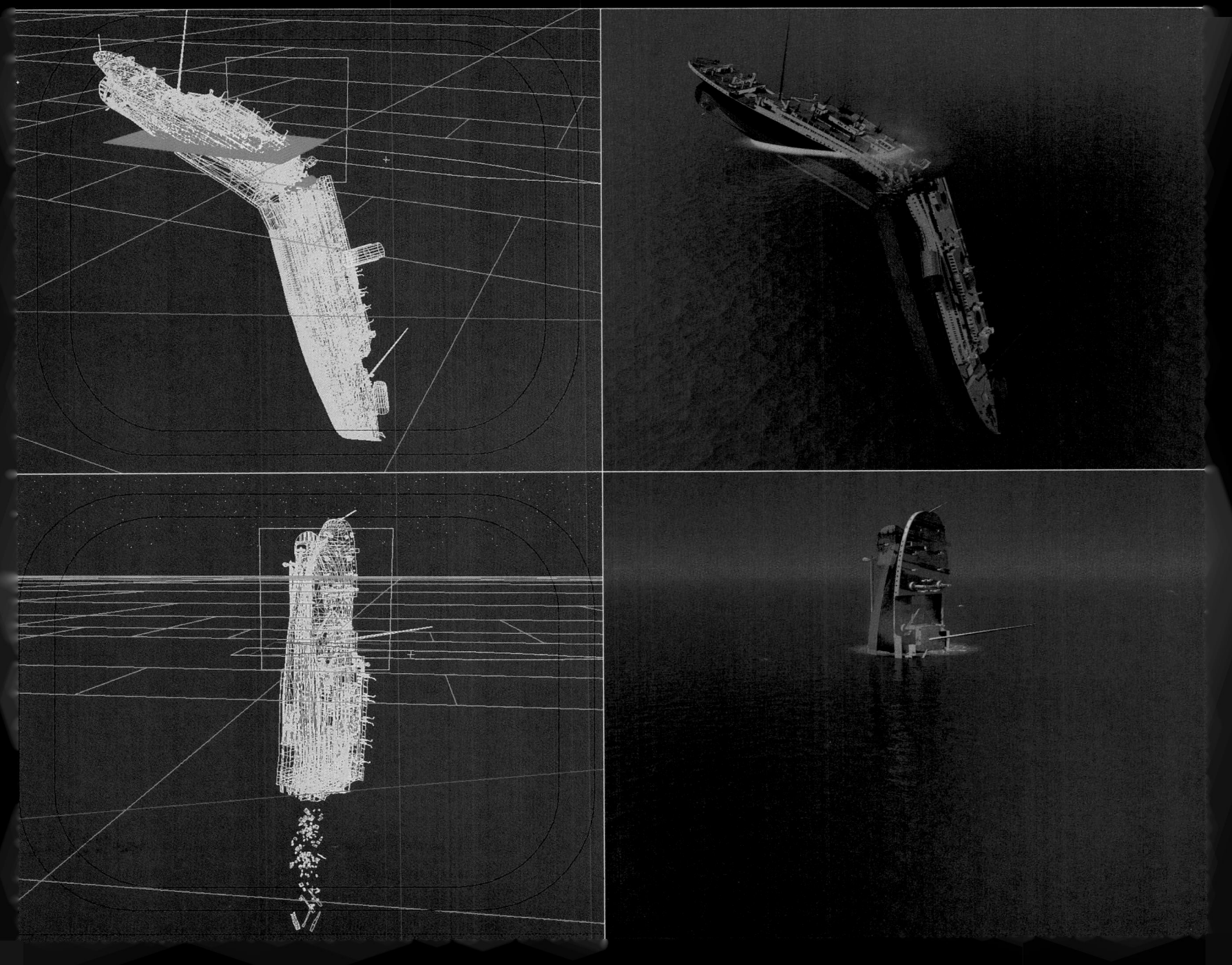

"Indian wrestling" on a staircase. The smallest motions of the human body are recorded in the unbounded virtual space of the computer, a breath of life for the digitally re-created person—Frankenstein on a floppy. "It's ironic that the only way to portray this chapter from the industrial era in all of its life and glory is with the digital technology of today," observes Legato. "We built this giant ship and the only way to sail her in certain shots is with the aid of a microprocessor small enough to fit in my palm."

Sail her . . . and sink her. Digital Domain provided its fair share of the chaos. Don Pennington, Inc., was commissioned to build a special sixty-five-foot model of the stern that could break in two repeatedly and descend below the waves. Digital Effects Supervisor Mark Lasoff and his team now face the task of populating this model with CG "victims," and are creating a growing library of faces, bodies and motion-captured action with which to work, a process that has involved every department, from Casting to Wardrobe to Stunts. "We motion-captured some falls from a height of about forty feet," recalls Simon Crane. "They were very tame falls, basically, but Digital Domain will use that information to create several people falling from a height of two hundred feet or more and smashing into things on the way down. Each department has its strengths, but working together allows us to extend the palette of what's possible."

"The film is primarily a kind of 'you are there' experience, involving the sinking of the *Titanic* in the presence of a very powerful love story. That's the goal," elaborates Cameron. "And we're using these big effects—computer-driven motion-control cameras, motion-capture systems, models and everything else—to create moments that function on an emotional level. The technology itself *has* to be invisible." Respected for pushing the technological envelope, Cameron also knows when to play it safe. He would not risk an important emotional climax in the film to the CG performances of a digital Leo or Kate. Instead, the actors now stand on the bow of the ship as it floats in a green-screen void. When they embrace, the whine of electric servo-motors kicks in and the motion-controlled camera retraces its exacting path. (The move was originally executed over the 1/20th-scale model of the ship and then scaled up to photograph the actors.) While everything around them is artificial, Leo and Kate's kiss is very real. "Throwing actors into a visual-effects setup before they've had a chance to connect with the scene is dangerous," remarks Cameron. "You may not get the full chromatic response good performers can create under the right circumstances. I've always found it's better to shoot the real situation first because an actor's reality comes from the inside out. Kate and Leo have kissed on the bow, and they've been fifty feet above the ocean and they've felt the wind in their hair. They know where they are both physically and emotionally and it keeps the moment alive."

LEFT: **Having saved himself, Ismay turns away from the inevitable. The American press condemned Ismay as an opportunistic coward, an accusation that followed him until his death in 1937.**

OPPOSITE: **Death throws of a Titan. The violent physics of the sinking (reenacted using the 1/8th-scale model) achieve a truly tragic dimension as visual effects artists composite hundreds of CGI passengers clinging to the railing and falling off the decks. In the script, Cameron describes the monstrous impact of the falling stern as "God's boot heel."**

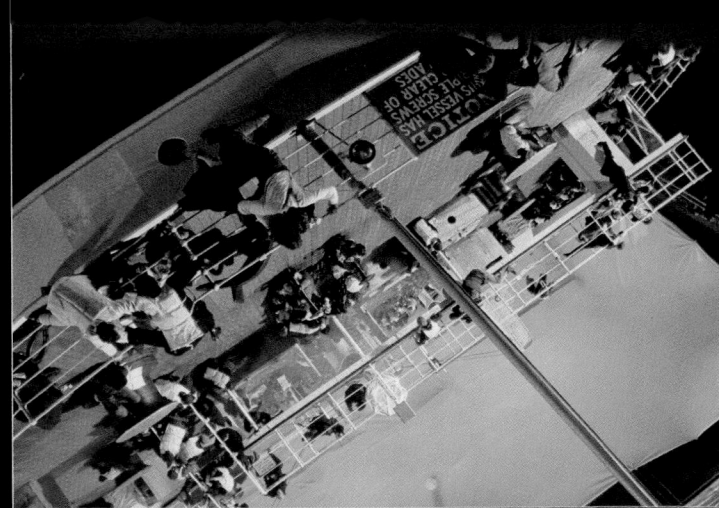

LEFT AND ABOVE: Technically an effects shot, the situation is still very real as Kate and Leo ride the tilting poop deck high above the ground. In addition to the ocean, Digital Domain added figures plunging to their deaths by combining motion-captured stunt data with surface textures and cyberscans.

BELOW: Stunt performer Joey Box bounces over the deck railing while infrared cameras track reference markers on his body. The stunt is recorded as three-dimensional data and will be utilized for the digital crowds that populate many of the effects shots.

Some jump, some fall, each dotting the water's surface like the period at the end of a sentence. Then, the stern slips under the water, plunging everyone into a coldness so intense it is indistinguishable from fire. Ten minutes. Twenty minutes. The inchoate wail of fifteen hundred souls slowly fades to individual cries from the darkness. *We know you can hear us! Save one life!* Seven hundred survivors stand by in lifeboats built for twelve hundred, afraid to act for fear of getting swamped. They tell themselves that the voices from the water do not belong to their husbands or their loved ones. They are merely the cries of the damned. "In all reality I think they believed that the people in the lifeboats would row back and rescue them," observes DiCaprio.

Cameron is pointing his lens into the dark heart of the *Titanic* myth, a place that more romantic interpretations of the legend have chosen to avoid. For as grand and tragic as the demise of the great ship was, it cannot compare with the cold, cold hell that followed. Cameras roll and the tank erupts in a whitewater of screaming, thrashing bodies. Men in tuxedos fight for scraps of floating debris. A third-class woman holds her baby above the fray (survivors will later see her frozen form bumping gently against the base of an iceberg, still clutching the infant in her

Cameron and crew members analyze playback from a scene in Tank 4. "Water adds a level of difficulty to every human endeavor," says Cameron, who is dealing with such varied concerns as crane movement, the positioning of a false horizon to replicate the open ocean, artificial wave machines, the lighting of an event in history during which there was technically *no* light and the well-being of sixty to seventy extras who, like the crew, spend most of their day floating in the water.

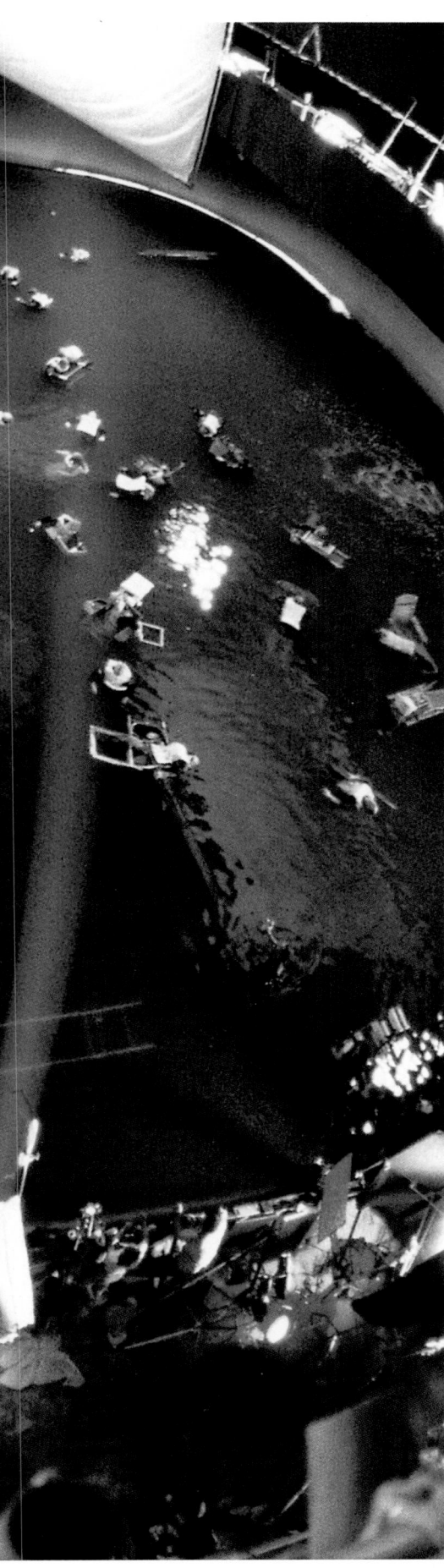

hands). On cue, Rose bursts to the surface in a flurry of air bubbles and joins the chaos. Jack is nowhere to be seen when suddenly a drowning man shoves her underwater in an attempt to save himself. Reviewing the take later, Kate smiles. "I've never acted underwater before. I'll have to put that on my résumé.

"It didn't really hit me until I'd stepped out of the tank for a while and watched a shot I wasn't in," remembers Winslet. "I cupped my hands around my eyes to block out all of the equipment and it looked so damn real. I had to cover my eyes."

Frances Fisher had a different reaction when observing a later portion of the same scene. "I remember watching the lifeboat push its way through the frozen bodies. Then Josh yelled, 'Cut! Fifteen-minute bathroom break!' and the corpses all got up and climbed out of the tank. Between setups they sat around talking in the hot tubs with their icy hair and frozen blue faces and fingernails. It was quite surreal."

"One of the problems with these scenes photographically is that historically there was absolutely no light other than starlight," explains Cameron. "It was a new moon. The stars were certainly brilliant, but what we've created is what I call the 'light of the mind,' a subtle, shadowless illumination that allows us to see action and emotion and photograph it unobtrusively. It's a tough call because you don't really know how far you can push it before the audience begins to question it. I've also added flashlights

LEFT: At a mere 350,000 gallons, Tank 4 is the smallest shooting tank created for the production. In this scene, lifeboat number fourteen makes its way slowly through bodies and debris.

BELOW: Cameron paints a mental picture for the passengers in Collapsible C (note the canvas sides). "With effects it can be hard to convey what's happening to the uninitiated. It helps to spell it out, like baseball on the radio."

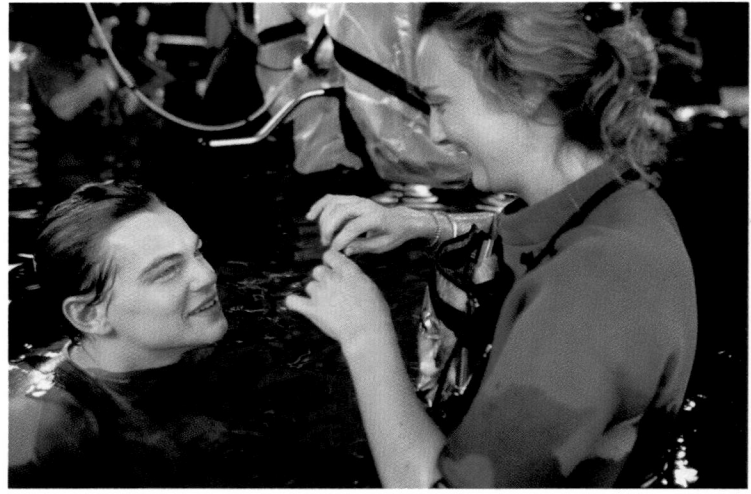

TOP: Cameron discusses the scene with Winslet and DiCaprio.

ABOVE AND RIGHT: Makeup Artists Sian Griegg (above) and Tina Earnshaw (right) keep Jack and Rose looking cold and miserable. Pool chemicals kept washing off the "waterproof" makeup.

to some of the lifeboats. It's one of our few historical inaccuracies but we have to light the scenes *somehow*."

Lifeboat number six was lowered from the port side of the ship with only twenty-eight on board. Cameron placed his fictional Ruth next to Molly Brown and used both characters as the "eyes" for the tragedy, painting complex word pictures for the actresses while he filmed their reactions. Now he has returned to the lifeboat to capture the emotional paralysis that prevented passengers from attempting rescues. "It's a brave thing to go back," says Cameron to Kathy Bates. "Molly wanted to go back. She did not care about getting swamped because there was no room for fear in her heart at that time, but she was overruled." Standing defiantly in the bottom of the boat, Molly confronts Quartermaster Hichens (Paul Brightwell), who has been instilling fear and pessimism for the better part of an hour, and admonishes her fellow passengers. "*I don't understand a one of you. It's your men back there!*" The oars remain motionless in the water.

Survivor Lawrence Beesley wrote: "Whoever reads the account of the cries that came to us afloat on the sea from those sinking in the ice-cold water must remember that they were addressed to him just as much as to those who heard them." Beesley's text continues to call for reforms that did, in fact, occur. For Frances Fisher, however, the reforms were too little, too late. "It was a disaster that didn't need to happen. It was about thinking with the ego instead of with the heart. And above all it was about arrogance. God is greater

Fifth Officer Lowe (Ioan Gruffudd, above) was the only
officer to return after the sinking and search for survivors.
Lowe and his crew saved three of the fifteen hundred souls
who went into the below-freezing water that night. Most of
Titanic's victims did not drown; they froze to death.

than all of us, and if you are so arrogant as to say something is unsinkable, you will get slapped in the face."

As the work progresses to the later part of the scene, the extras stand in a semicircle around Cameron as he outlines the stages of hypothermia. "Remember, the ocean water was below freezing, probably twenty-nine or thirty degrees. At a certain point, your shivering will stop and all of the blood will concentrate in your most vital organs. It's supposedly a very peaceful feeling." Nearby, Kate floats on a piece of debris, her face turned up to where the stars would be shining furiously (if this were the North Atlantic), encasing her in a bowl of night. Her cassette player is whispering Gregorian chants into her ears while makeup and hair artists coat her hair with ice-colored wax, freezing her bright red tresses to the surface of the wood.

Leo holds her hand, waiting patiently.

ABOVE: Collapsible A literally floated off the boat deck as the ship sank beneath it. Despite Cal's best efforts, more than a dozen survivors made it into the partially swamped boat after the ship had sunk.

RIGHT: Rose and Jack are reunited on the ocean's surface after the *Titanic*'s final death plunge.

She grips his hand and they lie with their heads together. It is quiet now, except for the lapping of the water. [From the screenplay.]

"One thing that's very important to me in life is, through having a relationship with somebody and loving that person and being allowed to feel the *whole* emotion of love despite all of the risks, you can find out who you are," observes Winslet. "And when Rose meets Jack she cuts through all of the class and money nonsense and connects with something real and alive and passionate in his soul. And when I read the script I was in floods of tears, because it takes you to the point where you would do anything— *absolutely anything*—to stop that ship from sinking."

EPILOGUE

On March 31, 1909, workers at Harland and Wolff began laying the keel for what would come to be called the unsinkable ship. Eighty-eight years later to the day, workers are dismantling the last traces of her cinematic twin, scrapping her parts for steel.

And yet, driving back to Los Angeles past the San Onofre nuclear power plant—built on the coastline of the earthquake capital of the world—one wonders if the old canoe has taught us its final lesson. In a line of dialogue that Cameron cut from the script before shooting began, Old Rose admonished Brock, "There's another iceberg out there, Mr. Lovett. I don't know what it is . . . but I *do* know the force driving us toward it."

Memories roll through time like the tide, echoing into the present. Old Rose finds herself on the stern of the *Keldysh*, floating two-and-a-half miles above the ship—and the life—she was rescued from long ago.

In a quiet moment of reflection Cameron mentions, "I sometimes wish I lived in a world where the *Titanic* was never a famous ship." Cast and crew would certainly agree, though it would mean never having come together to create something so opulent, so grand or so terrifying. For six months, thousands of artists and craftsmen willed the rust-fallen leviathan from its icy tomb and made it new again. Fragments of 1912 floated through the present like icebergs on the North Atlantic. How will they describe what they have seen?

It was a time of constant wonderment . . .

BELOW: "That's a good idea, Alex, but just so you know, I'm not going to share my directing credit with you."

CENTER: Documentary Director Ed Marsh with celebrity guest cameraman.

RIGHT: One of Russell Carpenter's reference Polaroids catches Kate and Leo out on a limb. Leo: "Every day we'd find ourselves in some weird situation and I'd turn to Kate and ask, 'How the hell did we get ourselves into this one?'"

A photo book cannot hope to contain everybody's contributions to a film of this magnitude—that's what the film itself is for—but I would like to specially thank the entire cast and crew for giving freely of their impressions. Six months is a long time to spend in a leaky boat with anybody but it was never unpleasant with so many friends around. I would also like to thank: my transcription team, Caroline L. Martinez and Danny Accomando; Historians Don Lynch, Ken Marschall, Ed and Karen Kamuda of the *Titanic* Historical Society (if there are factual errors regarding the ship or her passengers they cannot be held responsible); Geoff Burdick for his willingness and ability to dive into a project with fresh eyes; Kathy Grant, Carol Henry, Nancy Hobson, Al Rives, Mike Trainotti, Kim Troy and Ian Unterreiner of Lightstorm Entertainment for their help and support; Documentary Director of Photography Anders Falk for his second set of excellent eyes and ears; Jain Lemos, Joel Avirom, Meghan Day Healey and William Rus for their patience; Eileen Peterson for contributions too varied to list; Douglas Kirkland and Merie Wallace for their beautiful images; Jim Cameron, Rae Sanchini and Jon Landau for the once in a lifetime opportunity; and friends and family for their love and support; including Ree, who saw the iceberg coming and knew exactly what to do. —Ed W. Marsh

Special thanks to:

Charlie Arneson

Carole Bidnick

Paul Bishop

Elizabeth Bortz

Scott Browning

Johnny Buzzerino

David Carriere

Irmelin DiCaprio

Clay-Edward Dixon

Fernanda Echeverria

Ken Fund

Melissa Germaine

Marta Hallett

Bob Hoffman

Françoise Kirkland

Tom Lay

David le Vey

Michael McCaughan

Susan McDonough

Sandy Miller

Joseph Montebello

Patti O'Reilly

John Pemberton

Eileen Peterson

Amanda Roth

Jennifer Sebree

Amanda Selling

Joan Shepard

Studio Photo Service

Ulster Folk & Transport Museum

The *Virginian-Pilot*

Dianne Walber

George Wright

ABOVE: "How am I doing?" asks Leo. Cameron wryly responds, "Well, you know. It's only your first day. We can always recast."

LEFT: "Mmfff." A young acting coach makes adjustments to Kate's diction.

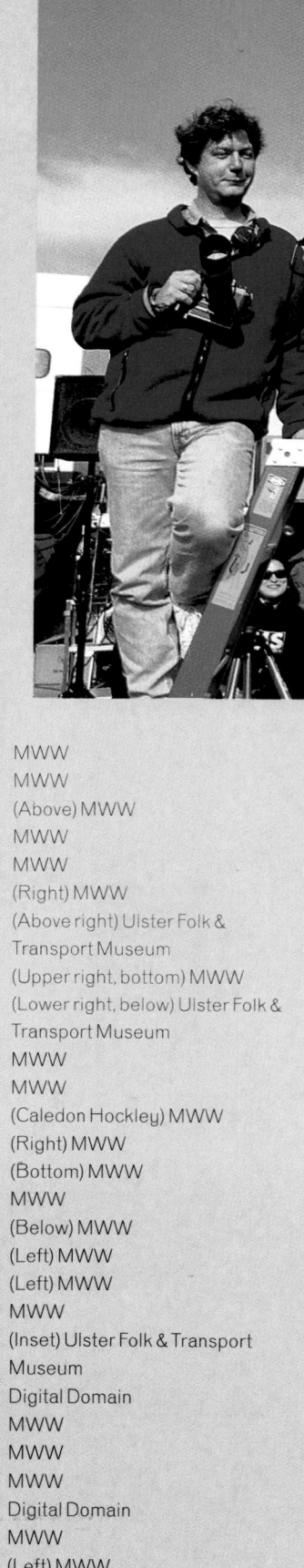

TOP: The photographic record of the real *Titanic* is largely incomplete. Not so on this project. Left to right: Tal Wallace, Unit Photographer Merie Wallace, Documentary Director of Photography Anders Falk, Photographer Douglas Kirkland, Project Editor Jain Lemos, and Polaroid enthusiast Billy Zane.

ABOVE: Photograph of David Warner at Southampton Pier by Billy Zane.

RIGHT: First Assistant Director Josh McLaglen with Jim Cameron and several pounds of radio communications gear. "I'm convinced that wireless communication is the next step in the evolution of human consciousness and that Josh and I are a couple of early mutations," jokes Cameron.

BELOW: Here's looking at you. Director of Photography Russell Carpenter (front row, left of slate) poses with many (but not all) members of the film's camera department.

Gloria Stuart shares a relaxing moment with Cameron on the set of Rose's Malibu home. "Shall we get back to the living hell we call film production?" he asks. "Well, the answer to that, of course, is 'It's a living,'" replies Stuart. When asked about her work on the project, she is thoughtful. "I don't think I'll act after this. After all the years and all my films, this one is the frosting on the cake."

Gifted

lovely little things
to knit + crochet

Gifted

lovely little things
to knit + crochet

mags kandis

 INTERWEAVE.
interweavestore.com

EDITOR
Ann Budd

ART DIRECTOR
Liz Quan

COVER & INTERIOR DESIGN
Pamela Norman

PHOTOGRAPHY
Joe Hancock

STYLISTS
Linda Takaha, Pamela Chavez

PRODUCTION
Katherine Jackson

Interweave Press LLC
201 East Fourth Street
Loveland, CO 80537
interweavestore.com

Printed in China by Asia Pacific Offset Ltd.

Library of Congress Cataloging-in-Publication Data

Kandis, Mags.
 Gifted : lovely little things to knit and crochet / Mags Kandis.
    p. cm.
 Includes index.
 ISBN 978-1-59668-178-1 (pbk.)
 1. Knitting--Patterns. 2. Crocheting--Patterns. 3. Felt work. I.
Title.

 TT820.K259 2010
 677'.02824--dc22

                2009053371

10 9 8 7 6 5 4 3 2 1

acknowledgments

I am grateful to all who contributed—big and small—
to making *Gifted* a reality.

Our fiber-filled lives would be lacking without lovely
yarns in luscious colors and thrilling textures. It was a
pleasure to work with some of the best yarns from the
best manufacturers. Without their collective passion for
knitting and crocheting, very few of us would be inspired
to create with needles and hooks.

It is only with the support, guidance, and generosity of
Ann Budd, Tricia Waddell, and all involved at Interweave
that my ideas have appeared on these pages as beauti-
fully as they have.

Ultimately, I wish to thank all the people in my life who
inspire me everyday to make and to share—family,
co-workers, friends, neighbors, friends of friends, and
even neighbors of neighbors! They are all **my** gift, and for
them I am most thankful.

contents

i love making stuff,

AND ONE OF MY GREATEST JOYS as a knitter and crocheter is to make special stuff for friends and family. I admit to a few late nights and more than one last-minute frenzied button-attaching session over the years. But ultimately, the expression of delight on the face of the "gifted" always makes it worth the effort.

While assembling the gifts in this book, I explored fun, quick, satisfying knitted and crocheted projects as well as simple recycled sewing ideas. The sewn projects are all crafted in whole or in part with scraps of felted knitting, be it repurposed machine-made sweaters that fell victim to moths (see the felted and stitched Arm Cozies on page 27) or a felting project that did not come out as envisioned (see the Cut-and-Sew Egg Cozies on page 105). In addition, I've included a few of my favorite treats from the kitchen. Who wouldn't enjoy a spicy Mexican Hot Chocolate mix (page 81) or a jar of refreshingly zippy and versatile Ginger Syrup (page 37)?

The projects in this book are organized in two groups. Gifts for the Body include wearable projects that are as easy as they are appealing. The Precious Baby Jacket (page 42), for example, is a simple first-knit for a baby embellished with cheerful appliqué and stitching. The Gilded Mesh Scarf (page 52) works up in a flash and is better than jewelry for a scarf junkie. The Granny Bag (page 30) is my interpretation of an old favorite with a hidden word of encouragement. The projects in Gifts for the Soul include a wide range of nonwearables, from Felted Heart Milagros (page 82), which are lovely on their own, in groups, or strung in a hanging, to a one-of-a-kind Scissor Sleeve and Heart Pincushion (page 110) to a bouquet of Colorful Crochet Flowers (page 90).

Don't be intimidated if a project calls for a technique that's unfamiliar—everything is clearly explained in the instructions and illustrated in the Glossary. And because they are small, the projects are ideal for learning and practicing new techniques. You can learn to felt with the Felted Trivet and Coasters (page 114), gain confidence with crochet with the Crochet Flower Brooch (page 47), practice intarsia colorwork with the Heart-in-Hand Mitts (page 68), explore and expand your sense of color with a Bevy of Bangles (page 62), master short-rows with the Ruby Foo Baby Cap (page 28), and perfect your embroidery with Felted Yule Bling (page 106).

I hope the projects on these pages inspire you to grab hook, needles, or spoon and share the joy of giving . . . even if you're giving to yourself!

✳ mags

gifts for the body

They warm hands, wrap necks, top heads, and toast up toes. Always a combination of function and form with a big sprinkle of personal style. Make someone warmer, add colored roses to their hair, or hug them with a scarf.

simple ribbed cap

FINISHED SIZE

About 19¾" (50 cm) circumference, slightly stretched. Will comfortably fit up to 22" (56 cm) circumference.

YARN

Chunky weight (#5 Bulky).

Shown here: Plymouth Yarn Baby Alpaca Grande (100% baby alpaca; 110 yd [100 m]/100 g): #403 gray heather, 1 skein.

NEEDLES

Size U.S. 10½ (6.5 mm): 4 or 5 double-pointed (dpn). Adjust needle size if necessary to obtain the correct gauge.

NOTIONS

Marker (m); tapestry needle.

GAUGE

13 stitches and 17 rounds = 4" (10 cm) in k3, p5 ribbing, slightly stretched.

100% alpaca guarantees two things—super softness and super warmth. Spun nice and thick, it becomes a triple threat when the project is super fast. This cap has it all— simple to make, simple to gift, and simple to wear. For a girlie gift, add a Colorful Crochet Flower (page 90), or two, to introduce color to an otherwise dreary winter day. Package the hat ***au natural,*** and the guy on your list will be toasty warm.

CAP

Loosely CO 64 sts. Place marker (pm) and join for working in rnds, being careful not to twist sts. Work in k3, p5 rib until piece measures 5" (12.5 cm).

Shape Crown

RND 1 *K2, ssk, p4; rep from *—56 sts rem.

RNDS 2 AND 3 *K3, p4; rep from *.

RND 4 *K2, ssk, p3; rep from *—48 sts rem.

RNDS 5 AND 6 *K3, p3; rep from *.

RND 7 *K2, ssk, p2; rep from *—40 sts rem.

RNDS 8 AND 9 *K3, p2; rep from *.

RND 10 *K2, ssk, p1; rep from *—32 sts rem.

RNDS 11 AND 12 *K3, p1; rep from *.

RND 13 *K2, ssk; rep from *—24 sts rem.

RNDS 14 AND 15 Knit.

RND 16 *K2tog; rep from *—12 sts rem.

RND 17 Knit.

RND 18 *K2tog; rep from *—6 sts rem.

Work rem 6 sts in I-cord (see Glossary) for 3½" (9 cm). BO all sts.

FINISHING

Weave in loose ends. Tie I-cord in an overhand knot.

linen summer wrap

Just like summer living, the knitting should be easy. This soft linen-blend wrap is a great treat that takes just a couple of evenings to create. Grab two skeins of yarn, follow the pattern while increasing merrily away until the tail of the first ball is uncomfortably close to your needles, then add the second ball and decrease to the other end. Voilà, a quick wrap with only a few inches of leftover yarn.

WRAP

CO 2 sts.

Work increase pattern (see Stitch Guide) until there are 40 sts, ending with Row 6 of patt—piece measures about 28½" (72.5 cm) from CO. Work decrease pattern (see Stitch Guide) until 2 sts rem, ending with Row 4 of patt. Loosely BO all sts.

FINISHING

Weave in loose ends. Block lightly if desired.

NEEDLES

Size U.S. 10½ (6.5 mm): straight. Adjust needle size if necessary to obtain the correct gauge.

NOTIONS

Tapestry needle.

GAUGE

13 stitches and 16 rows = 4" (10 cm) in pattern stitch.

cabled boot toppers

FINISHED SIZE
About 8" (20.5 cm) circumference, slightly stretched, and 8" (20.5 cm) long.

YARN
Sportweight (#2 Fine).

Shown here: Berroco Ultra Alpaca Light (50% alpaca, 50% wool; 144 yd [133 m]/50 g): #4294 turquoise heather, 2 skeins.

NEEDLES
Size U.S. 5 (3.75 mm): set of 5 double-pointed (dpn). Adjust needle size if necessary to obtain the correct gauge.

NOTIONS
Marker (m); cable needle (cn); tapestry needle.

GAUGE
32 stitches and 30 rows = 4" (10 cm) in k2, p2 rib, worked in rounds, slightly stretched.

I have always found it a shame that once boot weather starts, pretty handknit socks are sadly hidden until the next sock-showing season. Boot toppers are my answer to this problem. Let the boots hide the store-bought socks and allow the lushness of cables and frilly edges peek out where they can be enjoyed. Wrists a tad chilly? These can also be slipped over the hands to peek out from under coat sleeves. Add a Felted Leaf Brooch (page 23) for added flair.

STITCH GUIDE

RT Knit the second stitch on the left-hand needle, then knit the first stitch, then slip both sts off the needle.

T6R Slip next 4 sts (2 knit sts and 2 purl sts) onto cn and hold in back of work, k2, sl the 2 purl sts from cn onto left-hand needle and purl these 2 sts, k2 from cn.

T6L Slip next 4 sts (2 knit sts and 2 purl sts) onto cn and hold in front of work, k2, sl the 2 purl sts from cn onto left-hand needle and purl these 2 sts, k2 from cn.

BOOT TOPPER

Loosely CO 64 sts. Arrange sts evenly on 4 dpn, place marker (pm), and join for working in rnds, being careful not to twist sts. Work in k2, p2 rib until piece measures 4" (10 cm) from CO. Work cable as foll:

RNDS 1, 5, 7, AND 11 *RT (see Stitch Guide), p2, [k2, p2] 3 times; rep from *.

RND 2, 4, 6, 8, 10, AND 12 *K2, p2; rep from *.

RND 3 *RT, p2, T6R (see Stitch Guide), p2, k2, p2; rep from *.

RND 9 *RT, p2, k2, p2, T6L (see Stitch Guide), p2; rep from *.

Rep Rnds 1–12 for a total of 30 rnds (ending with Rnd 6)—piece measures about 8" (20.5 cm) from CO. BO in fringe as foll: BO 2 sts, *sl st from right-hand needle onto left-hand needle, use the cable method (see Glossary) to CO 3 sts, BO 5 sts; rep from *.

FINISHING

Weave in loose ends. Lightly steam.

✳ CABLED BOOT TOPPERS CHART

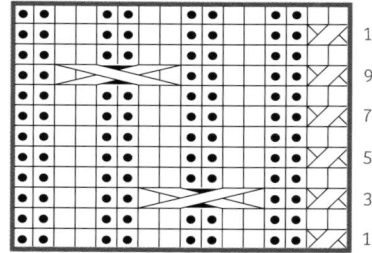

☐ knit

• purl

▧ RT: see Stitch Guide

T6R: see Stitch Guide

T6L: see Stitch Guide

☐ pattern repeat

SEE PAGE 23 FOR
THE FELTED LEAF
BROOCH.

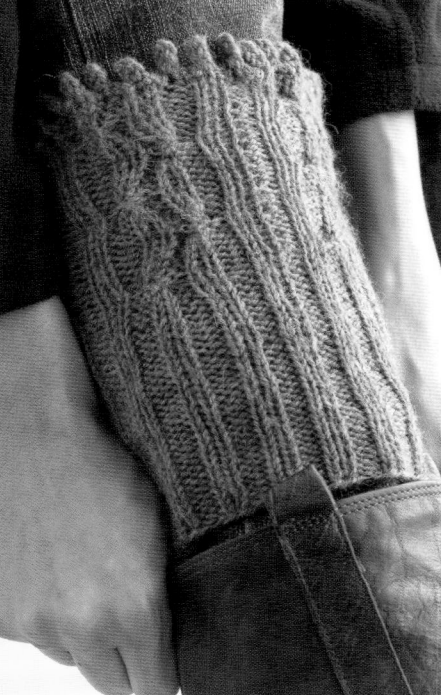

hazy frills neck wrap

FINISHED SIZE
About 6¼" (16 cm) wide
and 36" (91.5 cm) long.

YARN
Worsted weight (#4 Medium).

Shown here: Rowan Kidsilk Haze (70%
super kid mohair; 30% silk; 229 yd
[210 m]/25 g): #595 liqueur (dark red)
and #627 blood (medium red), 1 ball
each. *Note:* This is enough yarn to make
two neck wraps.

NEEDLES
Size U.S. 7 (4.5 mm): straight. Adjust
needle size if necessary to obtain the
correct gauge.

NOTIONS
Tapestry needle.

GAUGE
19 stitches and 22 rows = 4" (10 cm)
in garter stitch.

NOTE
✽ Use the garter ridges as a guide when
   picking up for frills.

It's the light loftiness of this yarn that creates all the allure—it's not known as Kid Silk **crack** for nothing. A few ruffles at each end is all that's needed to tart up a simple garter-stitch oblong. Even better, this project has twice the "gifting" in it! The two balls of yarn called for are enough to create *two* scarves—swap the base and ruffle yarns and a companion piece can be made for another deserving person. Maybe you?

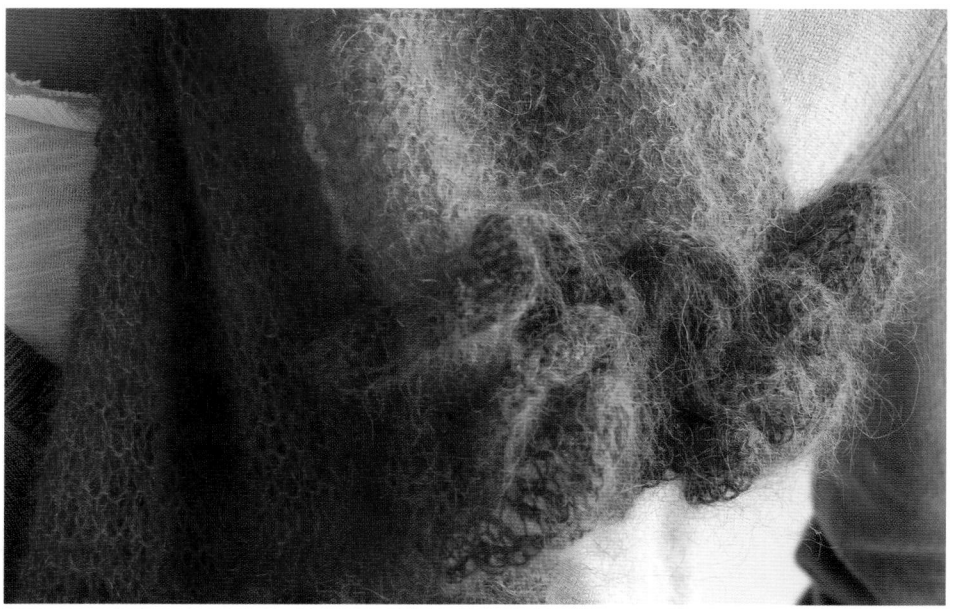

SCARF

With medium red, loosely CO 30 sts. Work even in garter st until piece measures about 36" (91.5 cm) from CO. Loosely BO all sts.

Frills

With dark red, RS facing, and using the garter ridges as a guide, pick up and knit 29 sts along the second garter ridge from the CO edge.

ROW 1 (WS) *K1f&b (see Glossary); rep from *—58 sts.

ROW 2 Knit.

ROW 3 Rep Row 1—116 sts.

ROW 4 Knit.

Loosely BO all sts.

**Skip 3 garter ridges and rep frill. Skip 2 garter ridges and rep frill. Rep from ** until a total of 7 frills have been completed.

Rep on BO edge, but work only 3 frills.

FINISHING

Weave in loose ends. Block lightly if desired.

felted leaf brooch

Nothing says autumn like falling leaves. Quickly knit with scraps of stash yarn, these leaves can be anything you wish them to be. Here, a pair is turned into a simple brooch (attach one to the Cabled Boot Toppers on page 16). But imagine one attached to a braided or crocheted cord wrapped around a jar of homemade jam or a whole bushel grouped together as a seasonal wreath.

FINISHED SIZE
About 3" (7.5 cm) long and 1½" (3.8 cm) wide, after felting.

YARN
Sportweight (#2 Fine).

Shown here: Berroco Ultra Alpaca Light (50% super fine alpaca, 50% Peruvian wool; 144 yd [131 m]/50 g): #4294 turquoise heather, less than 10 yd (9.5 m).

NEEDLES
Size U.S. 6 (4 mm): straight.

NOTIONS
Tapestry needle; embroidery needle, brooch back or safety pin.

GAUGE
About 20 stitches and 34 rows = 4" (10 cm) in garter stitch, before felting. Exact gauge is not crucial for this project.

LEAF
Loosely CO 3 sts.

ROWS 1, 2, AND 3 Knit.

ROW 4 K1f&b (see Glossary), k1, k1f&b—5 sts.

ROW 5 Knit.

ROW 6 K2, yo, k1, yo, k2—7 sts.

ROW 7 AND 8 Knit.

ROW 9 K3, yo, k1, yo, k3—9 sts.

ROW 10 AND 11 Knit.

ROW 12 K4, yo, k1, yo, k4—11 sts.

ROW 13, 14, 15, AND 16 Knit.

ROW 17 Ssk, k7, k2tog—9 sts rem.

ROW 18 AND 19 Knit.

ROW 20 Ssk, k5, k2tog—7 sts rem.

ROW 21 AND 22 Knit.

ROW 23 Ssk, k3, k2tog—5 sts rem.

ROW 24 AND 25 Knit.

ROW 26 Ssk, k1, k2tog—3 sts rem.

ROW 27 AND 28 Knit.

ROW 29 Sl 1, k2tog, psso—1 st rem.

Fasten off.

FINISHING
Weave in loose ends. Felt as described on page 118. With yarn threaded on embroidery needle, use backstitches (see Glossary) to add veins as shown in photo. Sew leaves firmly onto brooch back or safety pin.

shoulder cozy

FINISHED SIZE

About 35¼" (89.5 cm) wide at bottom edge and 11" (28 cm) deep.

YARN

Bulky weight (#5 Bulky).

Shown here: Brown Sheep Burly Spun (100% wool; 132 yd [121 m]/226 g): #BS03 gray heather, 1 skein.

NEEDLES

Size U.S. 15 (10 mm): straight. Adjust needle size if necessary to obtain the correct gauge.

NOTIONS

Tapestry needle with eye large enough to accommodate thick yarn.

GAUGE

8½ stitches and 10 rows = 4" (10 cm) in stitch pattern, slightly stretched.

NOTE

✲ There were only about 8 yards (7.3 m) of yarn left when the cozy was completed. Because of this, I have opted to start with the tie. Your shoulders will still be warm if you work 1 row more or less of the collar but without the tie . . . oh my!

Sometimes a scarf is just not enough. And sometimes jostling with the tails of a wrap is nothing more than a nuisance. Shoulders will keep warm and—well—cozy under a little capelet created in a big yarn on big needles. This quick project is a perfect whip-it-up-at-the-last-minute gift for any gal-on-the-go. Slip it over a jean jacket or sweater for a trip to the market or over pj's at home on a cool evening. For added "good thoughts," pin on a Felted Heart Milagros (page 82).

TIE

Using the backward-loop method (see Glossary), loosely CO 94 sts. Loosely BO all sts.

SHOULDER COZY

Using the long-tail method (see Glossary), loosely CO 75 sts.

SET-UP ROW (WS) K3, *p3, k3; rep from *.

ROW 1 (RS) K2, p1, sl 1, k2, psso, *p3, sl 1, k2, psso; rep from * to last 3 sts, p1, k2—62 sts rem.

ROW 2 K3, *p1, yo, p1, k3; rep from *—75 sts.

ROW 3 K2, p1, k3, *p3, k3; rep from * to last 3 sts, p1, k2.

ROW 4 K3, *p3, k3; rep from *.

ROWS 5–16 Rep Rows 1–4 three times.

ROW 17 (RS; dec row) K2, p1, sl 1, k2, psso, *p2tog, p1, sl 1 , k2, psso; rep from * to last 3 sts, p1, k2—52 sts rem.

ROW 18 (WS; eyelet row) K3, yo, p2tog, *k2, yo, p2tog; rep from * to last 3 sts, k3.

ROW 19 K2, p1, k2, *p2, k2; rep from * to last 3 sts, p1, k2.

ROW 20 K3, *p3, k3; rep from *.

Rep the last 2 rows until piece measures 11" (28 cm) from CO edge, ending with a WS row.

Loosely BO all sts in patt.

FINISHING

Weave in loose ends. Block lightly if desired. With RS facing and beg and end with the first and last eyelet, weave tie through eyelets.

✳ SHOULDER COZY CHART

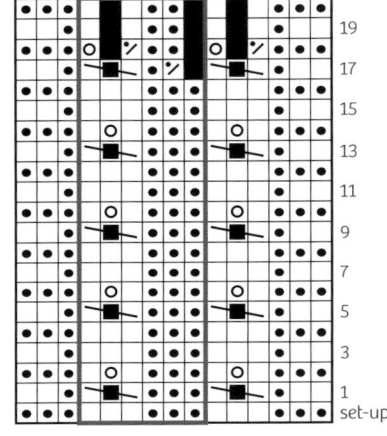

- ☐ knit on RS, purl on WS
- ● purl on RS, knit on WS
- ⊟ sl 1, k2, psso
- ⊙ yo
- ■ no stitch
- ☑ p2tog
- ☐ pattern repeat

arm cozies

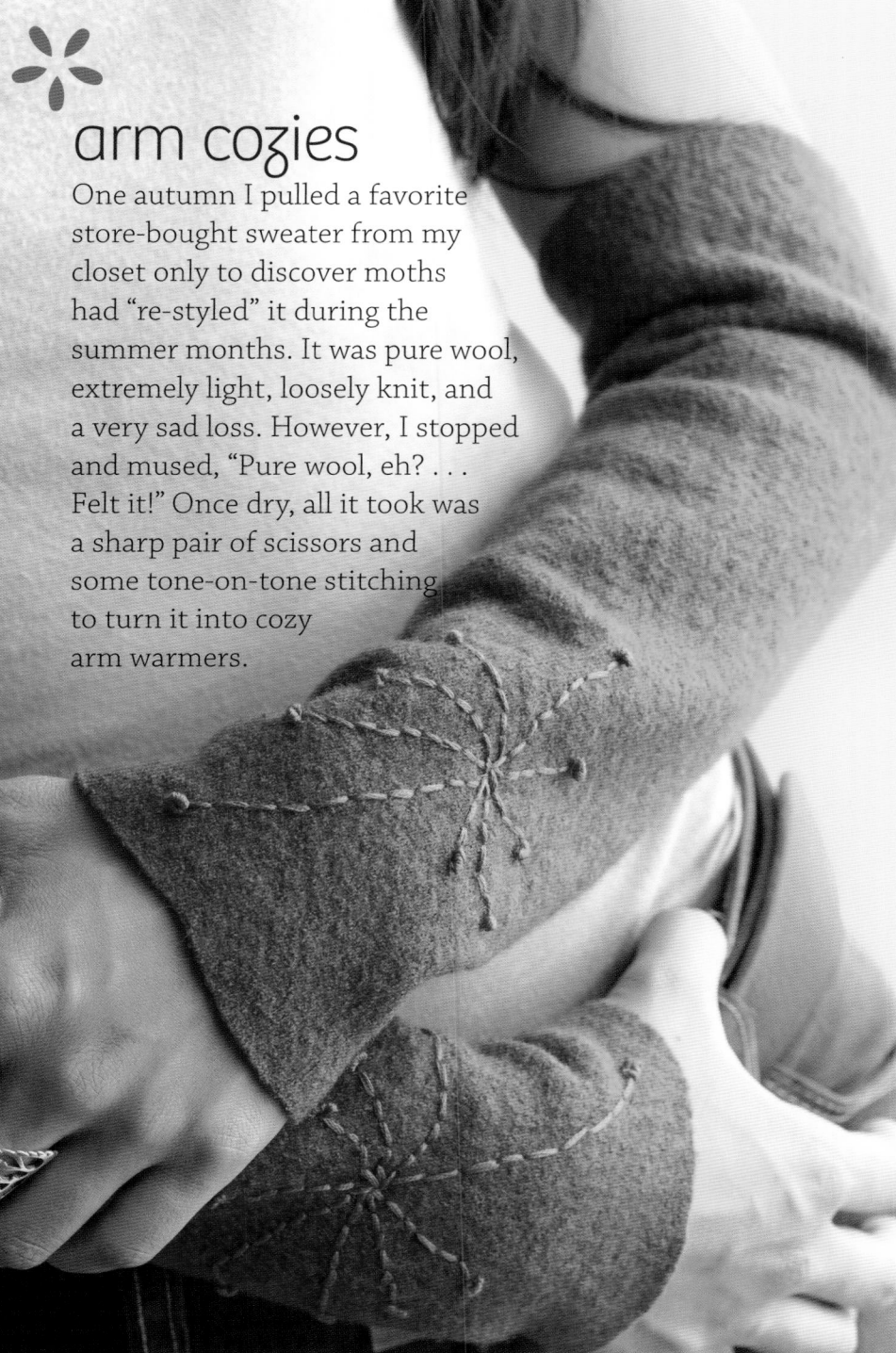

One autumn I pulled a favorite store-bought sweater from my closet only to discover moths had "re-styled" it during the summer months. It was pure wool, extremely light, loosely knit, and a very sad loss. However, I stopped and mused, "Pure wool, eh? . . . Felt it!" Once dry, all it took was a sharp pair of scissors and some tone-on-tone stitching to turn it into cozy arm warmers.

FINISHED SIZE

About 8" (20.5 cm) wrist circumference, 10" (25.5 cm) upper arm circumference, and 13½" (34.5 cm) long. *Note:* Actual measurements depend on shrinkage of sweater.

FABRIC

A recycled lightweight sweater that has been fully felted (see page 119).

NOTIONS

Sharp scissors; embroidery needle; coordinating embroidery cotton or fine yarn.

NOTES

✳ Look for a 100% wool sweater that is very lightweight for this project. If the original sweater is too heavy, the arm cozies will look like very lovely wooly casts.

✳ To prevent the cut edges from fraying, be sure to felt the fabric until the individual knit stitches are no longer visible.

ARM COZIES

Fully felt the sweater until the individual stitches are no longer visible. When completely dry, cut off the sleeves near the shoulders (save the body for other projects). Neatly cut off the cuff from each sleeve. Measure 13½" (34.5 cm) up from cuff edge, or desired total length, then cut off the upper portion of the sleeve (make sure your cuts are straight; use a ruler if necessary, so that the edges look neat). Trim edges as necessary.

FINISHING

With embroidery cotton or fine yarn threaded on an embroidery needle, use running stitches (see Glossary for embroidery instructions) as desired to create radiating star/flower shapes and work French knots at the ends of the radiating lines.

ruby foo baby cap

I have made variations of this cap in different yarns and gauges for years. The soft hand of this yarn will not bother baby's gentle brow in any way. Don't fret if you cannot find buttons just like the ones shown here. Most any small button will look lovely punctuating the dangly ends of the tassel. Just make certain to firmly attach whatever buttons you choose.

FINISHED SIZE

About 13½ (15¾)" (34.5 [40] cm) circumference; to fit ages 0–12 (12–24) months.

YARN

Worsted weight (#4 Medium).

Shown here: Louisa Harding Grace (50% wool and 50% silk; 110 yd [100 m]/50 g): #06 ruby, 1 ball.

NEEDLES

Size U.S. 6 (4 mm): straight *plus* one extra needle for three-needle bind-off. Adjust needle size if necessary to obtain the correct gauge.

NOTIONS

Tapestry needle with an eye big enough to thread yarn through yet small enough to pass through button's holes; seven ½" (1.3 cm) mother-of-pearl star-shaped buttons.

GAUGE

20 stitches and 28 rows = 4" (10 cm) in reverse stockinette stitch.

CAP

Using the crochet method (see Glossary), provisionally CO 46 sts.

Knit 1 row. Work short-rows (see Glossary) as foll:

SHORT-ROW 1 (RS) P42, wrap next st, turn.

SHORT-ROWS 2, 4, 6, 8, 10, 12, AND 14 Knit.

SHORT-ROW 3 P38, wrap next st, turn.

SHORT-ROW 5 P34, wrap next st, turn.

SHORT-ROW 7 P30, wrap next st, turn.

SHORT-ROW 9 P26, wrap next st, turn.

SHORT-ROW 11 P22, wrap next st, turn.

SHORT-ROW 13 P18, wrap next st, turn.

SHORT-ROWS 15 AND 16 Knit.

Rep Short-rows 1–16 four (five) more times, then rep Short-rows 1–14 once more—piece measures about 13½ (15¾)" (34.5 [40] cm) from CO, measured along long edge. With WS facing and using the three-needle method (see Glossary), BO all sts.

FINISHING

Tassel

Using the backward-loop method (see Glossary) CO 18 sts. *BO all sts until 1 st rem. Using the backward-loop method, CO 17 sts—18 sts total. Rep from * 5 more times, then BO all sts. Knot tail ends of yarn to form tassels.

With yarn threaded onto tapestry needle, sew top of cap closed. Sew star buttons firmly to the end of each tassel length. Firmly attach tassel to top of cap.

Lightly steam if needed, allowing opening to curl naturally.

FINISHED SIZE

About 13" (33 cm) wide and 14½" (37 cm) long, after felting and excluding handles.

YARN

Sportweight (#2 Fine).

Shown here: Brown Sheep Nature Spun Sport Weight (100% wool; 184 yd [168 m]/50 g): #225S brick road (A), #107S silver sage (B), #N17S French clay (C), #N80S mountain purple (D), #117S winter blue (E), #104S Grecian olive (F), #308S sunburst gold (G), #880S charcoal (H), #209 wood moss (I), #146S pomegranate (J), and #N18 plum line (K), 1 ball each.

HOOK

Size U.S. G/6 (4 mm). Adjust hook size if necessary to obtain the correct gauge.

NOTIONS

Tapestry needle; set of two rattan handles measuring 6" (15 cm) high and 7½" (19 cm) wide (handles shown here are style hr1 from tallpoppycraft.com); straight pins; about ½ yard (45 cm) lining fabric; matching thread. MAKINGS FOR PATCH (OPTIONAL): small scrap of fabric; iron-on adhesive; contrast thread; fabric ink pad in black; alphabet stamps.

GAUGE

Large square measures 5½" (14 cm) square before felting and 4" (10 cm) square after felting.

granny bag

Granny Squares have been in my life for as long as I can remember. They were probably the first thing I mastered as a fledging crafty-gal. I believe that a granny square throw is the ultimate gift, but a project of that size may be too much of a commitment. This bag condenses all the joy of a crazy patchwork throw into one compact, heartfelt package. When lining this type of bag, I like to add a little patch with a word of inspiration—"smile" in this case.

STITCH GUIDE

Large Square

Ch 5, sl st in first ch to form ring.

RND 1 Ch 2 (counts as 1 dc), 2dc in ring, ch 2, [3dc in ring, ch 2] 3 times, sl st in second ch of beg ch-2 to join—four ch-2 spaces.

RND 2 Ch 4 (counts as dc and ch 2), *(3dc, ch 2, 3dc) in next ch-2 sp, ch 2; rep from * 2 more times, 3dc, 2 ch, 2dc into last ch-2 sp, sl st in second ch of beg ch-4 to join—8 ch-2 sps.

RND 3 Ch 2 (counts as 1dc), 2dc in same ch-2 sp, ch 2, (3dc, ch 2, 3dc) in next ch-2 sp, ch 2, *3dc in next ch-2 sp, ch 2, (3 dc, 2 ch, 3dc) in the next ch-2 sp, ch 2; rep from * 2 more times, sl st in second ch of beg ch-2 to join—12 ch-2 sps.

RND 4 Ch 4 (counts as dc and ch 2), 3dc in next ch-2 sp, ch 2, (3dc, ch 2, 3dc) in next ch-2 sp, ch 2, *[3dc in next ch-2 sp, ch 2] 2 times, (3dc, ch 2, 3dc) in next ch-2 sp, ch 2; rep from * 2 more times, 2dc into the last ch-2 sp, sl st in second ch of beg ch-4 to join—16 ch-2 sps.

RND 5 Ch 2 (counts as 1 dc), 2 dc in same ch-2 sp, ch 2, 3 dc in next ch-2 sp, ch 2, (3 dc, 2 ch, 3dc) in next ch-2 sp, ch 2, *[3 dc in next ch-2 sp, ch 2] 3 times, (3 dc, ch 2, 3dc) in next ch-2 sp, ch 2; rep from * 2 more times, 3 dc into the last ch-2 sp, ch 2, sl st in second ch of beg ch-2 to join—20 ch-2 sps.

RND 6 Ch 4 (counts as dc and ch 2), [3dc in next ch-2 sp, ch 2] 2 times, (3dc, ch 2, 3dc) in next ch-2 sp, ch 2, *[3dc in next ch-2 sp, ch 2] 4 times, (3dc, ch 2, 3dc) in next ch-2 sp, ch 2; rep from * 2 more times, 3dc in next ch-2 sp, ch 2, 2dc into the last ch-2 sp, sl st in second ch of beg ch-4 to join.

Fasten off and secure.

Medium Square

Work Rnds 1–4 of large square. Fasten off and secure.

Small Square

Work Rnds 1 and 2 of Large Square. Fasten off and secure.

BAG

Following the list of color sequences at right, make 2 of each square (1 each for bag front and back).

FINISHING

Using a whipstitch (see Glossary), sew squares tog as shown at right for the bag front and back. Use a whipstitch to sew the front and back tog along the sides and bottom.

Edging

With A and RS facing, work a row of sc around bag opening, working 1 sc into each dc and 2 sc into each ch-2 sp. Fasten off and secure.

Gusset

Turn bag inside out and flatten base so that the fold is at the center of the base. With A threaded on a tapestry needle, sew a seam across each corner to form "ears" the depth of the small square as shown in photo at left. Fold "ears" toward center of bag base and lightly stitch in place.

Handle Tabs (make 4)

With A, ch 33.

ROW 1 Skip 3 ch, dc in next and all foll ch to end—31 dc.

ROW 2 Ch 3 (counts as 1 dc), dc in first and all foll dc to end.

Fasten off and secure.

✳ ASSEMBLY DIAGRAM FOR FRONT AND BACK

✳ COLOR SEQUENCE FOR SQUARES

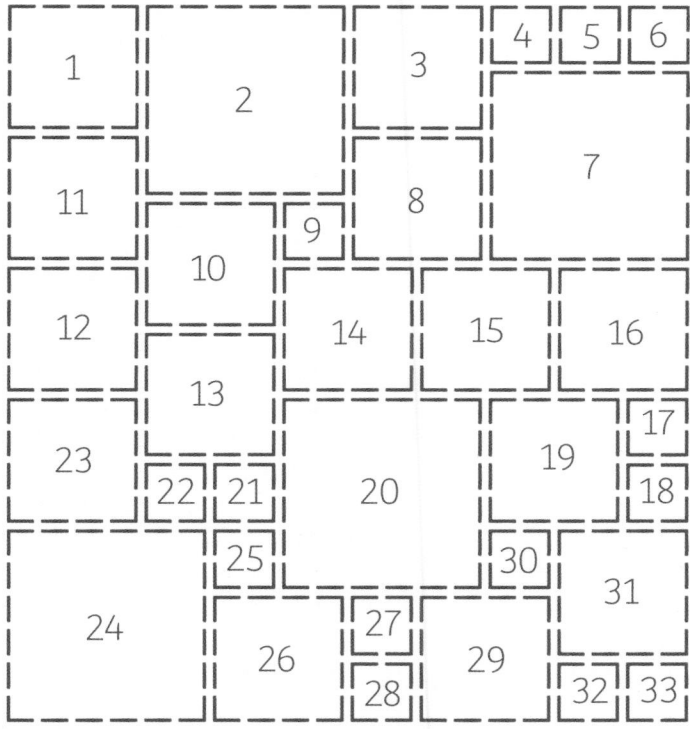

SQUARE	RND1	RND2	RND3	RND4	RND5	RND6
1	C	C	B	B		
2	G	F	F	F	L	L
3	D	D	C	C		
4	J	J				
5	B	L				
6	H	H				
7	L	J	J	J	F	F
8	I	I	I	G		
9	A	A				
10	B	E	E	E		
11	A	I	I	H		
12	D	J	J	J		
13	L	L	L	C		
14	I	I	D	D		
15	E	H	H	J		
16	A	G	G	E		
17	H	L				
18	C	C				
19	L	F	F	F		
20	A	A	I	I	B	B
21	E	E				
22	G	J				
23	B	B	H	H		
24	A	G	G	G	I	I
25	G	G				
26	E	D	D	J		
27	A	A				
28	F	L				
29	G	G	H	H		
30	H	J				
31	D	D	D	G		
32	C	C				
33	B	A				

Felting

Felt bag and tabs as described on page 118. Pin tabs to a firm surface so that they dry flat and straight.

Attach Handles

Pin handle tabs as desired at top edge of bag and insert handles. With A threaded on a needle, sew handle tabs securely to bag.

Lining

Measure bag for lining and add 1" (2.5 cm) to width measurement and 1½" (3.8 cm) to length measurement. Cut two pieces of lining fabric to these measurements. Iron optional patch fabric onto fusible adhesive following manufacturer's directions. Trim to size. Apply message using ink pad and alphabet stamps. Iron patch onto RS of lining fabric in desired location. With contrasting thread and using the buttonhole setting on a sewing machine, topstitch patch in place. With RS facing tog and using a ½" (1.3 cm) seam allowance, sew lining front and back tog along sides and bottom. Press seams. Make gussets as for bag. Fold opened end of lining down 1" (2.5 cm) to WS and press. Pin lining to bag with WS facing and sew in place by hand.

paper roses

"... paper roses ... oh, how real those roses seem to be ..." I can't help but hear Marie Osmond crooning as I whip up these lovelies. I first started making and sharing these when my desperate search for a bow came up short. It did not take long for me to think of roses made from papery Habu yarn. One skein of the yarn will make countless buds for wrapping, pinning, hair clipping, and napkin ringing.

USE A PAPER
ROSE BROOCH
TO FASTEN
A SHAWL

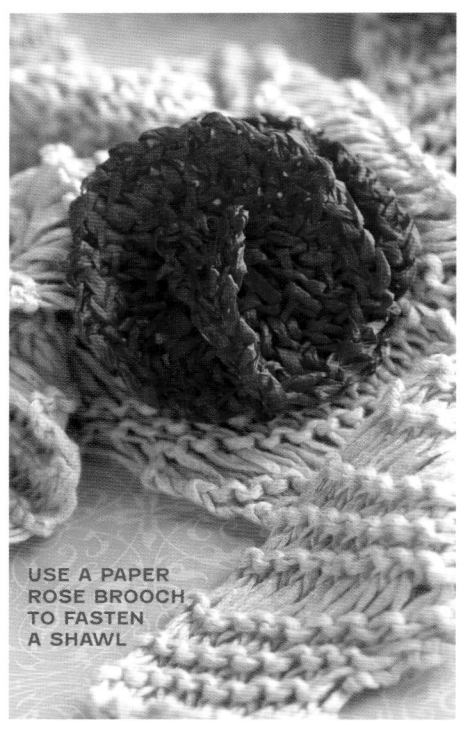

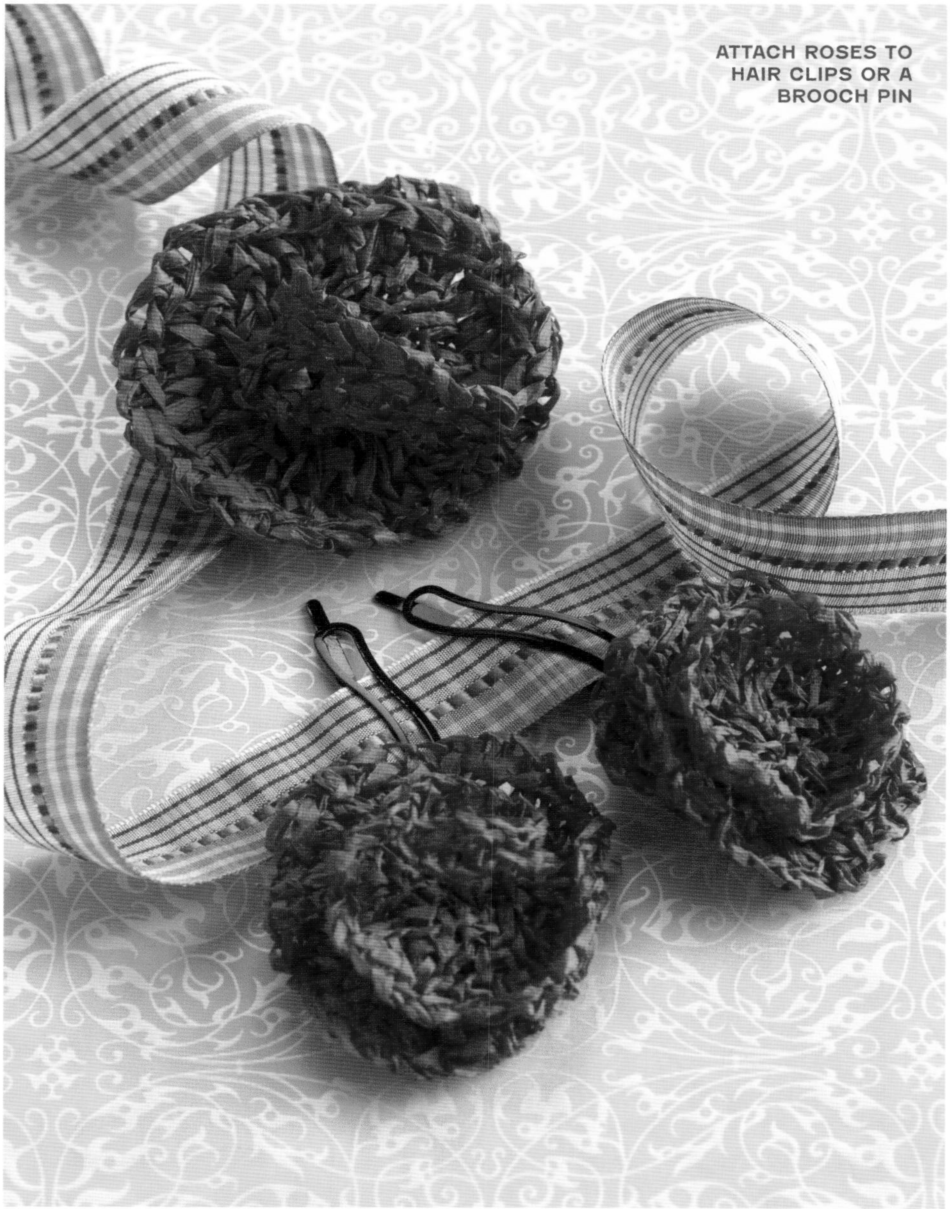
ATTACH ROSES TO
HAIR CLIPS OR A
BROOCH PIN

ROSE

Loosely CO 10 sts.

ROW 1 Knit.

ROW 2, 4, AND 6 Purl.

ROW 3 *K1f&b (see Glossary); rep from *—20 sts.

ROW 5 *K1f&b; rep from *—40 sts.

ROW 7 *K1f&b; rep from *—80 sts.

ROW 8 Purl.

Loosely BO all sts. Cut yarn, leaving a 15" (38 cm) tail for seaming.

FINISHING

Twist piece on itself into a spiral.

With the tail threaded on a tapestry needle, sew the spiral tog. Weave in loose ends.

NAPKIN RING

With smaller needles and single strand of yarn, CO 22 sts. Knit 4 rows. BO all sts. Cut yarn, leaving a 15" (38 cm) tail for seaming.

Thread tail on a tapestry needle and sew selvedge edges tog, overlapping them slightly, to form a ring. Thread tails of rose on a tapestry needle and sew to ring join. Weave in loose ends.

HAIRPINS

Attach to hair or bobby pin.

BROOCH

With matching thread, embroidery cotton, or strong fine yarn, attach rose firmly to brooch back or safety pin.

ginger syrup

Makes about 1½ cups

Ginger syrup adds a fresh taste to tea. Package it in a pretty bottle tucked inside a Felted Tea Cozy (page 74) or decorated with some Paper Roses (page 34) for anyone on your gift list.

WHAT TO GATHER

3 cups water
2 cups sugar
6 ounces fresh chopped gingerroot, unpeeled

WHAT TO DO

Combine all ingredients in a saucepan and bring to a boil stirring occasionally.

Simmer about 20 to 30 minutes until reduced by about half.

Remove from heat and let cool.

Strain into a pretty bottle and refrigerate until ready to give.

Include a note or label that says:

~ Add 1–2 tsp of ginger syrup in hot or cold tea

or

~ Add 1 tbsp of ginger syrup to a tall glass filled with ice, then add club soda to make real ginger ale.

~ Keep refrigerated, please.

recipe

petaled slouch cap

FINISHED SIZE
About 18¾" (47.5 cm) brim circumference.

YARN
Aran weight (#4 Medium).

Shown here: Elsebeth Lavold Silky Flamme (50% Peruvian wool, 30% alpaca, 20% silk; 82 yd [75 m]/50 g): #9 oliver, 2 balls.

NEEDLES
Size U.S. 7 (4.5 mm): 16" (40 cm) circular (cir). Size U.S. 10½ (6.5 mm): 16" (40 cm) cir and set of 4 double-pointed (dpn). Adjust needle size if necessary to obtain the correct gauge.

NOTIONS
Marker (m); tapestry needle.

GAUGE
14 stitches and 20 rounds = 4" (10 cm) in stockinette stitch worked in the round with larger needle; 16 stitches = 4" (10 cm) in brim pattern with smaller needle.

A little bit cloche and a little bit beret equals a whole bunch of lovely for the committed hat wearer on your gift list. With the pumped up yarn, this pattern quickly appears on the needles. The unconventional construction—worked from top knot down—contributes to the fun lessons this gift can teach. Learn a bit of lace and shaping while working in the round, all in one very satisfying project. Top it off with a Crochet Flower Brooch (page 47).

RND 8 *P1, k7, p1; rep from *
to end of rnd.

RND 9 *P1, k3, yo, k1, yo, k3, p1;
rep from * to end of rnd—55 sts.

RND 10 *P1, k9, p1; rep from *
to end of rnd.

RND 11 *P1, k4, yo, k1, yo, k4, p1;
rep from * to end of rnd—65 sts.

RND 12 *P1, k11, p1; rep from *
to end of rnd.

RND 13 *P1, k5, yo, k1, yo, k5, p1; rep from
* to end of rnd—75 sts.

RNDS 14–16 *P1, k13, p1; rep from *
to end of rnd.

RND 17 *P1, yo, ssk, k9, k2tog, yo, p1;
rep from * to end of rnd.

RND 18 *P2, k11, p2; rep from *
to end of rnd.

RND 19 *P2, yo, ssk, k7, k2tog, yo, p2; rep
from * to end of rnd.

RND 20 *P3, k9, p3; rep from *
to end of rnd.

RND 21 *P3, yo, ssk, k5, k2tog, yo, p3;
rep from * to end of rnd.

RND 22 *P4, k7, p4; rep from *
to end of rnd.

RND 23 *P4, yo, ssk, k3, k2tog, yo, p4;
rep from * to end of rnd.

CAP

With dpn, CO on 5 sts. Work 5-st I-cord
(see Glossary) until piece measures 3"
(7.5 cm) from CO.

INC ROW *K1f&b; rep from *—10 sts.

Divide sts onto 3 dpn, place marker (pm),
and join for working in rnds, being careful
not to twist sts. Cont as foll, changing to
cir needle when there are too many sts to
fit comfortably on dpn:

RND 1 *K1, k1f&b (see Glossary); rep from *
to end of rnd—15 sts.

RND 2 *P1, k1, p1; rep from *
to end of rnd.

RND 3 *P1, yo, k1, yo, p1; rep from *
to end of rnd—25 sts.

RND 4 *P1, k3, p1; rep from *
to end of rnd.

RND 5 *P1, [k1, yo] 2 times, k1, p1;
rep from * to end of rnd—35 sts.

RND 6 *P1, k5, p1; rep from * to end
of rnd.

RND 7 *P1, k2, yo, k1, yo, k2, p1;
rep from * to end of rnd—45 sts.

RND 24 *P5, k5, p5; rep from *
to end of rnd.

RND 25 *P5, yo, ssk, k1, k2tog, yo, p5;
rep from * to end of rnd.

RND 26 *P6, k3, p6; rep from *
to end of rnd.

RND 27 *P6, yo, sl 1, k2tog, psso, yo,
p6; rep from * to end of rnd.

RND 28 *P7, k1 through back loop (tbl),
p7; rep from * to end of rnd.

RND 29 *P6, p1f&b, k1tbl, p1f&b, p6;
rep from * to end of rnd—85 sts.

RND 30 *P8, k1tbl, p8; rep from *
to end of rnd.

RND 31 *P7, p1f&b, k1tbl, p1f&b, p7;
rep from * to end of rnd—95 sts.

RNDS 32–36 *P9, k1tbl, p9; rep from *
to end of rnd.

RND 37 *P7, p2tog, k1tbl, p2tog, p7;
rep from * to end of rnd—85 sts rem.

RNDS 38–42 *P8, k1tbl, p8; rep from *
to end of rnd.

RND 43 *P6, p2tog, k1tbl, p2tog, p6;
rep from * to end of rnd—75 sts rem.

Brim

Change to smaller cir needle.

RNDS 44–58 *P7, k1tbl, p7; rep from *
to end of rnd.

Loosely BO all sts knitwise.

FINISHING

Weave in loose ends. Lightly steam if
needed. Tie I-cord into an overhand knot.

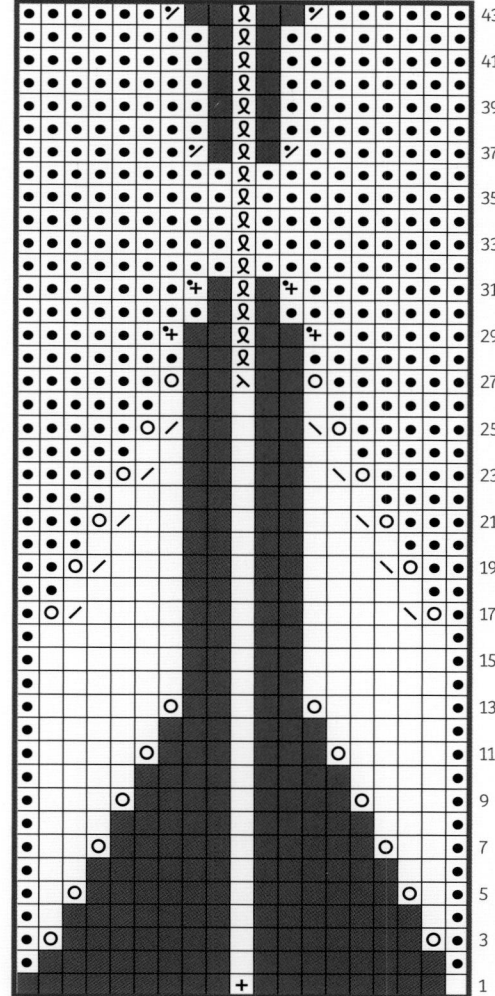

PETALED SLOUCH CAP CHART

□ knit
● purl
☑ k2tog
◩ ssk
⊞ k1f&b
⊙ yo
☒ sl1, k2tog, psso
⊠ k1 tbl
⊞ p1f&b
☑ p2tog
□ pattern repeat

precious baby jacket

There is no denying it—baby's first sweater has to be special! Knits for a baby compel us to embrace words such as "handmade" and "heirloom." This jacket is a quick-knit top-down raglan in seed stitch (no need to worry about unfinished edges curling). The addition of tone-on-tone felted appliqué and colorful stitching defines what a modern hand-crafted heirloom is all about—simple, practical, and special.

JACKET

With MC and straight needles, CO 58 sts. Knit 1 WS row.

SET-UP ROW (RS) K8, place marker (pm), k4, pm, k22, pm, k4, pm, k20.

Work 1 (WS) row in seed st (see Stitch Guide), slipping markers as you come to them.

INC ROW (RS) *Work in seed st to 1 st before m, (k1, p1) in next st, sl m, (k1, p1) in next st; rep from *—8 sts inc'd.

Rep the last 2 rows 11 (13, 15) times, ending with a WS row—154 (170, 186) sts.

Divide for Fronts and Back

(RS) Work 20 (22, 24) sts in seed st for left front, remove m, place next 28 (32, 36) sts onto waste yarn for left sleeve, remove m, work 46 (50, 54) sts in seed st for back, remove m, place next 28 (32, 36) sts onto waste yarn for right sleeve, remove m, work rem 32 (34, 36) sts in seed st for right front—98 (106, 114) sts rem.

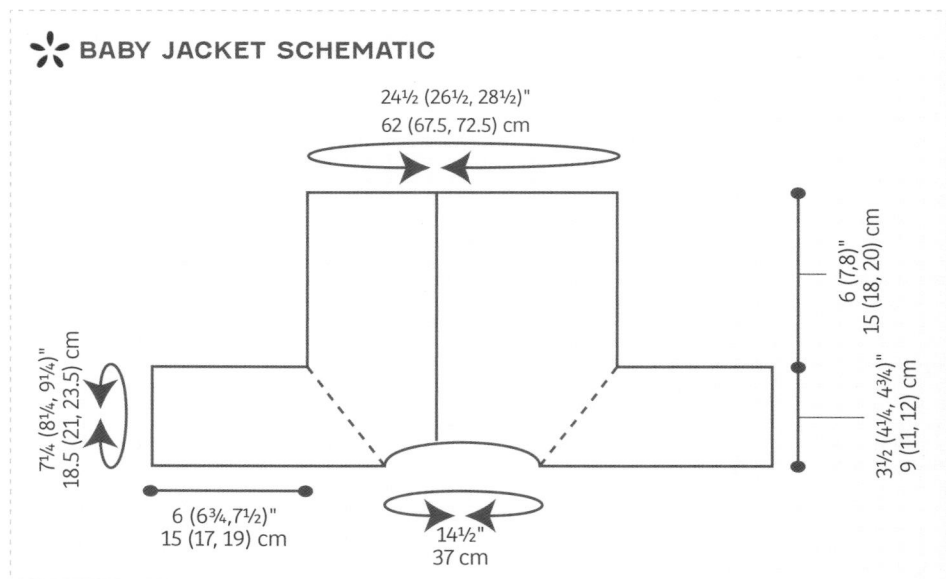

❈ BABY JACKET SCHEMATIC

24½ (26½, 28½)"
62 (67.5, 72.5) cm

6 (7,8)"
15 (18, 20) cm

3½ (4¼, 4¾)"
9 (11, 12) cm

7¼ (8¼, 9¼)"
18.5 (21, 23.5) cm

6 (6¾,7½)"
15 (17, 19) cm

14½"
37 cm

Lower Body

Cont even in seed st until piece measures about 6 (7, 8)" (15 [18, 20] cm) from armhole, or desired length. BO all sts in patt.

SLEEVES

Place 28 (32, 36) held sleeve sts onto dpn. With MC and RS facing, pick up and knit 1 st at base of armhole, work 28 (32, 36) sts in seed st as established—29 (33, 37) sts total. Pm and join for working in rnds. Work even in patt until piece measures 6 (6¾, 7½)" (15 [17, 19] cm) from pick-up rnd, or desired total length. BO all sts in patt.

FINISHING

Weave in loose ends. Block lightly or steam-block to measurements.

Felt Appliqué

With CC and straight needles, CO 36 sts. Work even in St st (knit RS rows; purl WS rows) until piece measures about 10" (25.5 cm) from CO. BO all sts. Felt the piece as described on page 118. Cut six circles varying in size from 1½" (3.8 cm) to 2" (5 cm). With embroidery cotton threaded on embroidery needle, use stem stitches (see Glossary) to embroider simple star shapes on the felt circles, working 2 circles each with copper, mauve, and gold. With CC threaded on embroidery needle, whipstitch (see Glossary) each circle firmly to jacket fronts as desired.

Braided Ties

Mark for first tie at top edge of right front. Cut 3 lengths of CC, each about 30" (76 cm) long. Thread all three lengths on a tapestry needle and make a single stitch at the marked position. Center the lengths to make 6 equal ends. Divide ends into three groups of 2 strands each and work a three-strand braid for about 11" (28 cm). Tie the end in an overhand knot to secure. Trim ends. Make another braided tie to correspond opposite the first tie, about 1" (2.5 cm) in from the left front edge.

FINISHED SIZE

About 3" (7.5 cm) wide and 5" (12.5 cm) tall.

YARN

Sportweight (#2 Fine).

Shown here: Elsebeth Lavold Silky Wool (45% wool, 35% silk, 20% nylon; 192 yd [175 m]/50 g): #51 eggshell, 1 skein.

HOOK

Size U.S. F/5 (3.75 mm).

NOTIONS

Tapestry needle; brooch back or safety pin; needle with an eye large enough to thread yarn and small enough to pass through beads; 43 size 6 silver-lined clear seed beads.

GAUGE

Each petal measures about 2" (5 cm) long and 1¼" (3.2 cm) wide. Exact gauge is not crucial for this project.

crochet flower brooch

Using a magical combination of white bread, glitter, and glue, my niece crafted a flower-shaped brooch for me. Her joy in the making and giving was inspiring. This crochet variation, worked in a crisp wool/silk yarn is a tad more practical with just the right amount of sparkle in the beads. Pin the flower to the Petaled Slouch Cap on page 38. Make three or four for a lapel and call it a bouquet.

FLOWER PETAL (MAKE 6)

Ch 12 to form spine of petal.

ROW 1 Sl st into second ch from hook, *sc into next ch, dc into next 2 ch, trc into next 3 ch, dc into next 2 ch, sc into next ch, sl st into last ch.

ROW 2 Working along the opposite side of the same ch base, sl st into first ch, rep from * of Row 1.

Fasten off and secure.

FLOWER CENTER BOBBLE

Ch 4. *Insert hook into back loop of next ch, yo and draw up a loop, yo, draw through 1 loop on hook—2 loops on hook. Rep from * to * 3 more times—5 loops on hook. Yo and draw through all 5 loops on hook. Fasten off.

Knot together tails of yarn to create a bobble.

FLOWER FRINGE

Ch 30. Skip first ch, sl st in each ch to end. [Ch 20, turn, skip first ch, sl st in each ch to end] 2 times. [Ch 25, turn, skip first ch, sl st in each ch to end] 2 times—5 fringes total. Fasten off.

FINISHING

Weave in loose ends. Arrange petals in a flower shaping, overlapping, and stitch them firmly into place at the center. Position flower center bobble and use tail ends to attach to joined petals. Thread yarn on needle and attach 11 beads on ch-30 fringe, 9 beads on each ch-25 fringe, and 7 beads on each ch-20 fringe. Position fringe at back of flower and firmly stitch into place. Attach firmly to brooch back or safety pin.

cheerful earmuffs

Those who live in cold climates know that combating chilly ears in a stylish way can take a lot of imagination—especially when avoiding "hat head." Ears will stay toasty and passersby will smile when these quirky muffs appear. I reclaimed the frame from fake fur muffs that had knocked around my closet for far too long. If you don't have your own old frame, take a trip to a local rummage shop. Who knows what else you can find there that will inspire you for other projects?

FINISHED SIZE

Inside frame measures 3" (7.5 cm) in diameter at the ears.

YARN

DK weight (#3 Fine).

Shown here: Classic Elite Miracle (50% alpaca, 50% Tencel; 108 yd [99 m]/50 g): #3318 olive, 1 skein. This yarn has been discontinued; substitute the DK weight yarn of your choice.

HOOK

Size U.S. G/6 (4 mm). Adjust hook size if necessary to obtain the correct gauge.

NOTIONS

Earmuffs frame (reclaimed, if possible); tapestry needle; small amount of polyester or bamboo fiber filling.

GAUGE

18 dc and 4 rows = 4" (10 cm).

MUFF INSIDE PIECE
(make 2)

RND 1 Ch 2, 6 sc in second ch from hook, sl st in first ch to join—6 sc.

RND 2 Ch 1 (counts as 1 sc), sc in same ch, [2 sc in next sc] 5 times, sl st in top of ch-1 to join—12 sc.

RNDS 3, 5, 7, AND 9 Ch 1, sc into each sc, sl st in top of ch-1 to join.

RND 4 Ch 1, sc in same ch, [2 sc in next sc] 11 times, sl st in top of ch-1 to join—24 sc.

RND 6 Ch 1, 1 sc into same ch, sc into next sc; *2 sc into next sc, sc into next sc; rep from * to end, sl st in top of ch-1 to join—36 sc.

RND 8 Ch 1, 1 sc into same ch, sc into the next 2 sc, *2 sc into next sc, sc into next 2 sc; rep from * to end, sl st in top of ch-1 to join—48 sc.

Fasten off and secure.

MUFF OUTSIDE PIECE
(make 2)

RNDS 1–8 Work as for inside piece.

RND 9 Ch 5, sl st in same ch-1 as join of previous rnd, *ch 5, sl st in next sc; rep from * to end.

Fasten off and secure.

BAND COVER

Ch 12, turn.

ROW 1 Skip 3 ch, dc in each ch to end, turn—10 dc.

ROW 2 Ch 2 (counts as dc), dc in each dc to end, turn.

Rep Row 2 until piece measures about 12½" (31.5 cm) from beg or long enough to cover band of earmuff frame.

Fasten off and secure.

FLOWERS
(make 6)

RND 1 Ch 2, 5 sc in second ch from hook, sl st in top of first sc.

RND 2 Ch 2, (3dc, ch 2, sl st) in the same sc as joining sl st, *ch 2, (3dc, ch 2, sl st) into next sc; rep from * 3 more times—5 petals.

Fasten off.

DANGLIES

Dangly 1

Work Rnds 1 and 2 of flower but do not fasten off. Ch 20, turn, skip first ch, sl st in each ch to end.

Fasten off.

Dangly 2

Work Rnds 1 and 2 of flower but do not fasten off. Ch 15, turn, skip first ch, sl st in each ch to end.

Fasten off.

Dangly 3

Work Rnds 1 and 2 of flower but do not fasten off. Ch 10, turn, skip first ch, sl st in each ch to end.

Fasten off.

FINISHING

Wrap band cover around earmuff frame band and, with yarn threaded on a

tapestry needle, use a mattress stitch (see Glossary) to join side edges tog. With WS facing, sew one inside piece to one outside piece, leaving about one-third of the distance open. Insert round wired part of earmuff frame, lightly stuff, then sew to end of seam. Rep for other side. Sew ends of band cover to earmuff sections. Sew flowers evenly spaced along band.

Attach danglies in a group near the band join at the top of one earmuff.

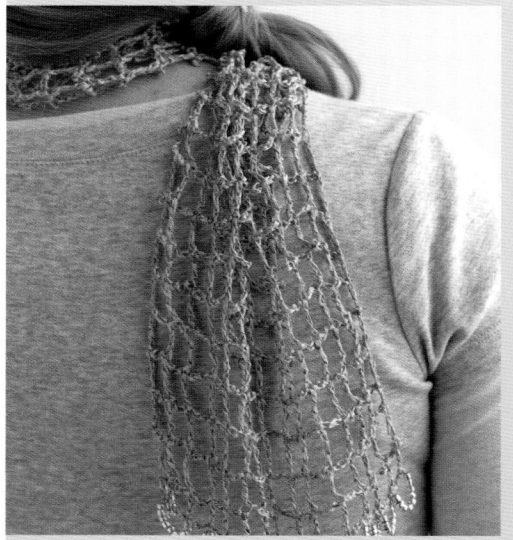

gilded mesh scarf

The simple stitch used for this project combined with the crisp ribbonlike silk yarn will make even a newbie crocheter look like a pro. In just a few easy evenings, a luscious length of spun gold will magically appear off of your hook. Add a scalloped edge of silver beads to take the opulence one step further. If your recipient is not a flashy gal, try a dry linen or a raw silk yarn and trim the ends with beads that have a subtle matte finish.

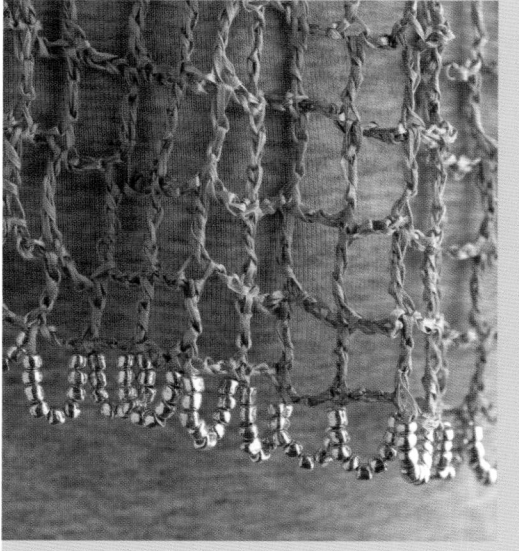

SCARF

Leaving a 30" (76 cm) tail (to use later to string beads), ch 63.

ROW 1 Trc into eleventh ch from hook, *ch 3, sk 3 ch, trc into next ch; rep from * to end, turn—14 grids.

ROW 2 Ch 7 (counts as 1 trc and 3 ch), *trc in top of the next trc, ch 3; rep from * to last grid, sk 3 ch, trc in next ch, turn.

Rep Row 2 until piece measures 66" (168 cm) or desired length, leaving a minimum of 30" (76 cm) of yarn for stringing beads.

Fasten off and secure.

FINISHING

Thread yarn still attached to piece onto tapestry needle. *Slide 9 beads onto yarn. Secure beaded "scallop" with a few stitches at the base of the next trc; rep from * to end. Fasten off securely and weave in end. Rep for opposite edge.

Block to measurements.

FINISHED SIZE

About 66" (168 cm) long and 8" (20.5 cm) wide.

YARN

Sportweight (#2 fine).

Shown here: Alchemy Silken Straw (100% silk; 260 yd [237 m]/40 g): #67e topaz, 1 skein.

HOOK

Size U.S. 7 (4.5 mm).

NOTIONS

Tapestry needle (with eye big enough to thread the yarn yet small enough for the beads to slide over); 252 size 6° silver-colored glass seed beads.

GAUGE

About 7 grids = 4" (10 cm) wide and 5" (12.5 cm) high. Exact gauge is not crucial for this project.

NOTES

✲ The pattern is a multiple of 4 stitches plus 11.

✲ Leave a length of yarn about 30" (76 cm) long at beginning of piece to use later for stringing beads.

FINISHED SIZE

About 8" (20.5 cm) foot circumference and 9" (23 cm) foot length from back of heel to tip of toe. To fit woman's U.S. shoe sizes 7 to 9. Length of foot can be altered to accommodate other shoe sizes.

YARN

Worsted weight (#4 Medium).

Shown here: Mirasol Qina (80% baby alpaca, 20% bamboo; 91 yd [83 m]/50 g): #915 (gray) 2 skeins, #900 (natural) and #903 (burnt orange), 1 skein each.

NEEDLES

Size U.S. 5 (3.75 mm): set of 4 double-pointed (dpn). Adjust needle size if necessary to obtain the correct gauge.

NOTIONS

Marker (m); stitch holder (optional for use during heel shaping); tapestry needle.

GAUGE

24 stitches and 24 rounds = 4" (10 cm) in stockinette charted pattern, worked in rounds.

NOTES

✶ To make it easier to hide the double wrapped stitches during the heel shaping on a purl row, turn the work so that the RS (knit side) is facing you, then pick up the wraps with the left-hand needle and place them on the right-hand needle (see Glossary). Turn work so that the WS (purl side) is facing you and purl the stitch together with the wraps.

✶ Lengthen or shorten foot as needed by working more or fewer rows of the dotted pattern (Rows 53 to 60 of chart) before you begin the toe shaping.

weekend socks

Tucked away in my sweater cupboard, I still have the ski sweater my mother knitted many years ago for my father based on traditional crisp, clean, two-color Norwegian motifs. Although the patterns have not changed over the years, the choice of yarns certainly has. The alpaca-bamboo blend used here creates the most scrumptious and decadent pair of socks—just perfect for weekend lounging. Think of them as après-ski sweaters for the feet!

LEFT SOCK

With gray, CO 48 sts. Divide sts as evenly as possible on 3 dpn. Place marker (pm) and join for working in rnds, being careful not to twist sts. Work in k4, p2 rib for 7 rnds. Work Rnds 1–36 of Weekend Socks chart.

Heel

Sl the previous st knitted onto the next needle, then slip the previous 22 sts onto a holder or waste yarn to work later for instep. Place rem 26 sts onto one needle to work heel.

Change to burnt orange and work short-rows (see Glossary) as foll:

SHORT-ROW 1 (RS) Sl 1, k23, wrap next st, turn.

SHORT-ROW 2 (WS) P22, wrap next st, turn.

SHORT-ROW 3 Knit to 1 st before gap created on previous RS row, wrap next st, turn.

SHORT-ROW 4 Purl to 1 st before gap created on previous WS row, wrap next st, turn.

SHORT-ROWS 5–14 Rep Short-rows 3 and 4 five more times—10 sts rem unwrapped in center.

SHORT-ROW 15 K10. Knit wrap tog with the next st (see Glossary), wrap the next stitch (this st has 2 wraps), turn.

SHORT-ROW 16 P11. Purl wrap tog with the next st, wrap the next st (this st has 2 wraps), turn.

SHORT-ROW 17 Knit to the first wrapped st, knit the 2 wraps tog with the next st, wrap the next st (this st has 2 wraps), turn.

SHORT-ROW 18 Purl to the first wrapped st, purl the 2 wraps tog with the next st (see Notes), wrap the next stitch (this st has 2 wraps), turn.

SHORT-ROWS 19–28 Rep Short-rows 17 and 18 five more times.

SHORT-ROW 29 K24, knit the 2 wraps tog with the next st, wrap the next st, turn—there is just 1 wrap on this row.

SHORT-ROW 30 P25, purl the 2 wraps tog with the next st, wrap the next st, turn—there is just 1 wrap on this row.

Rejoin for working in rnds (48 sts) and cont as charted until piece measures 6¾" (17 cm) from center of heel or about 2¼" (5.5 cm) less than desired total length (see Notes).

Shape Toe

Change to burnt orange and knit 1 rnd. Dec as folls:

RND 1 *K2tog, k20, ssk; rep from * to end of rnd—44 sts rem.

RNDS 2, 4, 6, 8, 10, AND 12 Knit.

RND 3 *K2tog, k18, ssk; rep from * to end of rnd—40 sts rem.

RND 5 *K2tog, k16, ssk; rep from * to end of rnd—36 sts rem.

RND 7 *K2tog, k14, ssk; rep from * to end of rnd—32 sts rem.

RND 9 *K2tog, k12, ssk; rep from * to end of rnd—28 sts rem.

RND 11 *K2tog, k10, ssk; rep from * to end of rnd—24 sts rem.

RND 13 *K2tog, k8, ssk; rep from * to end of rnd—20 sts rem.

RND 14 Knit.

FINISHING

Divide remaining 20 sts equally onto 2 needles. Using the Kitchener st (see Glossary), graft these sts tog. Weave in loose ends. Block lightly if desired.

RIGHT SOCK

CO and work as for left sock to beginning of heel. Set up for heel as foll: slip the first st onto the previous needle, then slip the next 22 sts onto a holder or waste yarn to work later for instep. Place rem 26 sts onto one needle to work short-row heel. Beg with Short-row 2, complete as for left sock.

✴ WEEKEND SOCKS CHART

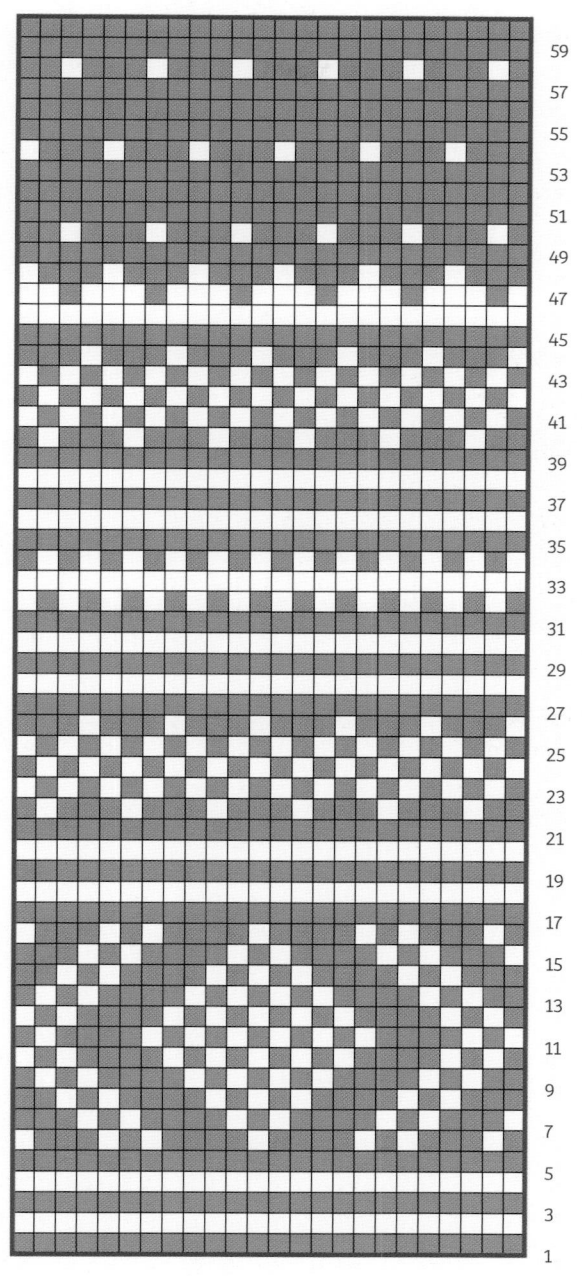

■ gray

□ natural

□ pattern repeat

modern mangas

FINISHED SIZE

About 7¾" (19.5 cm) wrist circumference, 11½" (29 cm) upper arm circumference, and 14" (35.5 cm) long, allowing cast-on edge to roll.

To fit an average-size woman.

YARN

Worsted weight (#4 Medium).

Shown here: Valley Yarns Stockbridge (50% alpaca, 50% wool; 109 yd [100 m]/50 g): soft grape (medium purple), terra cotta (soft orange), olive, wild rose (medium pink), stone blue (pale blue), periwinkle, and dark grey, 1 skein each.

NEEDLES

Size U.S. 6 (4 mm): set of 4 double-pointed (dpn). Adjust needle size if necessary to obtain the correct gauge.

NOTIONS

Marker (m); tapestry needle.

GAUGE

22 stitches and 24 rounds = 4" (10 cm) in stockinette charted pattern, worked in rounds.

Mangas is the Spanish word for "sleeves." The mountain people in the Andes wear the most wonderful ornately knitted sleeves over their clothing for warmth. They're like leg warmers for the arms. I fused this familiar Peruvian silhouette with traditional British Isle patterning, then added more color and texture with some not-so-afterthought embroidery. You don't have to live in the Andes to fight off the chill with stylish and thoroughly modern mangas.

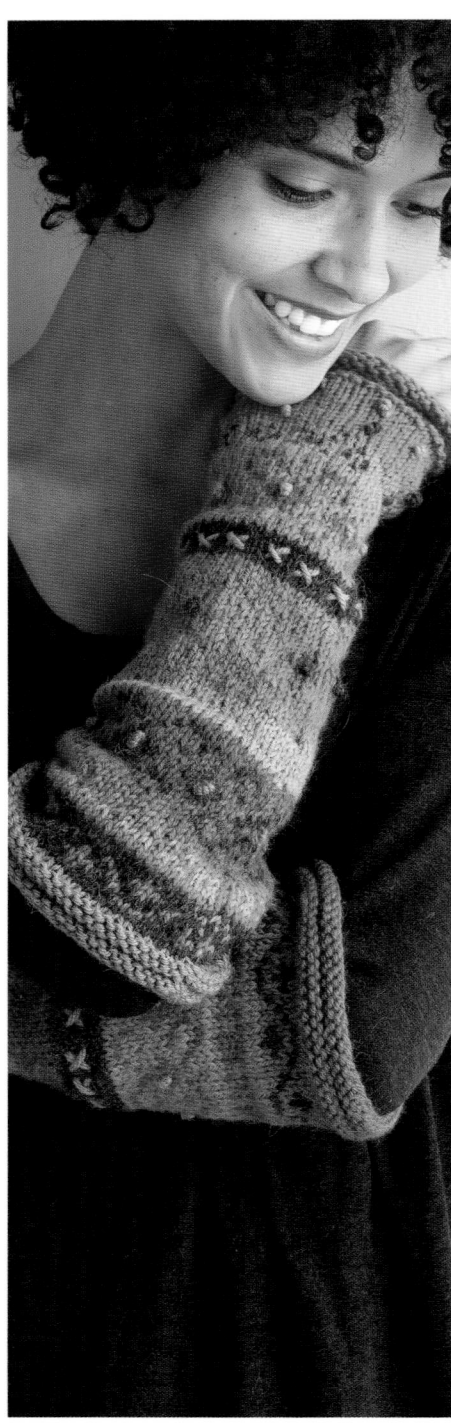

FIRST MANGA

With soft orange, CO 40 sts. Divide sts as evenly as possible on 3 dpn. Place marker (pm) and join for working in rnds, being careful not to twist sts.

RNDS 1–9 Knit.

RND 10 Purl.

RNDS 11–19 Knit.

Work Rnd 1 of First Manga chart and *at the same time* inc 3 sts evenly spaced—43 sts. Cont as charted, inc 1 st each end of needle on the 4th rnd, then every foll 7th rnd 9 more times—63 sts. Work through Rnd 72 of chart.

Change to periwinkle and work as foll:

RNDS 1, 2, 5, AND 6 Knit.

RNDS 3, 4, 7, AND 8 Purl.

BO all sts knitwise.

SECOND MANGA

With medium purple, CO 40 sts. Divide sts as evenly as possible on 3 dpn. Pm and join for working in rnds, being careful not to twist sts.

RNDS 1–9 Knit.

RND 10 Purl.

RNDS 11–19 Knit.

Work Rnd 1 of Second Manga chart and *at the same time* inc 3 sts evenly spaced—43 sts. Cont as charted, inc 1 st each end of needle on the 4th rnd, then every foll 7th rnd 9 more times—63 sts. Work through Rnd 72 of chart.

Change to olive and work as foll:

RNDS 1, 2, 5, AND 6 Knit.

RNDS 3, 4, 7, AND 8 Purl.

BO all sts knitwise.

FINISHING

Weave in loose ends. Lightly steam-block.

Embroidery

FIRST MANGA Scatter French knots (see Glossary) in different yarn colors on the soft orange area. With pale blue, work a French knot in the center of each diamond motif on chart Rnd 13. With pale blue, work a string of cross-sts (see Glossary) along the solid dark gray band between chart Rnds 20 and 24. With olive, work duplicate sts (see Glossary) center cross motifs beg on chart Rnd 31. With dark gray, work a French knot in the center of each cross motif on chart Rnd 33. With medium purple, work a French knot in the center of each diamond motif on chart Rnd 54.

SECOND MANGA Scatter French knots in different yarn colors on the medium purple area. With medium purple, work a French knot in the center of each diamond motif on chart Rnd 13. With pale blue, work duplicate sts in center cross motifs beginning on chart Rnd 31. With soft orange, work a French knot in the center of each cross motif on chart Rnd 33. With medium pink, work a string of cross-sts along the solid dark gray band between chart Rnds 42 and 47. With medium purple, work a French knot in the center of each diamond motif on chart Rnd 54.

First Manga

Second Manga

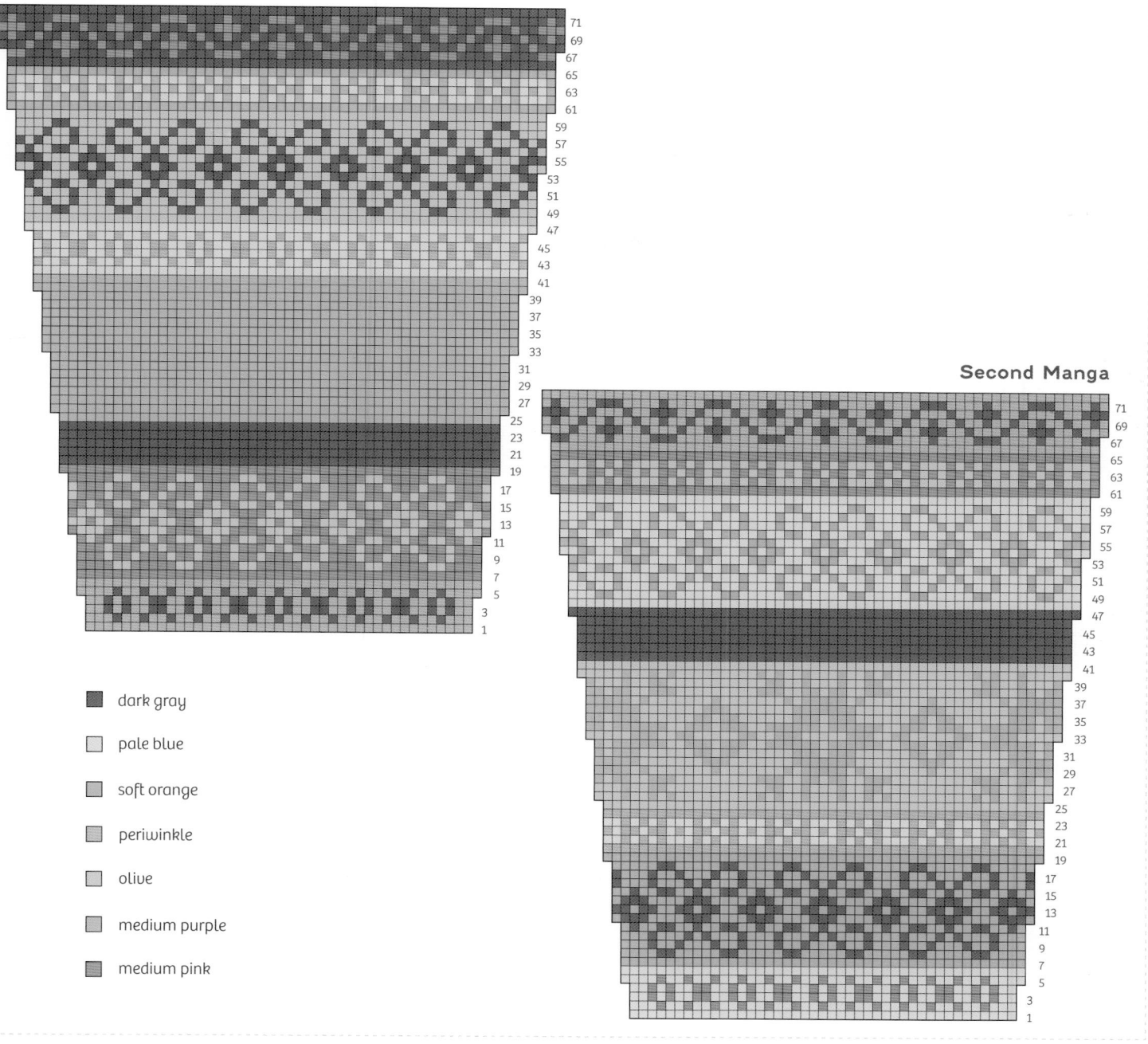

- ◼ dark gray
- ◻ pale blue
- ◻ soft orange
- ◻ periwinkle
- ◻ olive
- ◼ medium purple
- ◼ medium pink

FINISHED SIZE
About 7½" (19 cm) inside circumference.

YARN
Bulky (#5 Bulky) and sportweight (#2 Fine).

Shown here: FELTED BASES: Brown Sheep Lamb's Pride Bulky (85% wool, 15% mohair; 125 yd [114 m]/100 g): #m04 charcoal heather, #m162 mulberry, #m145 spice, #m173 wild violet, #m18 khaki, small amounts of each.

WRAPPING YARN: Brown Sheep Cotton Fine (80% cotton, 20% merino; 222 yd [203 m]/50 g): #cf930 candy apple, #cf005 cavern, #cf375 rue, #cf770 wisteria, #cf455 willow leaf, #cf450 oriental jade, and #cf860 Sedona red, small amounts of each.

NEEDLES
Size U.S. 11 (8 mm): straight *plus* 1 extra needle for three-needle bind-off.

NOTIONS
Size L/11 (8 mm) crochet hook and smooth waste yarn for provisional cast-on; tapestry needle.

GAUGE
About 10 stitches and 13 rows = 4" (10 cm) in stockinette stitch, before felting. Exact gauge is not crucial for this project.

NOTES
✢ The bangles are shown in two sizes based on the number of stitches cast-on. The pattern is written for the thinner size with the thicker size in parentheses.

✢ Some of the bangle bases are knitted in a single color, others are worked in two colors. Try different combinations, have fun, and savor your time playing with color.

✢ For thicker bands of color, double the yarn when wrapping the bangle; for thinner bands, use a single strand. Experiment to get the look you want.

✢ One skein of Brown Sheep Lamb's Pride Bulky is enough for at least a dozen bangle bases.

bevy of bangles

These silent bangles came to be because of my love of big, bold bracelets and my loathing of the clang, clang, clunk that almost always accompanies them. The first time I wore an armful to "girl's night," all my girlfriends wanted their own. I spent one evening knitting up a basket full of bases, then on the following afternoon, I tossed them all into the wash to felt them. I spent the next available evening surrounded by colorful cotton yarn, wrapping and playing to make each bangle unique.

FELTED BASE
With bulky yarn and using the crochet provisional method (see Glossary), CO 5 (7) sts. Work even in St st for 40 rows—piece measures about 12¼" (31 cm) from CO. Carefully remove the waste yarn from the provisional CO and place the live sts on a needle. Hold the needles parallel with RS of work facing tog to form a ring and use the three-needle method (see Glossary) to BO the sts tog.

Weave in loose ends.

FELTING
See page 118 for felting instructions.

FINISHING
Thread a length of wrapping yarn on a tapestry needle. Secure the yarn on the inside of the bangle, then wrap the yarn around the base ring, using even tension to ensure that the base ring doesn't compress too tightly or that the wraps aren't too loose and appear sloppy.

FINISHED SIZE

About 4½" (11.5 cm) foot circumference and 3½" (9 cm) foot length, after felting.

To fit size 0–6 months.

YARN

Sportweight (#2 Fine).

Shown here: Frog Tree Spun Alpaca Sport Weight (100% alpaca; 130 yd [119 m]/ 50 g): 1 ball (enough yarn for three pairs). Shown in #501 purple and #13 gold.

Fleece Artist Merino Sliver (100% merino; 50 g/reeling): red, 1 reeling.

NEEDLES

Size U.S. 6 (4 mm): straight. Adjust needle size if necessary to obtain the correct gauge.

NOTIONS

Tapestry needle; removable stitch markers or waste yarn; embroidery needle; plastic wrap or plastic bags to stuff into slipper while drying; 1 reeling of Fleece Artist Merino Sliver (100% merino; 1 reeling/50 g) in red for embellishment; 1 skein each of DMC 25 embroidery cotton (100% cotton; 8.7 yd [8 m]/skein) in #580 grass green and #3041 medium violet; medium-size needlefelting needle; dense foam pad for needlefelting.

GAUGE

18 stitches and 24 rows = 4" (10 cm) in stockinette stitch, before felting.

NOTE

✢ For needlefelting, cut a rectangular piece of foam to fit snuggly inside the dried bootie, then work the needlefelting against this base.

baby's first felted feet

What I adore most about dressing up baby is the pure whimsy of it all. When it comes to footwear, there is no need for sensible shoes on fresh little feet. The only concern is for the softness and warmth that this felted pure alpaca guarantees. Of course, the only other concern—the "cute" factor—can be achieved by the undeniable Seussian design sensibility of these little "awe" makers.

BOOTIES

Loosely CO 34 sts. Work in St st for 22 rows—piece measures about 3¾" (9.5 cm) from CO. Mark each end of the last row with removable stitch marker or waste yarn.

Shape Toe

ROW 1 K1, [k6, k2tog] 4 times, k1—30 sts rem.

ROW 2 AND ALL FOLL WS ROWS Purl.

ROW 3 Knit.

ROW 5 K1, [k5, k2tog] 4 times, k1—26 sts rem.

ROW 7 Knit.

ROW 9 K1, [k4, k2tog] 4 times, k1—22 sts rem.

ROW 11 Knit.

ROW 13 K1, [k3, k2tog] 4 times, k1—18 sts rem.

ROW 15 K1, [k2, k2tog] 4 times, k1—14 sts rem.

ROW 17 K1, [k1, k2tog] 4 times, k1—10 sts rem.

ROW 18 Purl.

Break yarn. Thread tail on a tapestry needle, draw through rem sts, pull tight to close hole, and secure on WS.

FINISHING

Fold CO edge of bootie in half so that WS face tog. With yarn threaded on a tapestry needle, use the mattress st (see Glossary) to sew edges tog to form back heel. Use a mattress st to join bootie from tip of toe to removable markers. Remove markers.

Weave in loose ends.

Felting

Felt according to the instructions on page 118. Stretch and shape wet booties as desired, stuff with plastic to hold the shape, and allow to air-dry completely.

Needlefelting and Embroidery

With small amounts of sliver, needlefelt (see page 119) small dots as desired. With embroidery cotton threaded onto embroidery needle, embroider a French knot (see Glossary) in the center of each needlefelted dot.

tomato jam

Makes about 2 pints

This spicy jam is guaranteed to warm you up! Include a jar with a pair of Weekend Socks (page 54) for someone who enjoys après ski.

WHAT TO GATHER

3 lbs ripe red tomatoes (Roma work well), cored, seeded, and coarsely chopped

2 cups white sugar

2 good-size limes, freshly squeezed

3" (7.5 cm) piece of gingerroot, peeled and freshly grated or minced

1 tbsp ground cumin

1 tsp salt

1 tsp ground cinnamon

¼ tsp ground cloves

2 good-size jalapeno peppers, seeded and minced

WHAT TO DO

Combine everything in a medium-size saucepan.

Bring to a boil, stirring often.

Reduce heat and simmer uncovered and stirring occasionally for about 1¼–1½ hours until sauce has consistency of thick jam.

Taste and adjust seasoning, then cool and refrigerate until using.

Include a note or label with the following:

> Great with Indian-style foods, on top of cream-cheese topped crackers, or swirled into a bowl of canned tomato soup.

> Will keep refrigerated two to three weeks.

heart-in-hand mitts

FINISHED SIZE
About 8" (20.5 cm) hand circumference
and 7¼" (18.5 cm) hand length.
To fit an average-size woman.

YARN
Chunky (#5 Bulky).
Shown here: Valley Yarns Berkshire Bulky
(85% wool, 15% alpaca;
108 yd [99 m]/100 g): #15 red,
2 balls; #12 orange, 1 ball.

NEEDLES
Size U.S. 10 (6 mm): straight and set of 4
double-pointed (dpn). Adjust needle size if
necessary to obtain the correct gauge.

NOTIONS
Marker (m); stitch holder; size L/11
(8 mm) crochet hook and smooth waste
yarn for provisional cast on; tapestry
needle.

GAUGE
14 stitches and 18 rounds = 4" (10 cm) in
stockinette stitch, worked in rounds.

The intarsia method of working with color strikes fear in many knitters. Oddly, I find it far easier and way more fun and manageable than two-color Fair Isle knitting. I guess, like everything else, it takes a first attempt followed up with a bit of practice. I hope that not only will there be a pair (or two) of quick and colorful mittens on your gift-making list, but also a sense of accomplishment in mastering this knitting technique—an added gift just for you.

LEFT MITTEN

With red, straight needles, and using the crochet chain method (see Glossary), provisionally CO 30 sts. Beg with a knit (RS) row, work 2 rows in St st. Work Rows 1–26 of Left Mitten chart and *at the same time* work thumb gusset on Rows 1–9 in orange as foll:

ROW 1 (RS) K13, M1 (see Glossary), k1, M1, knit to end of row—32 sts.

ROWS 2, 4, 6, AND 8 Purl.

ROW 3 K13, M1, k3, M1, knit to end of row—34 sts.

ROW 5 K13, M1, k5, M1, knit to end of row—36 sts.

ROW 7 K13, M1, k7, M1, knit to end of row—38 sts.

ROW 9 K13, slip next 10 sts onto holder or waste yarn, use the backward-loop method (see Glossary) to CO 2 sts over the gap, knit to end of row—30 sts rem.

Work even through Rnd 26 of chart.

Shape Top

With red only:

ROW 1 (RS) K1, [k2, k2tog] 7 times, k1—23 sts rem.

ROW 2 Purl.

ROW 3 K1, [k1, k2tog] 7 times, k1—16 sts rem.

ROW 4 Purl.

ROW 5 K1, [k2tog] 7 times, k1—9 sts rem.

Break yarn, thread tail through rem sts, pull tight to close hole, and secure on WS.

Cuff

Carefully remove waste yarn from provisional CO and place 30 exposed sts evenly spaced on 3 dpn. Place marker (pm) and join for working in rnds.

DEC RND K2tog, k1, [p2, k2] 6 times, p1, p2tog—28 sts rem.

Work in k2, p2 rib until cuff measures 4" (10 cm).

INC RND K2, [p1, M1P (see Glossary), p1] 7 times—35 sts.

Work in k2, p3 rib until cuff measures 8" (20.5 cm).

Loosely BO evenly in patt.

Thumb

With orange, dpn, and RS facing, k10 held thumb gusset sts, then pick up and knit 2 sts along CO edge at top of gusset—12 sts total. Knit 10 rnds.

SHAPE TOP

[K2tog] 6 times—6 sts rem.

Break yarn, thread tail through rem sts, pull tight to close hole, and secure on WS.

FINISHING

Weave in loose ends. With red threaded on a tapestry needle, sew side seam of hand. Lightly steam-block if needed.

RIGHT MITTEN

With red, straight needles, and using the crochet chain method (see Glossary), provisionally CO 30 sts. Beg with a knit (RS) row, work 2 rows in St st. Work Rows 1–26 of Right Mitten chart and *at the same time* work thumb gusset on Rows 1–9 in orange as foll:

ROW 1 (RS) K16, M1, k1, M1, knit to end of row—32 sts.

ROWS 2, 4, 6, AND 8 Purl.

ROW 3 K16, M1, k3, M1, knit to end of row—34 sts.

ROW 5 K16, M1, k5, M1, knit to end of row—36 sts.

ROW 7 K16, M1, k7, M1, knit to end of row—38 sts.

ROW 9 K16, slip next 10 sts onto holder or waste yarn, use the backward-loop method (see Glossary) to CO 2 sts over the gap, knit to end of row—30 sts rem.

Complete as for left mitten.

 MITTEN CHARTS

Left Mitten

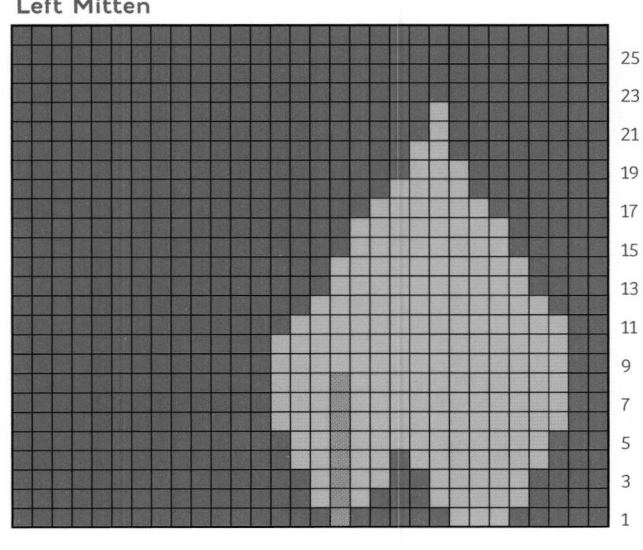

Right Mitten

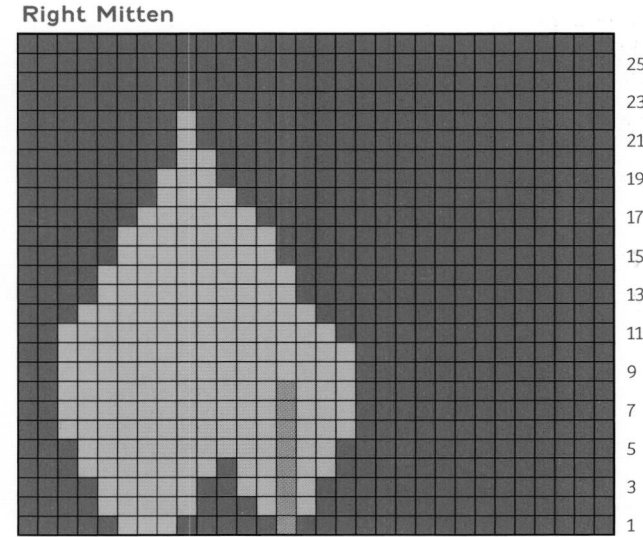

■ red ☐ orange ■ work thumb gusset with orange

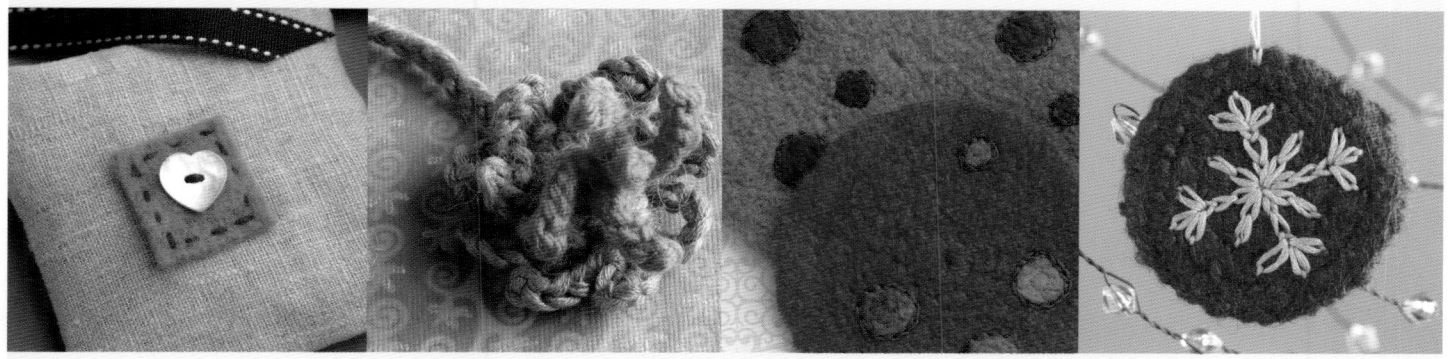

gifts for the soul

They celebrate passions, infuse color, add zest, and lift spirits. Never meant to be serious, they add pleasure to the simple moments of the day. Why save them for big events? The best gifts are the ones that are least expected.

FINISHED SIZE
About 21½" (54.5 cm) circumference, stretched, and 9" (23 cm) tall.

YARN
Worsted weight (#4 Medium) and fingering weight (#1 Super Fine).

Shown here: TEA COZY: Classic Elite La Gran Mohair (78.4% mohair, 17.3% wool, 4.3% nylon; 106 yd [97 m]/50 g): #61555 tangerine, 1 ball.

TIE AND FOB: Frog Tree Alpaca Fingering (100% alpaca; 215 yd [196 m] /50 g): #42 teal, a walnut-size amount.

NEEDLES AND HOOK
TEA COZY: Size U.S. 10 (6 mm): 16" (40 cm) circular (cir).
TIE AND FOB: Size G/6 (4 mm) crochet hook. Adjust needle and hook size if necessary to obtain the correct gauge.

NOTIONS
TEA COZY: Markers (m); stitch holders or waste yarn; tapestry needle.
TIE AND FOB: Embroidery needle; one 8.7 yd (8 m) skein of DMC embroidery cotton in #580 (moss green).

GAUGE
TEA COZY: 13 stitches and 20 rows/ rounds = 4" (10 cm) in rib pattern, stretched.

tea cozy + felted tie fob

I can't think of a better gift on a cool, dark, dreary day than sharing a cup of tea with a friend. With a brightly colored, simply ribbed, mohair "turtleneck" gracing the pot, the time spent will be even brighter. Consider a personal touch by replacing the graphic swirl on the fob with a monogram. When wrapping it all up for the intended, tuck in a few bags of your favorite tea. Even if you can't be there, your warm thoughts will be.

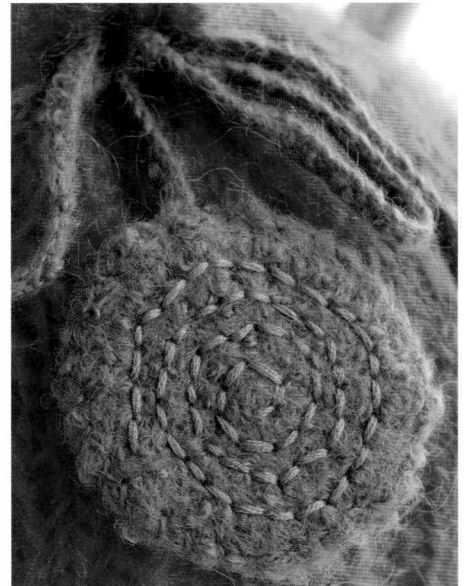

COZY

CO 70 sts. Place marker (pm) and join for working in the rnd, being careful not to twist sts.

RNDS 1–6 K1, *p2, k3; rep from * to last 4 sts, p2, k2.

RND 7 Cont in rib patt as established, placing a marker between the 35th and 36th sts.

Divide for Handle and Spout Openings

INC ROW (RS) K1f&b (see Glossary), *p2, k3; rep from * to 4 sts before m, p2, k2—36 sts for first half.

Place rem 35 sts on holder, removing m.

First Half

Working back and forth in rows, work 36 sts as foll:

ROW 1 (WS) P2, k2, *p3, k2; rep from * to last 2 sts, p2.

ROW 2 (RS) K2, p2, *k3, p2; rep from * to last 2 sts, k2.

Cont in rib as established until piece measures 5½" (14 cm) from CO, ending with a WS row. Place sts on holder. Do not cut yarn.

Second Half

Return 35 held sts to needle with RS facing and rejoin yarn to beg of sts. Work back and forth in rows as foll:

INC ROW (RS) K1f&b, *p2, k3; rep from * to last 4 sts, p2, k2—36 sts.

ROW 1 (WS) P2, k2, *p3, k2; rep from * to last 2 sts, p2.

ROW 2 (RS) K2, p2, *k3, p2; rep from * to last 2 sts, k2.

Cont in rib as established until second half matches first half. Leave sts on needle. Cut yarn.

Join Halves

With RS of second half facing, return held sts of first half onto needle to the right of the second half.

JOINING RND Using yarn still attached to first half, work first half sts as foll: *k2, p2, k1; rep from * to last st of first half, k2tog (last st of first half with first st of second half), k1, p2, **k3, p2; rep from ** to last 2 sts, k1, k2tog (last st of second half with first st of first half, pm to mark beg of rnd—70 sts.

Work even as established for 2 rnds, ending last rnd 1 st before m. Sl last st, remove m, return slipped st to left needle, replace m.

DEC RND *K2tog, p2, k1; rep from * to end of rnd—56 sts rem.

NEXT RND *K1, p2, k1; rep from * to end of rnd.

EYELET RND *K1, p2, k2, p2tog, yo, k1; rep from * to end of rnd—7 eyelets completed.

NEXT RND *K1, p2, k1; rep from * to end of rnd.

Rep last rnd until piece measures about 9" (23 cm) from CO. Loosely BO all sts.

FINISHING

Weave in loose ends.

Tie

With jade and crochet hook, loosely work a crochet chain (see Glossary) that measures 36" (91.5 cm) long. Turn, skip 1 ch, sc in each ch to end. Fasten off.

Fob

With teal and crochet hook, make two circles as described for Felted Yule Bling on page 108.

Felting

Felt the two circles and tie as described on page 118.

EMBROIDERY

With embroidery cotton threaded onto needle and working outward from the center, use running stitches (see Glossary) to form a spiral pattern on the fob.

Hold the two circles with WS facing together. With jade threaded on embroidery needle, use whipstitches (see Glossary) to join the outer edges of the two circles tog, leaving a small opening. Insert one end of tie between the two circles, then sew to end of seam, catching the tie as you go. Thread tie through eyelets of cozy, knot the free end, and trim.

FINISHED SIZE
About 7¼" (18.5 cm) circumference and 2½" (6.5 cm) tall, after felting.

YARN
Shown here: Fingering weight (#1 Super Fine). Frog Tree Alpaca Fingering Weight (100% alpaca; 215 yd [196 m]/50 g): #0011 heathered gray or #46 lime green, 1 ball.

NEEDLES
Size U.S. 6 (4 mm): set of 4 or 5 double-pointed (dpn). Adjust needle size if necessary to obtain the correct gauge.

NOTIONS
Marker (m); tapestry needle; embroidery needle; one 8.7 yd (8 m) skein each of DMC 25 Embroidery Cotton in #902 (deep wine) or #347 (red), #3740 (purple), and #501 (teal).

GAUGE
22 stitches and 28 rounds = 4" (10 cm) in stockinette stitch worked in rounds, before felting.

NOTES
✴ One ball will make cozies for at least a half-dozen eggs.

✴ Wrap the embroidery thread around the needle four times to create chunkier French knots.

felted egg cozies

Here's a warm and fuzzy way to serve up some true green eggs with that ham! Basically constructed like little hats, these toppers will keep eggs at an optimum temperature while you enjoy a leisurely breakfast. Stitch up a motif that reflects the season or the personality of the recipient. When invited for a weekend visit, bring along a collection of these as a hostess gift—you will leave behind smiles for years to come.

COZY

Loosely CO 48 sts. Place marker (pm) and join for working in the rnd, being careful not to twist sts. Work in St st until piece measures 3" (7.5 cm) from CO.

Shape Top

RND 1 *K2tog; rep from *—24 sts rem.

RND 2 Knit.

RND 3 *K2tog; rep from *—12 sts rem.

RND 4 Knit.

RND 5 *K2tog; rep from *—6 sts rem.

RND 6 K2tog, k2, k2tog—4 sts rem.

Work rem 4 sts in I-cord (see Glossary) for 4" (10 cm). Fasten off.

FINISHING

Weave in loose ends. Felt as described on page 118.

FOR THE GRAY COZIES

With embroidery cotton threaded onto embroidery needle, work French knots (see Glossary) randomly as desired (see Notes). Tie the I-cord in an overhand knot.

FOR THE GREEN COZIES

With embroidery cotton threaded onto embroidery needle, work stem stitches (see Glossary) and French knots as shown in photograph. Tie the I-cord in an overhand knot.

mexican hot chocolate mix

*Enough for about 12 servings

This easy-to-use mix will satisfy the hot chocolate lover on your gift list. Package the mix along with a bundle of cinnamon sticks tied up with Felted Heart Milagros (page 82) for a heartfelt gift.

WHAT TO GATHER

½ cup unsweetened cocoa

½ cup granulated sugar

1 tbsp ground cinnamon

1 tsp chili powder

WHAT TO DO

Mix everything together and pour into a jar.

Include a note or label with the following:

~Place 2 tbsp of mix in a cup.

~Add ¼ cup of milk, ¾ cup of boiling water, and a good squirt of chocolate syrup (optional).

~Stir and enjoy!

recipe

felted heart milagros

FINISHED SIZE

About 2" (5 cm) high and 2" (5 cm) wide, after felting.

YARN

Sportweight (#2 Fine).

Shown here: Brown Sheep Nature Spun Sport Weight (100% wool; 184 yd [168 m]/50 g): less than 10 yards (9.1 m) for each heart. Shown in #880s charcoal, #N17s French clay, #335s brick road, #109s spring break, #107s silver sage, and #146s pomegranate.

Frog Tree Alpaca Sport Weight (100% alpaca; 130 yd [118 m]/50 g): less than 10 yd (9.1 m) for each heart. Shown in #28 plum.

NEEDLES

Size U.S. 6 (4 mm): straight.

NOTIONS

Tapestry needle; small amount of polyester or bamboo fiberfill.

GAUGE

About 21 stitches and 30 rows = 4" (10 cm) in stockinette stitch, before felting. Exact gauge is not crucial for this project.

These little hearts bring me such joy that I can't stop myself from making and sharing them! Knitted in one piece with a bit of short-rowing for shape, there is just one quick seam and a little stuffing before you shout, "Everyone in the pool!" Well, the "pool" may be the washing machine or a basin, but I do promise it will be fun. These hearts can be used for anything you can imagine—pins, bookmarks, place markers, welcome garlands, good-luck charms, etc.

SHORT-ROWS 2, 4, AND 6 Purl to last st, p1f&b (see Glossary)—1 st inc'd.

SHORT-ROW 3 K7, wrap next st, turn—13 sts.

SHORT-ROW 5 K6, wrap next st, turn—14 sts.

SHORT-ROW 7 K5, wrap next st, turn—15 sts.

SHORT-ROWS 8 AND 10 Purl.

SHORT-ROW 9 K4, wrap next st, turn.

SHORT-ROW 11 K3, wrap next st, turn.

SHORT-ROWS 12, 14, AND 16 Purl to last 2 sts, p2tog.

SHORT-ROW 13 K5, working wraps tog with wrapped sts when you come to them, wrap next st, turn—14 sts rem.

SHORT-ROW 15 K6, working wraps tog with wrapped sts when you come to them, wrap next st, turn—13 sts rem.

SHORT-ROW 17 Knit to end, working wraps tog with wrapped sts when you come to them—12 sts rem.

SHORT-ROW 18 Purl.

Rep Short-Rows 1–18 three more times—piece measures about 9½" (24 cm) from CO at widest point. Loosely BO all sts.

FINISHING

With yarn threaded on a tapestry needle, sew the CO and BO edges tog. Stitch top of heart closed, leaving 1" (2.5 cm) open for stuffing. Stuff with fiberfill until lightly firm but not bursting. Stitch closed.

Weave in loose ends. Felt as described on page 118.

HEART

Loosely CO 12 sts. Work short-rows (see Glossary) as foll:

SHORT-ROW 1 (RS) K8, wrap next st, turn.

heart milagros door hanger

LET'S FACE IT, sometimes you just won't have the time to gather the *exact* supplies needed for an *exact* project to gift. Often I am left digging through my stash and sifting through drawers for inspiring bits and bobs. This project is a perfect example of using what you have floating about for last-minute giving. The leftover yarn from the Modern Mangas (page 58) provided the yarn for the Felted Heart Milagros (page 82), and the beads from the Crocheted Flower Brooch (page 47) offered the shiny little spacers.

All that is needed to complete the project is some strong fishing line to thread the pieces together and a sharp needle with a good-size eye that is long enough to pass through the hearts. Tada—a way to parlay that joyful bowl or basket full of milagros into another gift idea!

FINISHED SIZE

About 10" (25.5 cm) wide and 7½"
(19 cm) long; see Notes for adjusting
the size.

FABRIC

Gray wool suiting (looks fabulously
felty) measuring the desired width and
depth and 1" (2.5 cm) wide (11" [28 cm]
shown) and the desired height and depth
and 1" (2.5 cm) long (8½" [21.5 cm]
shown); lining fabric measuring the
same dimensions (dark red douppioni silk
shown here).

NOTIONS

Ruler; pencil; felt scraps cut into squares
varying in size from ¾" to 1" (2 to 2.5 cm);
fabric glue; straight pins; matching
thread; contrasting thread; embroidery
needle; six 28" (71 cm) lengths of
fingering-weight yarn (Brown Sheep
Cotton Fine shown here) for braided ties.

NOTES

✴ To make a cozy for any size notebook
  (or netbook or laptop), cut the fabric
  the width and depth and 1" (2.5 cm)
  wide (W) and the length and depth and
  1" (2.5 cm) long (L).

✴ Use a drop of fabric glue or a few
  basting stitches to keep the bits of felt
  secure prior to stitching.

✴ If you know the make and model, you
  can find the exact dimensions of any
  netbook or laptop online.

✴ When pressing the wool fabric, be sure
  to use a steam setting on your iron that
  is appropriate for wool and use a damp
  pressing cloth on top of the wool to
  protect it.

notebook or netbook cozy

Whether the recipient is high tech or low, a personalized cozy will be happily received. Originally conceived with a Netbook in mind, just a small square of wool-blend suiting offers up the majority of the felty feel of this project. The shots of color and interest are achieved through contrasting thread that top-stitches small scraplets of cut-up knitted felt onto the background. It is headshaking how little bits of nothing can make such a colorful difference. Waste not, want not!

NETBOOK COZY

Cut two pieces of wool fabric and two pieces of lining, all measuring W" × L" (see Notes). Arrange the felt bits on the right (long) side of one of the pieces of wool fabric and pin in place (use a drop of fabric glue or a few basting sts if necessary). Topstitch the felt in place with contrasting thread, taking several passes with the sewing machine from short edge to short edge. Work free-form lines of additional machine stitching as desired.

Hold the two wool fabric pieces tog with RS facing tog and sew along the short sides and bottom (non-embellished long side), using a ½" (1.3 cm) seam allowance. Trim the corners close to the stitching to lessen the bulk. Press seams open. Turn RS out and use a knitting needle to gently shape the corners into points. Press flat.

Hold the two lining pieces tog with RS facing tog and sew both short sides tog using a ½" (1.3 cm) seam allowance. Sew across the bottom, leaving about a 3" (7.5 cm) opening. Press seams open. With the lining still inside out, pull it up around the wool bag (RS will be tog) and pin lining to wool fabric along top opening. Sew tog along top opening, using a ½" (1.3 cm) seam allowance. Turn RS out by gently easing the wool bag through the lining opening, then turn in the seam allowances at the opening and sew closed by hand or machine. Push the lining down into the wool bag.

FINISHING

Topstitch ⅛" (3 mm) from opening edge. Mark placement of tie in the center of the front and back, about ⅛" (3 mm) below open edge. Cut three lengths of fingering-weight yarn, each about 28" (71 cm) long. Thread all three lengths on a tapestry needle and make a single stitch through both thicknesses at the marked position—6 working lengths.

Center the lengths and divide them into three groups of two strands each. Work a three-strand braid for about 10" (25.5 cm). Tie the ends in an overhand knot to secure. Trim ends. Rep for other side. Use the braided strands to tie a bow, securing the notebook inside the cozy.

vanilla sugar

*Makes 3 cups

This flavored sugar is a great way to say "I think you're sweet." Include a jar with the Linen Summer Wrap (page 14) to welcome the sunny season or wrap a jar with a Colorful Crochet Flower bookmark (page 90) for an avid reader.

WHAT TO GATHER

1 vanilla bean, cut in 1" (2.5 cm) pieces

3 cups extra-fine sugar

WHAT TO DO

Add vanilla bean pieces to the sugar.

Cover and let sit for two weeks before using.

Do not remove vanilla bean pieces.

Store in an airtight container.

Include a note or label with the following:

~Serve with fresh-picked strawberries.

~Use in Darjeeling tea.

~Sprinkle on crepes.

recipe

FINISHED SIZE

From about 1¼" (3.2 cm) to 2" (5 cm) across, size varies depending on yarn used.

YARNS

Sportweight (#2 Fine) and worsted weight (#4 Medium).

Shown here: KEY RING AND BOOK-MARK OR GIFT TIE: Brown Sheep Nature Spun Sport Weight (100% wool; 184 yd [168 m]/50 g): Small amounts of assorted colors (yarn shown is leftover from Granny Bag on page 30).

BROOCH: Frog Tree Alpaca Sport Weight (100% alpaca; 130 yd [119 m]/50 g), Nashua Handknits Creative Focus Worsted Wool (75% wool, 25% alpaca; 220 yd [201 m]/100 g), and Mirasol Sulka (60% merino, 20% alpaca, 20% silk; 55 yd [50 m]/50 g).

HOOK

Size F/5 to G/6 (3.75 to 4 mm) for sportweight yarn; size H/7 to I/9 (4.5 to 5.5 mm) for worsted-weight yarn.

NOTIONS

Metal ring and clip for key ring; brooch back or safety pin.

GAUGE

Not crucial for project. The bigger the yarn, the bigger the hook, the bigger the gauge, the bigger the flower; and vice-versa.

NOTES

✴ For key ring, begin and end each part leaving about a 12" (30.5 cm) tail.

✴ For brooch, begin and end each part leaving about a 6" (15 cm) tail.

✴ For brooch, work Part 1 in Frog Tree Alpaca Sport Weight, Part 2 in Nashua Handknits Creative Focus Worsted Wool, and Part 3 in Mirasol Sulka.

✴ For bookmark or gift tie, begin and end each part leaving about an 18" (45.5 cm) tail.

colorful crochet flowers

If you're like me, you have little scraps of luscious yarns far too pretty to throw away. These little gems of crochet whimsy use up yarn bits too small for anything useful, and they give you the added enjoyment of experimenting with colorways as you go. Make up a bunch of each of the pieces and then mull all the color-mixing possibilities—you'll be amazed by how wonderful some of the oddest color combinations look! Use them for key fobs, bookmarks, and brooches.

FLOWER

Part 1: Cluster

*Ch 8, turn, sl st to end; rep from * 4 times more—5 "stamen" total. Knot tails tog to form cluster.

Part 2: Small Petals

Ch 5, sl st into first ch to form ring. *Ch 6, sc into ring; rep from * 5 more times—6 petals.

Part 3: Large Petals

Ch 5, sl st into first ch to form ring. *Ch 8, sc into ring; rep from * 7 more times—8 petals.

FINISHING

Assemble parts by inserting the tails of the small petals through the center of the large petals, then inserting the tails of the cluster through the center of the petals. Knot ends tog to secure in place.

Braid

Divide tails into three groups of two strands each and work 3-strand braid as follows for your project.

KEY RING

Work braid for ½" to 1½" (1.3 to 3.8 cm), slide ring onto one group, then cont to braid for desired length. Secure ends with an overhand knot. Trim ends.

BROOCH

Work braid for ½" to 1" (1.3 to 2.5 cm). Secure ends with an overhand knot. Trim ends.

BOOKMARK OR GIFT TIE

Work braid for or 12" (30.5 cm) or desired length. Secure ends with an overhand knot. Trim ends.

Lavender sachets

Sachets have always been a gift-giving staple for me. Inspired by whatever is floating around my work space at the time, they are always changing and always unique. I like to tuck one or two into a pair of socks or a folded scarf to give the gifted a whiff that something good is about to happen.

FINISHED SIZE
About 4" (10 cm) square.

FABRIC
Two piece of natural linen measuring 5" (12.5 cm) square for each sachet.

NOTIONS
Sharp scissors; sharp-point sewing needle and matching thread; pieces of scrap felt cut into squares varying in size from 1" to 1½" (2.5 to 3.8 cm); straight pins; embroidery needle with eye small enough to penetrate button holes; embroidery cotton; assorted buttons; about 15 grams (0.5 ounce) of lavender for each sachet.

NOTES
✧ Add all embellishments before sewing the pieces together.

✧ Begin sewing the seams at the center of an edge so that all of the corners will look the same and to facilitate pressing and handstitching.

✧ To help fill the pouch with lavender, insert the small end of a funnel or paper cone into the opening and pour into the wide end.

SACHET

With embroidery needle and cotton, sew felt to right side of one linen square, using a running stitch around the inner perimeter of the felt, at least ¾" (2 cm) away from each edge (sachets shown have the squares placed near the center). Sew button on top of felt.

Hold two linen squares tog with right sides facing tog. With sharp-point sewing needle, matching thread, and beg at the center of one edge, sew the square tog with a ½" (1.3 cm) seam allowance, leaving a 1½" (3.8 cm) opening on one side for filling with lavender. Trim the corners close to the stitching to lessen the bulk. Turn bag right side out by easing it gingerly through the opening. Use a knitting needle to nudge the corners into points. Press flat, being careful not to touch the iron to the button.

Fill with lavender (see Notes), then turn in the seam allowances at the opening and stitch closed.

FINISHED SIZE
About 4½" (11.5 cm) wide and 6½"
(16.5 cm) long.

FABRIC
Piece of fabric from lightweight sweater
that has been *lightly* felted or fabric
rescued from a well-loved T-shirt or
sweatshirt, cut to measure 8" (20.5 cm)
wide and 12" (30.5 cm) long; remnant of
green felt or felted sweater fabric for leaf
accent, cut to measure 2" (5 cm) wide
and 4" (10 cm) long.

NOTIONS
Sharp-point sewing needle and matching
thread; lightweight paper for wrist-rest
template; card stock for leaf template;
pencil or washable marker to trace
templates; sharp scissors; straight pins;
embroidery needle and six-strand cotton
embroidery floss to match green felt;
about 250 grams (9 ounces) of whole
flax seed.

NOTES
✣ To help fill the pouch with seeds, insert
the small end of a funnel or paper cone
into the opening and pour the seeds
into the wide end.

✣ For maximum comfort, do not
appliqué anything exactly where your
wrist will lie.

wrist rest

A lightweight wool sweater (this one
was snagged on a nail) tossed in the wash
created the perfect felted fabric for this
organically shaped wrist rest. For this project,
it is best for the felt to be firm enough to hold
its shape but supple enough to pass easily
through a sewing machine. Filled with whole
flax seed, all it takes is a quick zap in the
microwave to make a soothing place to rest
a wrist that has had too much mouse action.

WRIST REST

Fold the fabric in half with RS facing together. Trace the wrist-rest template onto lightweight paper, cut out, and place the pattern on the folded fabric. Cut shape through both layers of fabric.

With RS facing tog, sew around the edge of the shape by hand or machine, allowing a ½" (1.3 cm) seam allowance and leaving a 1½" (3.8 cm) opening for filling with seeds. Press. Trim seam and clip curves, being careful not to cut through stitching. Turn the pouch RS out.

Fill with flax seeds (see Notes), then handstitch the opening securely closed.

FINISHING

Trace the leaf template onto green felt and cut out. Pin leaf as desired onto wrist rest (see Notes). With cotton embroidery floss and embroidery needle, sew the leaf in place as shown, using a backstitch (see Glossary) for the center of the leaf and adding straight stitches (see Glossary) for stem and veins.

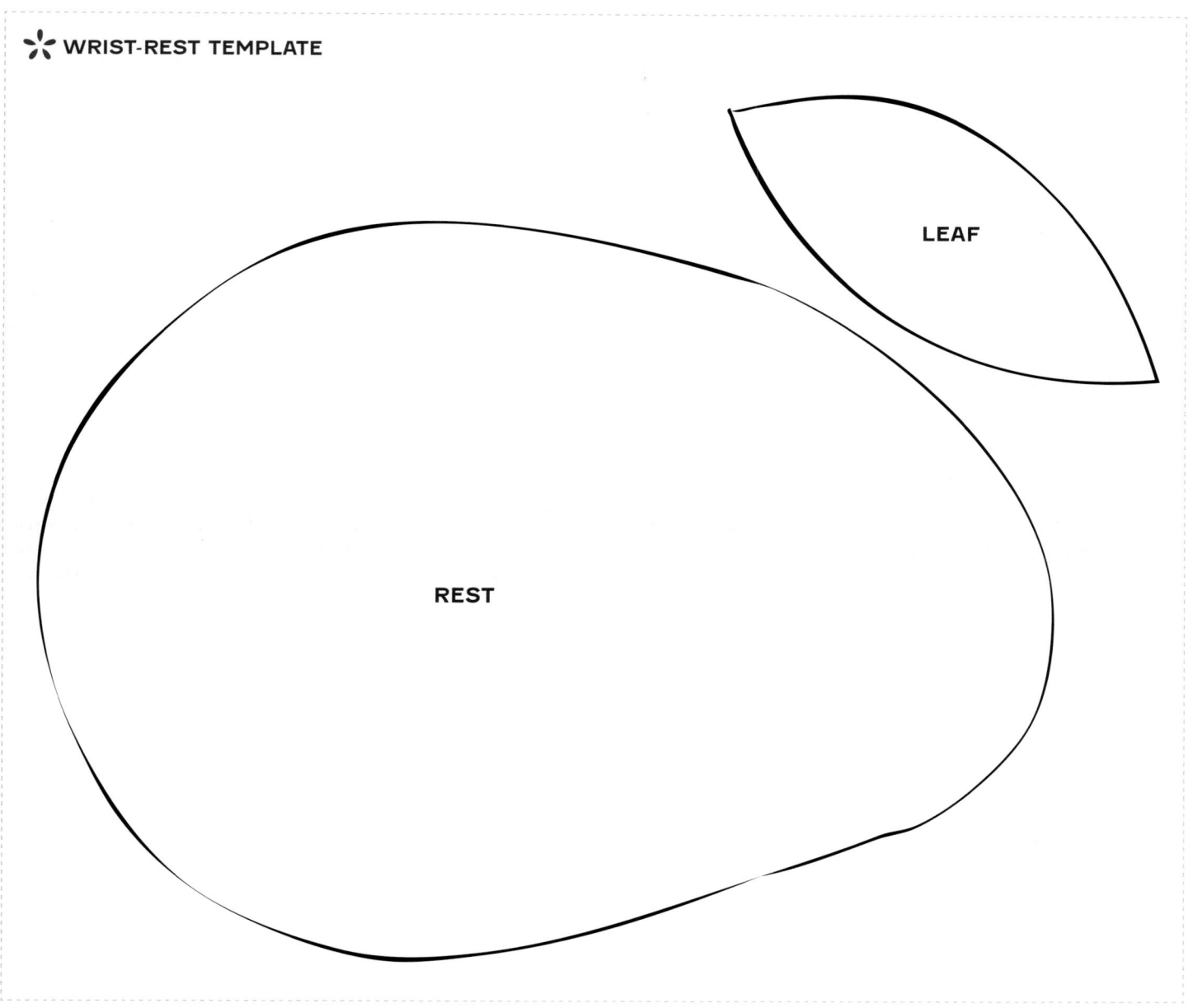

WRIST-REST TEMPLATE

LEAF

REST

gift bag

Whipping up your own gift bags does take a bit of time, but they are always well received. When I have the time, I add gussets to make a square base so that after the gifting, the bag can be used to tote portable projects. It doubles the gifting!

FINISHED SIZE
About 11½" (29 cm) wide and 13" (33 cm) deep.

FABRIC
Douppioni silk measuring 15" (38 cm) wide and 26" (66 cm) long (about ½ yd [45 cm] if buying off the bolt).

NOTIONS
Sharp scissors; straight pins; sharp-point sewing needle matching thread; Felted Heart Milagros pin (page 82); 3 lengths of yarn, each 36" (91.5 cm) long for braided tie.

NOTES
✲ The yarn for the felted Milagros pin and braided tie is Classic Elite Miracle in #3388 prairie sunset and #3332 gamay.

✲ Instead of a Felted Heart Milagros, decorate the bag with a Colorful Crocheted Flower (page 90) or a Paper Rose (page 34).

✲ You can make this project simple by cutting scraps of fabric to size, stitching the side and bottom seams, pinking or zig-zagging the seams, and adding a quick double-fold hem at the top. I chose to use French seams to protect the silk fabric from fraying, and I made a gusset to create a flat bottom.

BAG

Cut two pieces of fabric to the desired dimensions, adding about 1½" (3.8 cm) to the width and 2" (5 cm) to the height for seam allowances and hem (for a bag that measures 11½" × 13" [29 × 33 cm], cut each piece of fabric 13" × 15" [33 × 38 cm]).

Sew the side seams in a French seam to neatly enclose the seam allowances on the inside of the bag: Beginning with *wrong* sides tog, pin the two pieces tog along one long side. By hand or machine, sew ¼" (6 mm) seam. Press and trim the seam allowance to ⅛" (3 mm). Rep for other side seam. Turn bag so WS is facing out. Press seamline flat. Pin and sew each side seam again, enclosing the original seam in a wider seam (about ½" [1.3 cm]). Turn bag RS out and press. Sew the bottom seam in the same manner.

To make the gussets, turn the bag inside out, flatten the bottom, and sew a diagonal seam at each corner as for Granny Bag shown on page 30. Fold the top edge down about ½" (1.3 cm) to the WS and press. Fold again to enclose raw edge. Stitch close to lower folded edge by hand or machine.

FINISHING
Tie

Hold three lengths of yarn tog and knot at one end. Work a 3-strand braid. Knot the other end. With sharp-point sewing needle and matching thread, sew one end of the braid to the top of the bag. Tie braid into a bow to close the bag.

Decorate with a felted heart, crocheted flower, or paper rose, if desired.

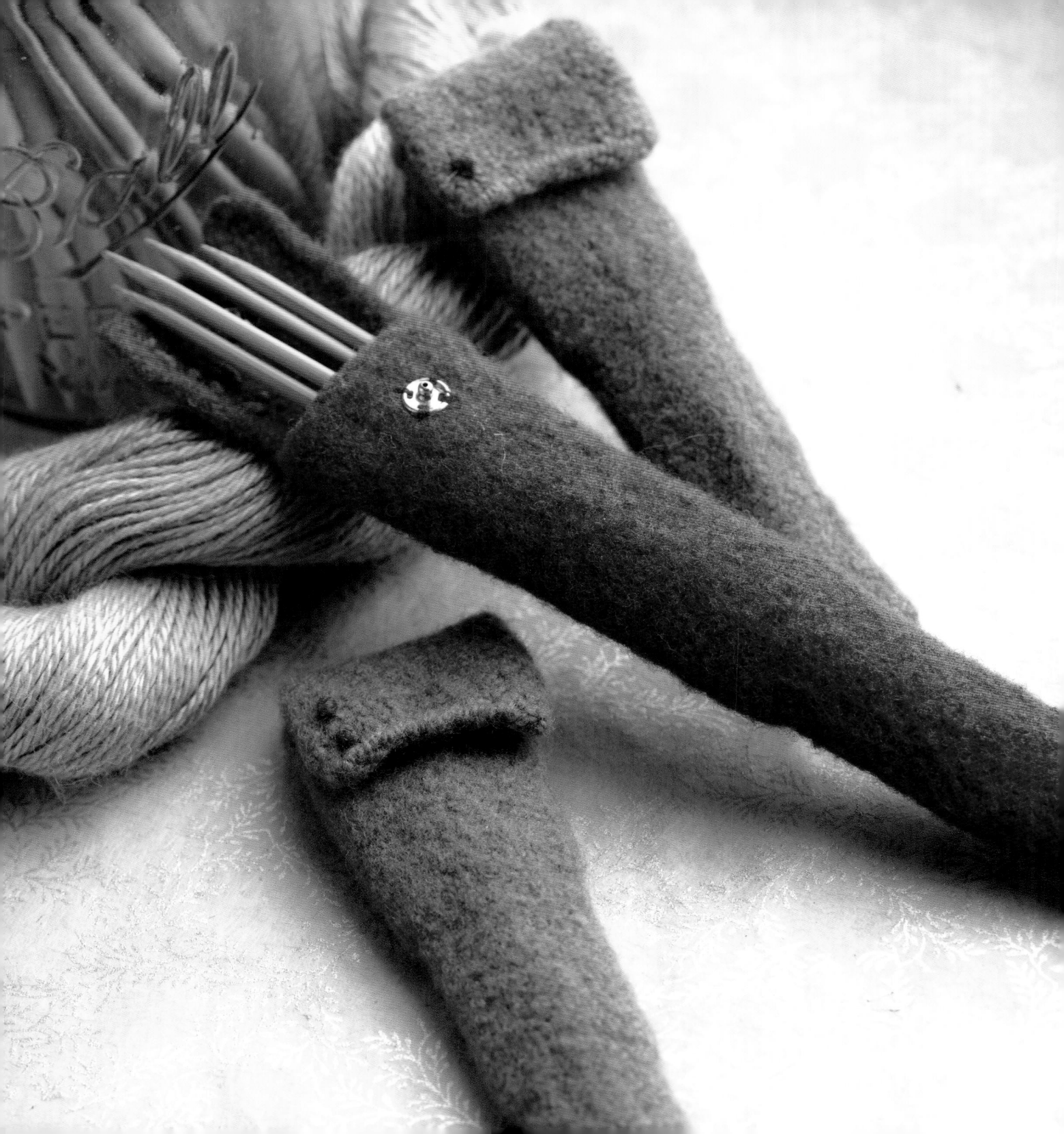

double-point needle case

The committed and disorganized sock knitter knows the frustration of hunting down sets of matching double-pointed needles. A selection of needle cases, each holding a single set, will make for an easier and far more colorful life. Clearly mark the flap with French knots to denote the size needles—one knot for size 1, two knots for size 2, and so on. Or, add some small buttons or beads or use silky floss to embroider the needle size.

FINISHED SIZE

About 5¼ (7)" (13.5 [18] cm) long from base to fold of flap. To fit needles up to 5 (7)" (12.5 [18] cm) long.

YARN

DK weight (#3 Light).

Shown here: Reynolds Soft Sea Wool (100% wool; 162 yd [147 m]/50 g): #910 raspberry (shown for large cozy) and #521 teal (shown for small cozies), 1 skein each.

NEEDLES

Size U.S. 6 (4 mm): set of 4 or 5 double-pointed (dpn). Adjust needle size if necessary to obtain the correct gauge.

NOTIONS

Marker (m); tapestry needle; sewing needle; one 9-mm snap set for each cozy; sharp-point sewing needle and matching thread.

GAUGE

20 stitches and 28 rounds = 4" (10 cm) in stockinette stitch, before felting.

CASE

CO 12 sts. Place marker (pm) and join for working in the rnd, being careful not to twist sts.

RNDS 1–12 Knit.

RND 13 K1f&b (see Glossary), k4, [k1f&b] 2 times, k4, k1f&b—16 sts.

RNDS 14–25 Knit.

RND 26 K1f&b, k6, [k1f&b] 2 times, k6, k1f&b—20 sts.

Knit even until piece measures 6 (8½)" (15 [21.5] cm) from CO.

Flap

Loosely BO 10 sts—10 sts rem. Working back and forth in rows, cont in St st (knit RS rows; purl WS rows) until flap measures 2" (5 cm). Loosely BO all sts.

FINISHING

Thread CO tail onto a tapestry needle and sew base of case closed. Weave in loose ends.

Felting

Felt as described on page 118.

Embroidery

With contrasting yarn, work French knots (see Glossary) to indicate needle size: one knot for size U.S. 1 (2.25 mm) needles, two knots for size U.S. 2 (2.75 mm) needles, and so on.

With sharp-point sewing needle and matching thread, sew one half of snap to underside of flap and the other half to the corresponding position on the cozy.

FINISHED SIZE

About 7" (18 cm) circumference at base and 5" (12.5 cm) tall. To fit an average large egg.

FABRIC

Felt scraps from a recycled lightweight sweater that has been fully felted (page 119).

NOTIONS

Card stock for template; pencil or washable marker to trace template; sharp scissors; embellishments—cotton embroidery floss, needlefelting gear, felt scraps, buttons, bells, etc.; embroidery or crewel needle; a length of matching or coordinating fine yarn or embroidery floss to stitch together the cozy.

EGG COZIES

Trace the cozy template onto the felted fabric and cut out. Personalize the cozy any way you like. Keep in mind that it is easiest to do all the embroidery, needlefelting, stitching, etc., before sewing the side seam. Align the two straight edges with WS facing tog (seam will show on outside of cozy).

Thread the length of fine yarn or floss on an embroidery or crewel needle and sew the straight edges tog in a ⅛" (3 mm) seam with a running stitch or use a blanket stitch (see Glossary) for a more decorative effect.

cut-and-sew egg cozies

If you don't quite have the time to make custom-fitted cozies from scratch (page 78), you can still brighten up the breakfast table with this quick cut-and-handstitched option. Dig through your odds and sods of felted scraps, create a template out of card stock, and start tracing away. For one, I chose a bit of needlefelting and stitching that mimics the Felted Trivets and Coasters (page 114). For the other, I was inspired by the leaf appliqué found on the Wrist Rest (page 96). Decorate in any manner that makes your heart sing.

✳ **EGG-COZY TEMPLATE**

felted yule bling

Unwrapping all the little bits and bobs that are brought out every year to adorn the tree is a tradition in many homes. Finding that some of the fragile treasures did not survive storage is never a happy discovery. A modern take on traditional Swedish cut-felt ornaments, these bits of bling will last from year to year. Crochet circles worked in the softest fingering-weight alpaca are felted, stitched, stacked, and held together in a neat package with a simple braided ribbon.

FINISHED SIZE

About 2½" (6.5 cm) in diameter, after felting.

YARN

Fingering weight (#1 Super Fine).

Shown here: Frog Tree Alpaca Fingering (100% alpaca; 215 yd [196 m]/50 g): #204 red, 1 ball.

HOOK

Size U.S. G/6 (4 mm) hook.

NOTIONS

Embroidery needle; DMC 25 Embroidery Cotton in #453 (pale silver grey), two (8.7 yd [8 m]) skeins.

GAUGE

2 rounds = about 1¾" (4.5 cm) in diameter, before felting. Exact gauge is not crucial for this project.

CIRCLES

(make 2 for each bling)

Ch 4. Sl st in first chain to form a ring.

RND 1 Ch 2 (count as 1 dc here and throughout), dc into ring 11 times, sl st in top of second ch—12 dc.

RND 2 Ch 2, dc in same ch, work 2 dc in each of the next 11 dc, sl st into top of second ch—24 dc.

RND 3 Ch 2, dc in same ch, work 1 dc in next dc, *work 2 dc in next dc, work 1 dc in following dc; rep from * to end of rnd, sl st in top of second ch—36 dc.

RND 4 Rep Rnd 3—54 dc.

Fasten off.

FINISHING

Weave in loose ends.

Felting

Felt as described on page 118.

Embroidery

With embroidery cotton threaded on a needle and using the photos as a guide, embroider (see Glossary for embroidery instructions) the traditional snowflake pattern in chain stitches or the modern snowflake pattern in long stitches that are anchored in the center and topped with 4-wrap French knots.

Assembly

Hold two circles tog with WS facing together. With yarn threaded on a tapestry needle, use whipstitches (see Glossary) to join the outer edges of the circles tog. Cut embroidery cotton into 12" (30.5 cm) lengths. Fold each length in half and tie ends tog in an overhand knot. Attach loop to edge of circle with a half-hitch knot.

Braided "Ribbon" (optional)

Cut 9 lengths of embroidery cotton, each 36" (91.5 cm) long. Tie one end of the bundle in an overhand knot. Divide into 3 groups of 3 lengths each and braid for desired length. Tie end with an overhand knot. Trim ends.

mulling spice mix

*Makes 4 sachets

Include a few sachets of this traditional mix with some Yule Bling (page 106) to ensure a happy holiday.

WHAT TO GATHER

8 squares of cheesecloth cut into 4" (10 cm) squares

4 lengths of string, each 8" (20.5 cm) long

8 slices of gingerroot, each about ⅛" (3 mm) thick

6 strips each of lemon and orange rind, each about 1" (2.5 cm) thick

¼ cup whole cloves

2 tbsp whole allspice

2 cinnimon sticks, each about 3"– 4" (7.5 – 10 cm) long, broken in small pieces

WHAT TO DO

Arrange gingerroot, lemon rind, and orange rind on rack.

Let stand for about a day until dry and brittle.

Break gingerroot, lemon rind, and orange rind into ¼" (6 mm) pieces and place in mixing bowl.

Add cloves, allspice, and cinnamon and mix thoroughly.

Scoop one-quarter of the mix onto center of a double layer of cheesecloth. Pull up the corners and tie with string. Repeat with remaining mix.

Include a note or label with the following:

~Mulled Wine: In a medium saucepan, combine a bottle of red wine, ⅓ cup of sugar, and 1 sachet. Simmer until warm and fragrant.

~Mulled Juice: In a medium saucepan, combine 6–8 cups of apple cider or cranberry juice and 1 sachet. Simmer until warm and fragrant.

~Room Fragrance: Simmer 1 sachet in a few cups of water. Keep a careful eye on the stove.

recipe

FINISHED SIZE

SCISSORS SLEEVE: About 7½" (19 cm) long without flap and 2¼" (5.5 cm) wide at top, after felting.

PINCUSHION: About 4" (10 cm) high and 4" (10 cm) wide, after felting.

YARN

Fingering weight (#1 Super Fine).

Shown here: Brown Sheep Nature Spun Fingering Weight (100% wool; 310 yd [283 m]/50 g): #N80 mountain purple (purple) and #N48 scarlet (red), 1 ball each.

NEEDLES

Sizes U.S. 6 and 10 (4 and 6 mm): straight. Adjust needle size if necessary to obtain the correct gauge.

NOTIONS

Tapestry needle; embroidery needle; polyester or bamboo fiberfill.

GAUGE

SCISSORS SLEEVE: 21 stitches and 30 rows = 4" (10 cm) in stockinette stitch with smaller needles, before felting.

PINCUSHION: 16 stitches and 22 rows = 4" (10 cm) in stockinette stitch with larger needles and yarn doubled, before felting.

NOTE

✳ The scissors sleeve will accommodate scissors measuring up to 5" (12.5 cm) from tip to beginning of finger holes. If your scissors are considerably smaller, trim the top to the desired length after felting.

scissors sleeve + heart pincushion

When I entertained the notion of a knitted gift for a sewing friend, my first thought was of a scissors sleeve. After a wee bit of mulling, I concluded that I could use short-rows to create a cone shape that would accommodate scissors blades of various lengths. By adding some simple stitching on the flap the gift is that much more special. The pincushion? Just a variation of one of my very favorite Felted Heart Milagros (page 82) all pumped up.

SCISSORS SLEEVE

With purple and smaller needles, loosely CO 45 sts. Work short-rows (see Glossary) as foll:

SHORT-ROW 1 (RS) K40, wrap next st, turn.

SHORT-ROWS 2, 4, 6, 8, 10, 12, 14, AND 16 Purl.

SHORT-ROW 3 K35, wrap next st, turn.

SHORT-ROW 5 K30, wrap next st, turn.

SHORT-ROW 7 K25, wrap next st, turn.

SHORT-ROW 9 K20, wrap next st, turn.

SHORT-ROW 11 K15, wrap next st, turn.

SHORT-ROW 13 K10, wrap next st, turn.

SHORT-ROW 15 K5, wrap next st, turn.

SHORT-ROW 17 Knit, working wraps tog with wrapped sts when you come to them.

SHORT-ROW 18 Purl.

Rep Rows 1–18 two more times—piece measures about 7¼" (18 cm) from CO along long edge. Loosely BO all sts.

Flap

With purple, loosely CO 18 sts. Work even in St st until piece measures about 5¾" (14.5 cm) from CO. Loosely BO all sts.

FINISHING

With purple threaded on a tapestry needle, sew the CO and BO edges of sleeve tog to form a cone. Weave in loose ends. Felt as described on page 118.

Stitching

With red threaded on an embroidery needle, work running stitches (see

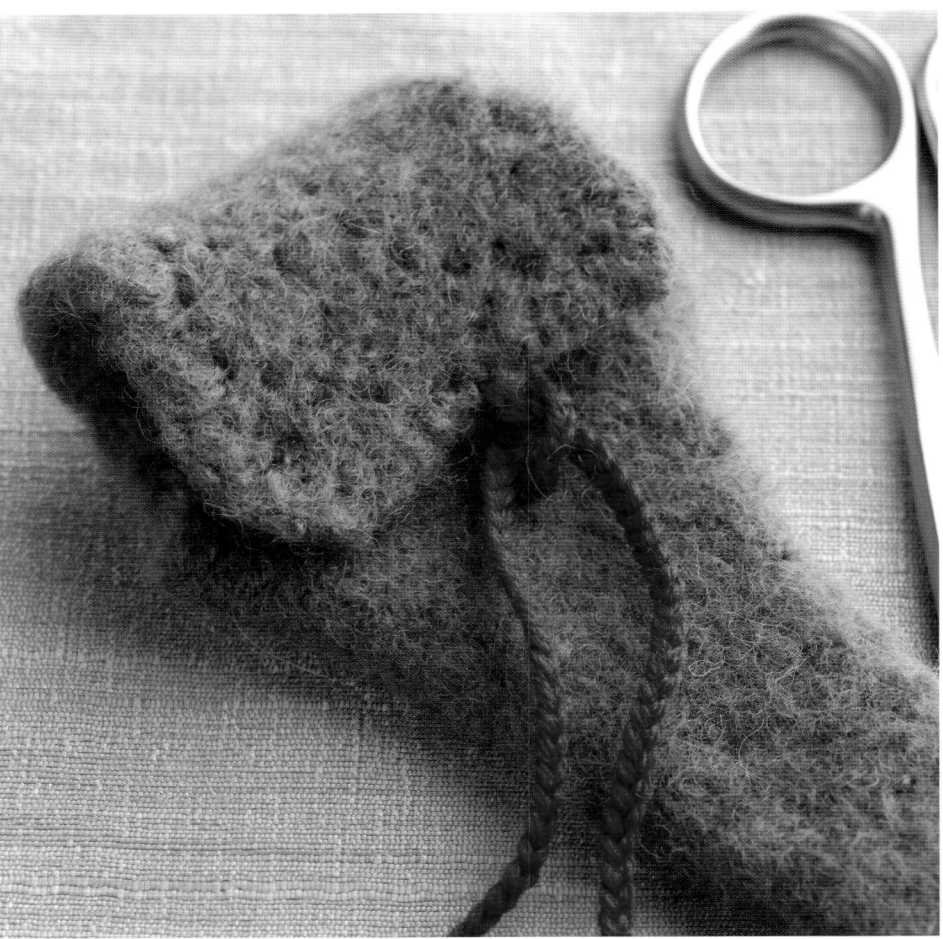

Glossary) to create free-form loops as shown. With purple, use backstitches (see Glossary) to sew flap to sleeve.

Braided Ties

Mark for first tie at center of flap just above the edge. Cut three lengths of red,

each about 18" (45.5 cm) long. Thread all three lengths onto a tapestry needle and make a single stitch at the marked position—6 lengths. Center the lengths and divide them into three groups of two strands each. Work a three-strand braid for about 6" (15 cm). Tie the ends in an overhand knot to secure. Trim ends. Make another braided tie at the center of the sleeve, opposite the first tie.

PIN CUSHION

With two strands of purple held tog and larger needles, loosely CO 18 sts. Work short-rows (see Glossary) as foll:

SHORT-ROW 1 (RS) K14, wrap next st, turn.

SHORT-ROWS 2, 4, 6, AND 8 Purl to last st, p1f&b (see Glossary)—1 st inc'd.

SHORT-ROW 3 K13, wrap next st, turn—15 sts.

SHORT-ROW 5 K12, wrap next st, turn—16 sts.

SHORT-ROW 7 K11, wrap next st, turn—17 sts.

SHORT-ROW 9 K10, wrap next st, turn—18 sts.

SHORT-ROWS 10 AND 12 Purl.

SHORT-ROW 11: K8, wrap next st, turn.

SHORT-ROW 13 K5, wrap next st, turn.

SHORT-ROWS 14, 16, 18, AND 20 Purl to last 2 sts, p2tog.

SHORT-ROW 15 K6, working wraps tog with wrapped sts when you come to them, wrap next st, turn—17 sts rem.

SHORT-ROW 17 K7, working wraps tog with wrapped sts when you come to them, wrap next st, turn—16 sts rem.

SHORT-ROW 19 K10, working wraps tog with wrapped sts when you come to them, wrap next st, turn—15 sts rem.

SHORT-ROW 21 Knit to end, working wraps tog with wrapped sts when you come to them—14 sts rem.

SHORT-ROW 22 Purl.

SHORT-ROWS 23–43 Rep Short-Rows 1–21.

SHORT-ROW 44 With two strands of red held tog, purl all sts.

With red, rep Short-Rows 1–22 twice.

Loosely BO all sts.

FINISHING

With either yarn threaded on a tapestry needle, sew the CO and BO edges tog. Sew top closed, leaving a 1" (2.5 cm) gap for stuffing. Stuff with fiberfill until lightly firm but not bursting. Stitch closed. Weave in loose ends. Felt as described on page 118. With purple threaded on an embroidery needle, work running stitches (see Glossary) to create free-form loops as shown.

felted trivet + coasters

Crochet is the way to go if you want perfectly felted circles. These circles are great practice for a crochet and needlefelting newbie—any "imperfections" will disappear in the wash, and dots are easy to master with a felting needle. Add a loop, and the trivet can be hung near the stove and double as a quirky and convenient pot holder!

FINISHED SIZE

TRIVET: About 7½" (19 cm) in diameter, after felting.

COASTERS: About 4¾" (12 cm) in diameter, after felting.

YARN

Worsted weight (#4 Medium).

Shown here: Paton's Classic Wool (100% wool; 223 yd [204 m]/100 g): #240 leaf green, #238 paprika, and #218 peacock, 1 ball each.

Fleece Artist Merino Sliver (100% merino; 50 g/reeling): cosmic dawn, 1 reeling.

HOOK

Size J/10 (6 mm). Adjust hook size if necessary to obtain the correct gauge.

NOTIONS

Tapestry needle; embroidery needle; one 8.7 yd (8 m) skein of DMC 25 embroidery cotton in #844 (dark gray); medium-sized needlefelting needle; dense foam pad for needlefelting.

GAUGE

2 rounds = 2½" (6.5 cm) in diameter, before felting.

work 1 dc in next 2 dc; rep from * to end of rnd, sl st in top of second ch to join—72 dc.

RND 6 Rep Rnd 5—96 dc.

RND 7 Ch 2, work 1 dc in each dc, sl st into top of second ch to join.

RND 8 Rep Rnd 7.

Fasten off.

COASTERS

Make 2 each in peacock and paprika. Work as for trivet, ending with Rnd 5.

FINISHING

Weave in loose ends.

Felting

Felt as described on page 118. Pin to shape on a flat surface and allow to air-dry. Once dry, steam-press if necessary.

Needlefelting and Embroidery

With small amounts of sliver, needlefelt (see page 119) small dots as desired. With embroidery cotton threaded on an embroidery needle, work chain stitches (see Glossary) around each dot.

TRIVET

With leaf green, ch 4. Sl st in first ch to form a ring.

RND 1 Ch 2 (count as 1 dc here and throughout), dc into ring 11 times, sl st in top of second ch to join—12 dc.

RND 2 Ch 2, dc into same ch, work 2 dc in each of the next 11 dc, sl st in top of second ch to join—24 dc.

RND 3 Ch 2, dc into same ch, work 1 dc in next dc, *work 2 dc in the next dc, work 1 dc in foll dc; rep from * to end of rnd, sl st in top of second ch to join—36 dc.

RND 4 Rep Rnd 3—54 dc.

RND 5 Ch 2, dc into same ch, work 1 dc in next 2 dc, *work 2 dc in the next dc,

make it special ✺

WHEN it comes to embellishments and finishing, I'm not a big fan of step-by-step instructions. To me, they encourage "cookie cutter crafting" that defeats the whole purpose of making things by hand. Instead, I hope that *Gifted* will inspire you to create gifts that reflect your passion and personality as well as the personality of the recipient. Keep in mind that the only rule to creativity is that there are no rules! There may be *momentary* better ways of doing things, but in general, new ideas arise from mistakes. To paraphrase a dear friend, there are no mistakes—just opportunities! That said, there are a number of tips that will simplify the process, whether it's embroidery, beading, or felting.

embroidery

As with most creative endeavors, when it comes to embroidery, you are only limited by your imagination. Although I used cotton embroidery floss for many of the *Gifted* projects, the choice is all yours. Embroidery is a perfect way to make use of leftover bits of thread and yarn that may be in your scrap basket.

* You do not need to knot the end of the thread when you begin embroidery. Simply thread the needle, enter the work from front (right side) to back (wrong side) a few inches (2.5 cm) away from where the stitching is to begin, leaving a tail about 3" to 4" (7.5 to 10 cm) on the right side. After the stitching is complete, pull that tail to the wrong side and weave it in.

* Use manageable lengths of stitching thread—36" (91.5 cm) is more than enough length. Don't be fooled into thinking that you'll save time weaving in multiple ends by using one overly long length. You'll end up spending more time straightening tangles and getting frustrated.

* Be sure that the stitching yarn can be laundered the same as the knitted project. Check colorfastness before stitching it on the knitted or crocheted base.

* Consider splitting the plies of thick yarn to create a suitable yarn for embroidery. I commonly work with two plies of four-ply yarn.

make it special

beading

Instead of knitting or crocheting beads in place as I work, I often prefer to add them after the fact. This gives me complete freedom to place the beads exactly where I think they will look best.

* Attach the beads with thread or yarn that matches the base fabric.

* If the size of needle necessary to accommodate the thickness of the yarn is too big for the bead to pass over, thread the beads on an auxiliary thread and a smaller needle. Thread a 10" (25.5 cm) length of strong thread through the smaller needle, fold the string in half and knot the ends to form a ring. Loop the yarn through the thread ring, pass the bead over the needle, along the thread, and onto the yarn.

* When adding beads in close clusters, simply weave the needle through stitches on the wrong side to where the next bead is to be placed instead of knotting and cutting the yarn after each bead.

felting

When it comes to felting, you don't have to limit yourself to pure wool. Alpaca, camel, yak, cashmere, mohair, and angora all have great felting potential. But because every yarn felts differently, it is important that you knit and felt a generous swatch to understand how a particular yarn will behave. Try felting blends of these fibers with nonfelting fibers—silk, Tencel, rayon, or soy—for an inspiring adventure. Swatch and wash to discover the possibilities.

There is no magical formula when it comes to the shrinking factor of a felted project. Therefore, it's always a good idea to take the time to knit and wash a swatch. Every yarn felts differently—even different colors of the same yarn can have very different results. Small projects are best handfelted.

BEADING

* Be careful not to let the inside of a project fuse together. I had to gently pry apart the sides of my first felted egg cozy and the crease never went away. Check the progress periodically and never underestimate how quickly an item can go from floppy to felted.

* When felting in the washing machine, place the project in a lingerie bag or pillowcase to reduce the amount of fiber that can escape and clog the machine or attach to the next load of laundry.

* Keep in mind that what appears to be a felting disaster may in fact be a wonderful opportunity. I have had more than my share of mishaps when felting. The boo-boos that I've collected over the years have become inspiring materials for other projects.

FELT APPLIQUÉ

Working with felt appliqué is one of my favorite ways to embellish gifts. I love the handcrafted quality of appliqué.

* I prefer that the stitch definition of the felted fabric is completely obscured before I cut the fabric for appliqué. That way, I'm sure that the fabric will not fray when cut.

* Use sharp scissors to cut the felt pieces and use a sharp needle with the appropriate size eye to stitch the pieces in place. Your work is only as good as your tools.

FELTING READY-MADE KNITS

The art of felting ready-made knits is a whole bunch of known-knowns (superwash wool will not felt and lambswool almost certainly will), unknown-knowns (a 50% wool 50% silk blend will felt, but we don't know exactly how well until we try), and unknown-unknowns (a 70% rayon 30% alpaca inexplicitly felts like a dream with thrilling, lustrous little loops of rayon that raise above the felted background).

✳ When felting reclaimed sweaters, etc., assume nothing and be prepared to be pleasantly surprised or disappointed.

✳ Take solace in the fact that you did not spend hours knitting the piece to begin with. The odds are good that it wasn't wearable when you began or why would you want to felt it in the first place?

✳ Read the content label to increase your chances of success. If the garment is made of pure wool, 100% wool, lambswool, 100% alpaca, or 50% wool and 50% alpaca, you can expect good results. Blends of these fibers with silk, Tencel, rayon, or soy may also work. Avoid superwash wool, which has been treated not to felt.

✳ If the care label says handwash, dry flat, or dry-clean only, the chances are good that it will felt.

✳ I prefer to felt reclaimed sweaters, etc., that are lightweight. Lightweight garments produce a finer and more pliable

felted fabric that suit many project ideas. Besides, it's better that a machine to do all the fine, time consuming work and you stick to the quicker, chunkier handknitting. I also find that simple stitch patterns such as stockinette stitch are best. Lace patterns often get lost during felting, Fair Isle patterns can distort and blur, cable patterns can become too bulky.

✳ Don't worry about rips or holes—the felting process will prevent them from raveling.

NEEDLEFELTING

When needlefelting, it's important to mind your fingers. Needlefelting needles are sharp and painful if stabbed into flesh. It's better to be cautious than learn the hard way.

✳ You may wish to dig up some thimbles for protection for at the very least your first few projects.

✳ Always have a few needlefelting needles on hand. You are almost guaranteed to break a needle on your first go.

✳ Most needlefelters work against a dense foam pad. Not knowing any better when I started, I used a 2" (4 cm) pad of Styrofoam covered with muslin (to hold the pieces that would inevitably crumble off). I still prefer this to a dense foam pad. This is a creative process—use whatever works for you!

NEEDLEFELTING

Have fun when making it special!

glossary

ABBREVIATIONS

beg(s)	begin(s); beginning
BO	bind off
CC	contrasting color
cm	centimeter(s)
cn	cable needle
CO	cast on
cont	continue(s); continuing
dec(s)	decrease(s); decreasing
dpn	double-pointed needles
foll	follow(s); following
g	gram(s)
inc(s)	increase(s); increasing
k	knit
k1f&b	knit into the front and back of same stitch
kwise	knitwise, as if to knit
m	marker(s)
MC	main color
mm	millimeter(s)
M1	make one (increase)
p	purl
p1f&b	purl into front and back of same stitch
patt(s)	pattern(s)
psso	pass slipped stitch over
pwise	purlwise, as if to purl
rem	remain(s); remaining
rep	repeat(s); repeating
rev St st	reverse stockinette stitch

rnd(s)	round(s)
RS	right side
sl	slip
sl st	slip st (slip 1 stitch purlwise unless otherwise indicated)
ssk	slip 2 stitches knitwise, one at a time, from the left needle to right needle, insert left needle tip through both front loops and knit together from this position (1 stitch decrease)
st(s)	stitch(es)
St st	stockinette stitch
tbl	through back loop
tog	together
WS	wrong side
wyb	with yarn in back
wyf	with yarn in front
yd	yard(s)
yo	yarnover
*	repeat starting point
* *	repeat all instructions between asterisks
( )	alternate measurements and/or instructions
[ ]	work instructions as a group a specified number of times

BIND-OFFS

Standard Bind-Off

Knit the first stitch, *knit the next stitch (2 stitches on right needle), insert left needle tip into first stitch on right needle (**figure 1**) and lift this stitch up and over the second stitch (**figure 2**) and off the needle (**figure 3**). Repeat from * for the desired number of stitches.

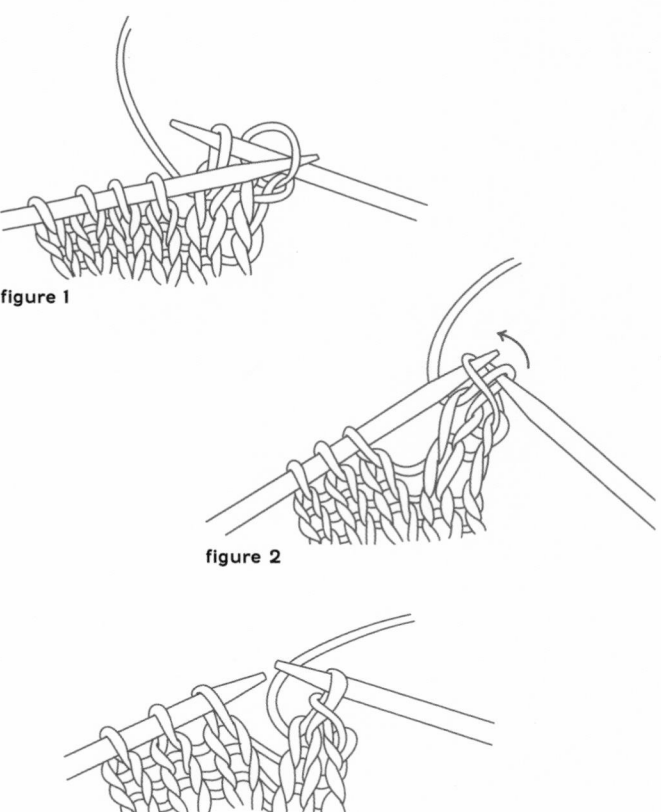

figure 1

figure 2

figure 3

Three-Needle Bind-Off

Place the stitches to be joined onto two separate needles and hold the needles parallel so that the right sides of the knitting face together. Insert a third needle into the first stitch on each of the two needles (**figure 1**) and knit them together as a single stitch (**figure 2**). *Knit the next stitch on each needle the same way, then use the left needle tip to lift the first stitch over the second and off the needle (**figure 3**). Repeat from * until no stitches remain on the first two needles. Cut the yarn and pull the tail through the last stitch to secure it.

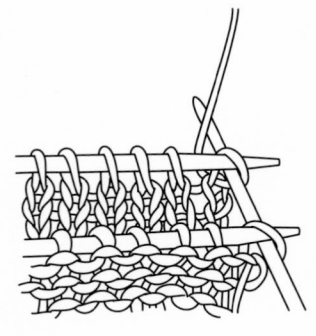

figure 1

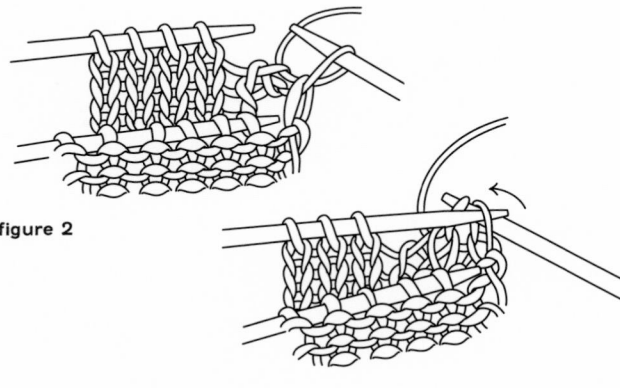

figure 2

figure 3

CAST-ONS

Backward-Loop Cast-On

*Loop working yarn and place it on needle backward so that it doesn't unwind. Repeat from *.

Cable Cast-On

Hold needle with working yarn in your left hand with the wrong side of the work facing you. *Insert right needle *between* the first 2 stitches on left needle (**figure 1**), wrap yarn around needle as if to knit, draw yarn through (**figure 2**), and place new loop on left needle (**figure 3**) to form a new stitch. Repeat from * for the desired number of stitches, always working between the first 2 stitches on the left needle.

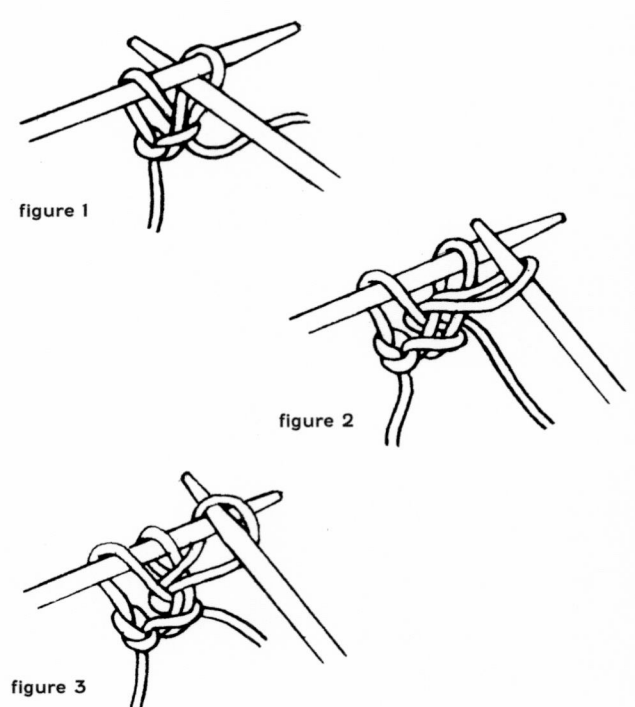

figure 1

figure 2

figure 3

Crochet Chain Provisional Cast-On

With waste yarn and crochet hook, make a loose crochet chain (see page 124) about 4 stitches more than you need to cast on. With knitting needle, working yarn, and beginning 2 stitches from end of chain, pick up and knit 1 stitch through the back loop of each crochet chain **(figure 1)** for desired number of stitches. When you're ready to work in the opposite direction, pull out the crochet chain to expose live stitches **(figure 2)**.

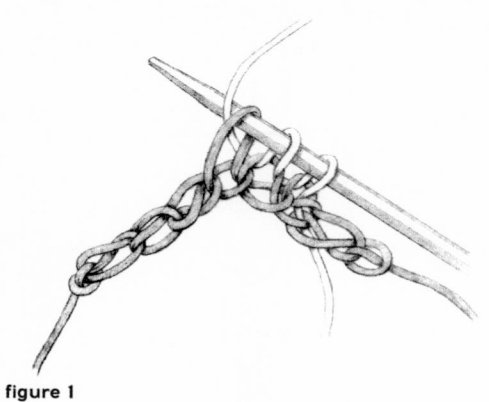

figure 1

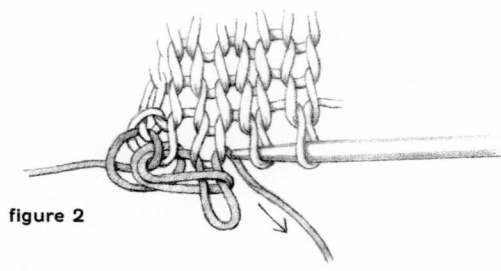

figure 2

Long-Tail (Continental) Cast-On

Leaving a long tail (about ½" [1.3 cm]) for each stitch to be cast on), make a slipknot and place on right needle. Place thumb and index finger of your left hand between the yarn ends so that working yarn is around your index finger and tail end is around your thumb and secure the yarn ends with your other fingers. Hold your palm upward, making a V of yarn **(figure 1)**. *Bring needle up through loop on thumb **(figure 2)**, catch first strand around index finger, and go back down through loop on thumb **(figure 3)**. Drop loop off thumb and, placing thumb back in V configuration, tighten resulting stitch on needle **(figure 4)**. Repeat from * for the desired number of stitches.

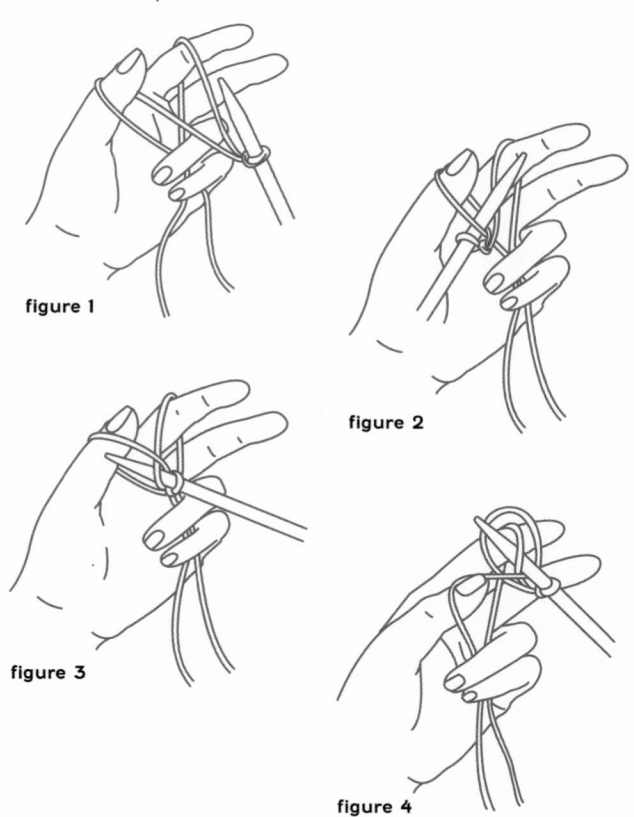

figure 1

figure 2

figure 3

figure 4

CROCHET

Crochet Chain (ch)

Make a slipknot and place it on crochet hook if there isn't a loop already on the hook. *Yarn over hook and draw through loop on hook. Repeat from * for the desired number of stitches. To fasten off, cut yarn and draw end through last loop formed.

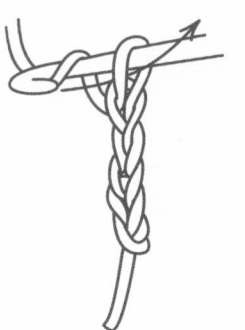

Slip-Stitch Crochet (sl st)

*Insert hook into stitch, yarn over hook and draw a loop through both the stitch and the loop already on hook. Repeat from * for the desired number of stitches.

Single Crochet (sc)

*Insert hook into the second chain from the hook (or the next stitch), yarn over hook and draw through a loop, yarn over hook (**figure 1**), and draw it through both loops on hook (**figure 2**). Repeat from * for the desired number of stitches.

figure 1

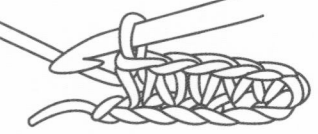

figure 2

Double Crochet (dc)

*Yarn over hook, insert hook into a stitch, yarn over hook and draw a loop through (3 loops on hook), yarn over hook (**figure 1**) and draw it through 2 loops, yarn over hook and draw it through remaining 2 loops (**figure 2**). Repeat from * for the desired number of stitches.

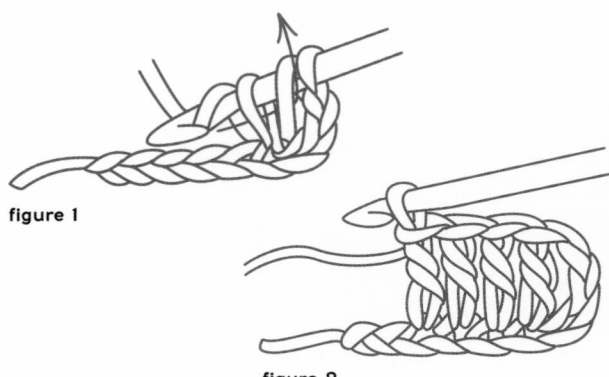

figure 1

figure 2

Treble Crochet (trc)

*Wrap yarn around hook two times, insert hook into a stitch, yarn over hook and draw a loop through (**4 loops on hook; figure 1**), yarn over hook and draw a loop through 2 loops (**figure 2**), yarn over hook and draw a loop through the next 2 loops, yarn over hook and draw it through the remaining 2 loops (**figure 3**). Repeat from * for the desired number of stitches.

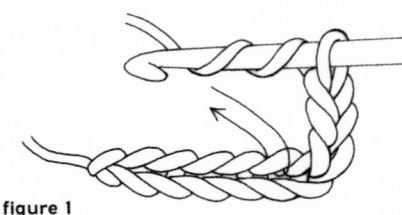

figure 1

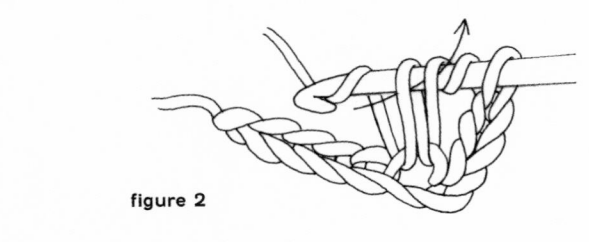

figure 2

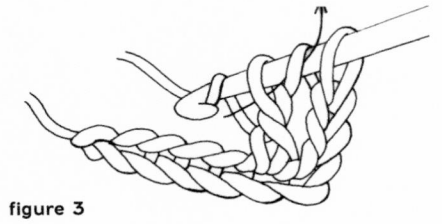

figure 3

EMBROIDERY
Backstitch

Bring threaded needle out from back to front between the first 2 knitted stitches you want to cover. *Insert the needle at the right edge of the right stitch to be covered, then bring it back out at the left edge of the second stitch. Insert the needle again between these 2 stitches and bring it out between the next 2 to be covered. Repeat from *.

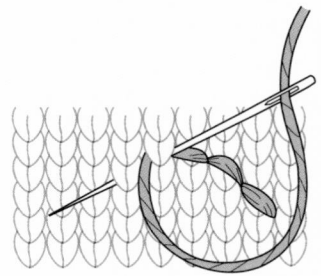

Chain Stitch

Bring threaded needle out from back to front, form a short loop, then insert needle back in where it came out. Keeping the loop under the needle, bring the needle back out a short distance to the right.

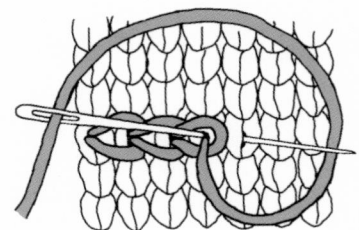

Cross-Stitch

Bring threaded needle out from back to front at lower left edge of the knitted stitch to be covered. Working from left to right, *insert needle at the upper right edge of the same stitch and bring it back out at the lower left edge of the adjacent stitch, directly below and in line with the insertion point. Work from right to left to work the other half of the cross.

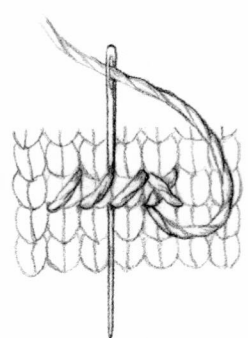

Duplicate Stitch

Bring threaded needle out from back to front at the base of the V of the knitted stitch you want to cover. *Working right to left, pass needle in and out under the stitch in the row above it and back into the base of the same stitch. Bring needle back out at the base of the V of the next stitch to the left. Repeat from * for desired number of stitches.

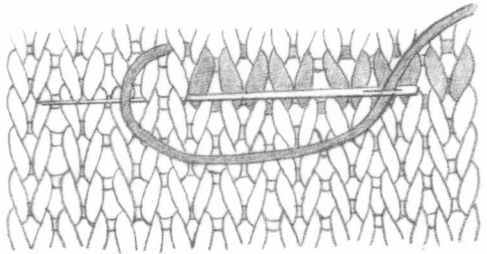

French Knot

Bring threaded needle out of knitted background from back to front, wrap yarn around needle 1 to 3 times, and use your thumb to hold the wraps in place while you insert needle into background a short distance from where it came out. Pull the needle through the wraps into the background.

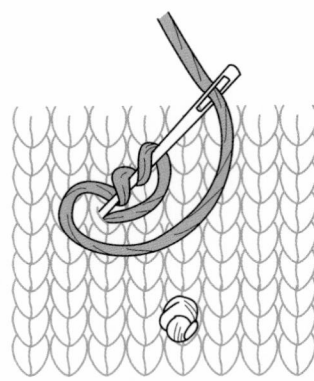

Running Stitch

Bring threaded needle in and out of background to form a dashed line.

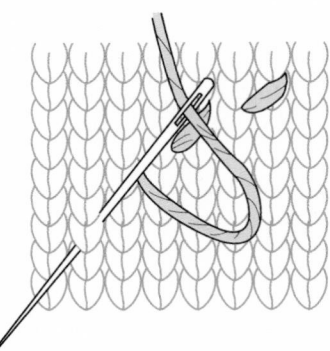

Stem Stitch

*Bring threaded needle out of knitted background from back to front at the center of a knitted stitch. Insert the needle into the upper right edge of the next stitch to the right, then out again at the center of the stitch below. Repeat from * as desired.

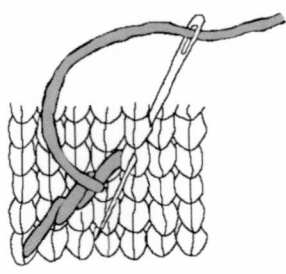

Straight Stitch

*Bring threaded needle out of knitted background from back to front at the base of the stitches to be covered, then in from front to back at the tip of the stitches to be covered. Repeat from *, working in straight lines or radiating from a point as desired.

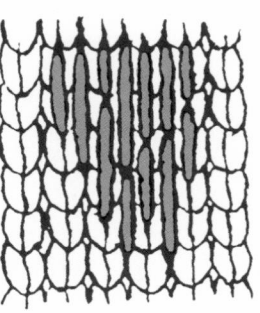

I-Cord (also called Knit-Cord)

Using two double-pointed needles, cast on the desired number of stitches (usually 3 to 4). *Without turning the needle, slide stitches to other end of needle, pull the yarn around the back, and knit the stitches as usual. Repeat from * for desired length.

Attached I-Cord: As I-cord is knitted, attach it to the garment as follows: With garment right side facing and using a separate ball of yarn and circular needle, pick up and knit the desired number of stitches along the garment edge. Slide these stitches down the needle so that the first picked-up stitch is near the opposite needle point. With double-pointed needle, cast on the desired number of I-cord stitches. *Knit across the I-cord to the last stitch, then knit the last stitch together with the first picked-up stitch on the garment, and pull the yarn behind the cord. Repeat from * until all picked-up stitches have been used.

GRAFTING

Kitchener Stitch

Arrange stitches on two needles so that there is the same number of stitches on each needle. Hold the needles parallel to each other with wrong sides of the knitting together. Allowing about ½" (1.3 cm) per stitch to be grafted, thread matching yarn on a tapestry needle. Work from right to left as follows below.

Repeat Steps 3 and 4 until 1 stitch remains on each needle, adjusting the tension to match the rest of the knitting as you go. To finish, bring tapestry needle through the front stitch as if to knit and slip this stitch off the needle, then bring tapestry needle through the back stitch as if to purl and slip this stitch off the needle.

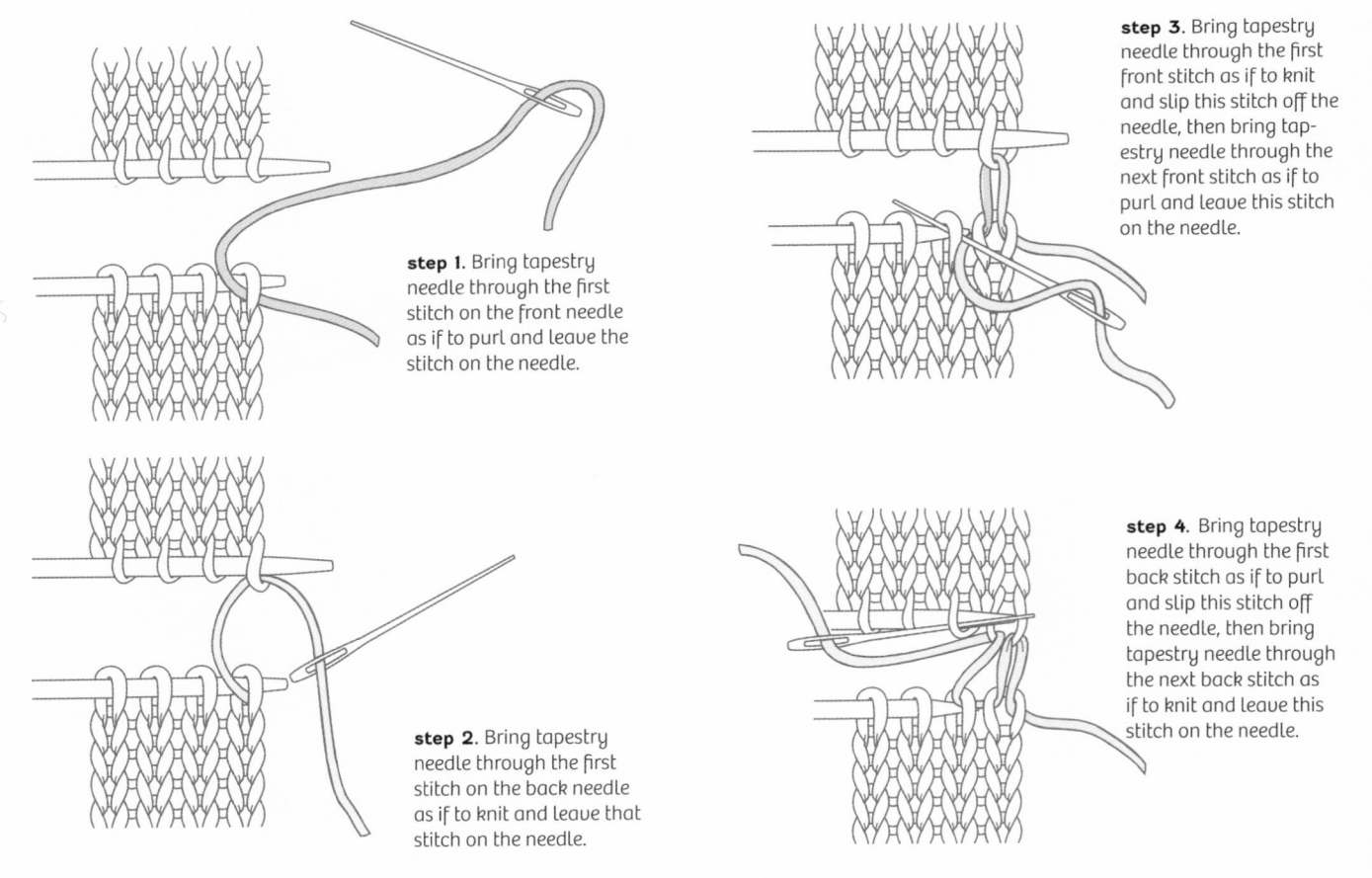

step 1. Bring tapestry needle through the first stitch on the front needle as if to purl and leave the stitch on the needle.

step 2. Bring tapestry needle through the first stitch on the back needle as if to knit and leave that stitch on the needle.

step 3. Bring tapestry needle through the first front stitch as if to knit and slip this stitch off the needle, then bring tapestry needle through the next front stitch as if to purl and leave this stitch on the needle.

step 4. Bring tapestry needle through the first back stitch as if to purl and slip this stitch off the needle, then bring tapestry needle through the next back stitch as if to knit and leave this stitch on the needle.

INCREASES

Bar Increase Knitwise (k1f&b)

Knit into a stitch but leave it on the left needle (**figure 1**), then knit through the back loop of the same stitch (**figure 2**) and slip the original stitch off the needle (**figure 3**).

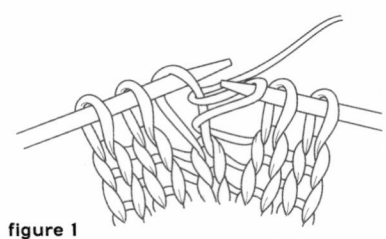

figure 1

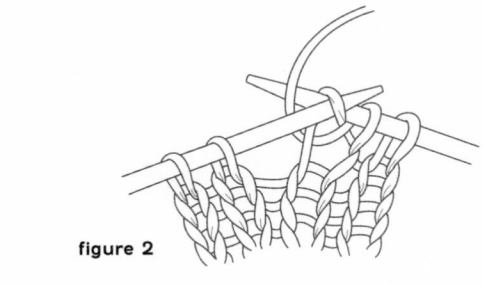

figure 2

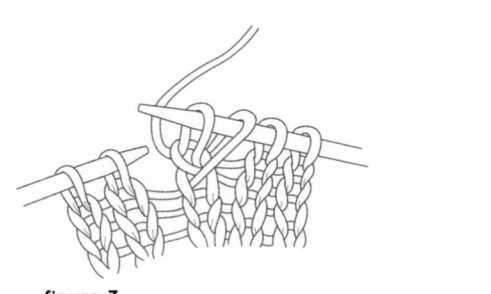

figure 3

Bar Increase Purlwise (p1f&b)

Purl into a stitch but leave it on the left needle (**figure 1**), then purl through the back loop of the same stitch (**figure 2**) and slip the original stitch off the needle.

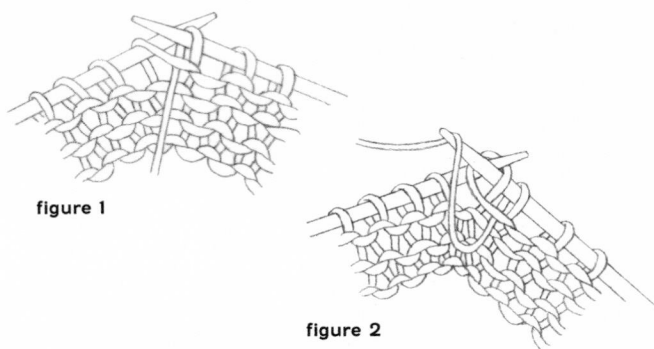

figure 1

figure 2

Raised Increase Knitwise (M1)

With left needle tip, lift the strand between the needles from front to back (**figure 1**), then knit the lifted loop through the back (**figure 2**).

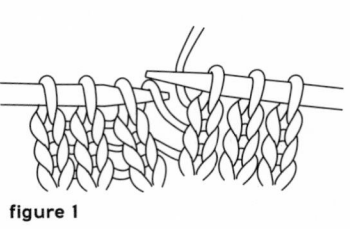

figure 1

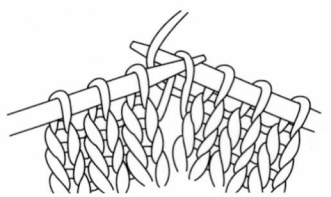

figure 2

Raised Increase—Purlwise (M1P)

With left needle tip, lift the strand between the needles from front to back (**figure 1**), then purl the lifted loop through the back (**figure 2**).

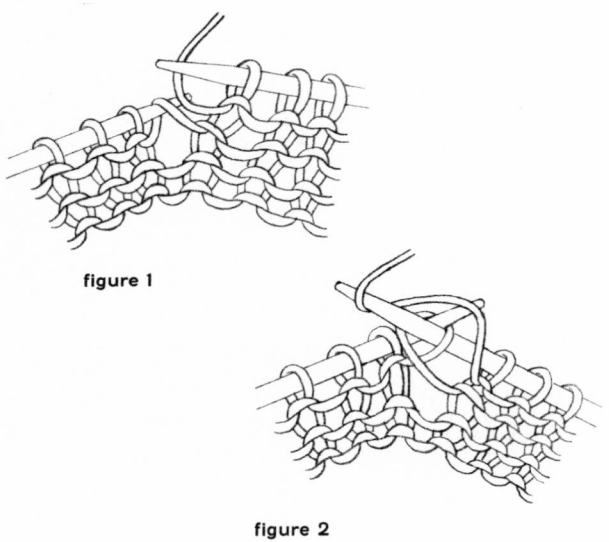

figure 1

figure 2

NO STITCH

Many charted stitch patterns involve increases or decreases that cause the stitch count, and consequently the number of boxes in a chart, to vary from one row to the next. When adding or subtracting boxes at the edge of a chart disrupts the vertical alignment of symbols in the chart, "no stitch" symbols may be used. "No stitch" symbols are placed within the borders of a chart so that stitches that are aligned vertically in the knitting will appear aligned vertically in the chart. The no stitch symbol accommodates a "missing" stitch while maintaining the vertical integrity of the pattern. In this book, missing stitches are represented by gray shaded boxes. When you come to a shaded box in a chart, simply skip over it and continue to the end of the row as if it doesn't exist.

SEAMS

Backstitch

Pin pieces to be seamed with right sides facing together. Working from right to left into the edge stitch, bring threaded needle up between the next 2 stitches on each piece of knitted fabric, then back down through both layers, 1 stitch to the right of the starting point (**figure 1**). *Bring the needle up through both layers a stitch to the left of the backstitch just made (**figure 2**), then back down to the right, through the same hole used before (**figure 3**). Repeat from *, working backward 1 stitch for every 2 stitches worked forward.

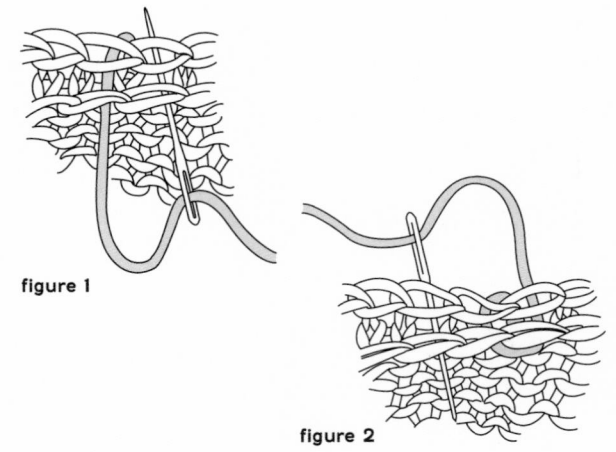

figure 1

figure 2

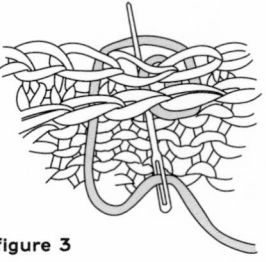

figure 3

Mattress Stitch

Place the pieces to be seamed on a table, right sides facing up. Begin at the lower edge and work upward as follows for your stitch pattern:

STOCKINETTE STITCH with 1-Stitch Seam Allowance

Insert threaded needle under one bar between the 2 edge stitches on one piece, then under the corresponding bar plus the bar above it on the other piece (**figure 1**). *Pick up the next 2 bars on the first piece (**figure 2**), then the next 2 bars on the other (**figure 3**). Repeat from *, ending by picking up the last bar or pair of bars on the first piece.

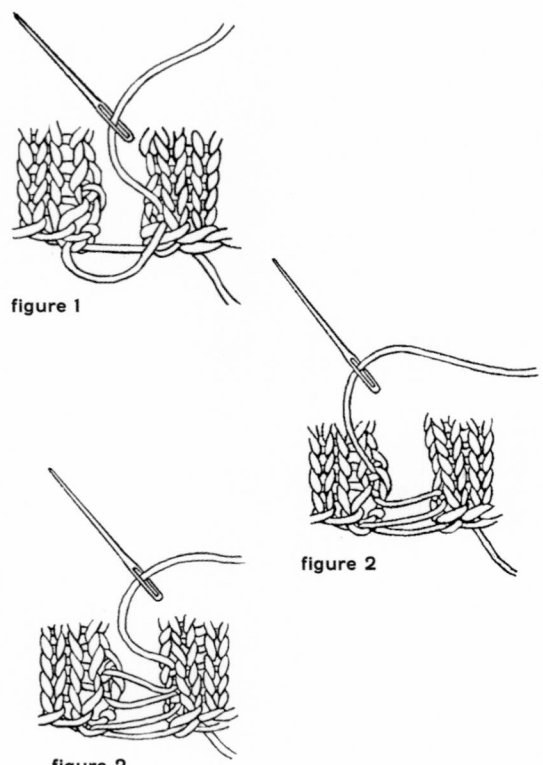

figure 1

figure 2

figure 2

STOCKINETTE STITCH with ½-Stitch Seam Allowance

To reduce bulk in the mattress-stitch seam, work as for the 1-stitch seam allowance but pick up the bars in the center of the edge stitches instead of between the last 2 stitches.

Whipstitch

Hold pieces to be seamed so that the edges are even with each other. With yarn threaded on a tapestry needle, *insert needle through both layers from back to front, then bring needle to back. Repeat from *, keeping even tension on the seaming yarn.

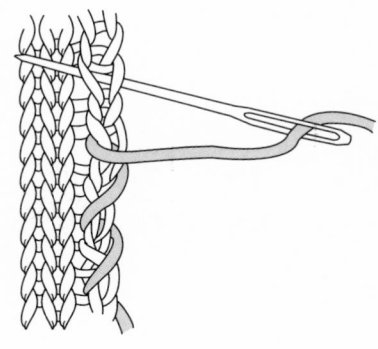

SHORT-ROWS

Short-Rows Knit Side

Work to turning point, slip next stitch purlwise **(figure 1)**, bring the yarn to the front, then slip the same stitch back to the left needle **(figure 2)**, turn the work around and bring the yarn in position for the next stitch—1 stitch has been wrapped and the yarn is correctly positioned to work the next stitch. When you come to a wrapped stitch on a subsequent row, hide the wrap by working it together with the wrapped stitch as follows: Insert right needle tip under the wrap (from the front if wrapped stitch is a knit stitch; from the back if wrapped stitch is a purl stitch; **figure 3**), then into the stitch on the needle, and work the stitch and its wrap together as a single stitch.

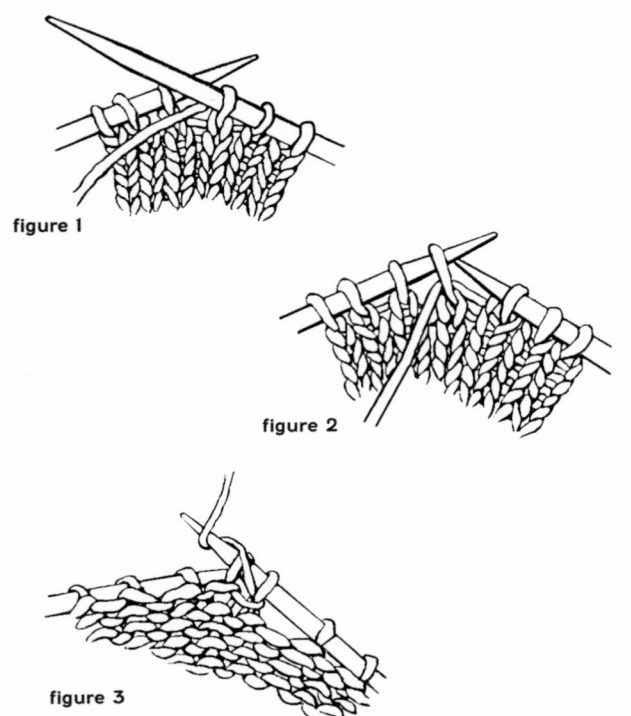

figure 1

figure 2

figure 3

Short-Rows Purl Side

Work to the turning point, slip the next stitch purlwise to the right needle, bring the yarn to the back of the work **(figure 1)**, return the slipped stitch to the left needle, bring the yarn to the front between the needles **(figure 2)**, and turn the work so that the knit side is facing—1 stitch has been wrapped and the yarn is correctly positioned to knit the next stitch. To hide the wrap on a subsequent purl row, work to the wrapped stitch, use the tip of the right needle to pick up the wrap from the back, place it on the left needle **(figure 3)**, then purl it together with the wrapped stitch.

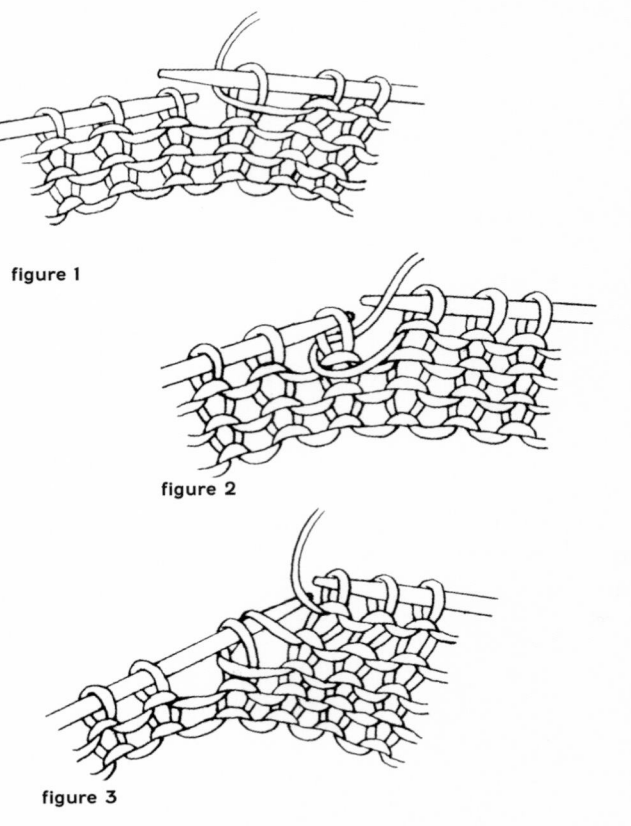

figure 1

figure 2

figure 3

SOURCES FOR SUPPLY

**ALCHEMY YARNS
OF TRANSFORMATION**
PO Box 1080
Sebastopol, CA 95473
alchemyyarns.com

BERROCO INC.
PO Box 367
14 Elmdale Rd.
Uxbridge, MA 01569
berroco.com
in Canada: S. R. Kertzer Ltd.

BLUE SKY ALPACAS INC.
PO Box 88
Cedar, MN 55011
blueskyalpacas.com

BROWN SHEEP COMPANY
100662 County Rd. 16
Mitchell, NE 69357
brownsheep.com

CLASSIC ELITE YARNS
122 Western Ave.
Lowell, MA 01851
classiceliteyarns.com

DIAMOND YARN
9697 St. Laurent, Ste. 101
Montréal, QC
Canada H3L 2N1
155 Martin Ross, Unit 3
Toronto, ON
Canada M3J 2L9
diamondyarn.com

FLEECE ARTIST
fleeceartist.com

HABU TEXTILES
135 W. 29th St., Ste. 804
New York, NY 10001
habutextiles.com

**JCA INC./ARTFUL/
JO SHARP/REYNOLDS**
35 Scales Ln.
Townsend, MA 01469
jcadrafts.com

**KNITTING FEVER INC./
ELSBETH LAVOLD/LOUISA
HARDING/MIRASOL**
PO Box 336
315 Bayview Ave.
Amityville, NY 11701
knittingfever.com
in Canada: Diamond Yarn

PATONS/SPINRITE
320 Livingstone Ave. South
Listowel, ON
Canada N4W 3H3
patons.com

PLYMOUTH YARN CO.
PO Box 28
Bristol, PA 19007
plymouthyarn.com

S. R. KERTZER LTD.
50 Trowers Rd.
Woodbridge, ON
Canada L4L 7K6
kertzer.com

**T&C IMPORTS/
FROG TREE YARNS**
PO Box 1119
East Dennis, MA 02641
frogtreeyarns.com

WEBS/VALLEY YARNS
75 Service Center Rd.
Northampton, MA 01060
yarn.com

**WESTMINSTER FIBERS/
JAEGER/NASHUA HAND-
KNITS/ROWAN**
165 Ledge St.
Nashua, NH 03060
westminsterfibers.com
in Canada: Diamond Yarn

INDEX

Find even more designs for *year-round giving*
in these delightful resources from Interweave

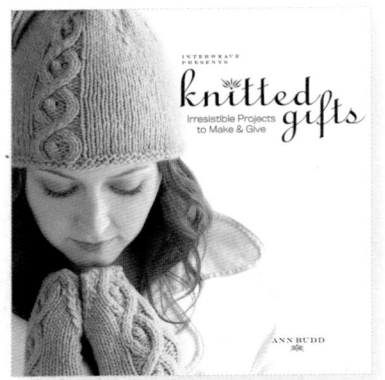
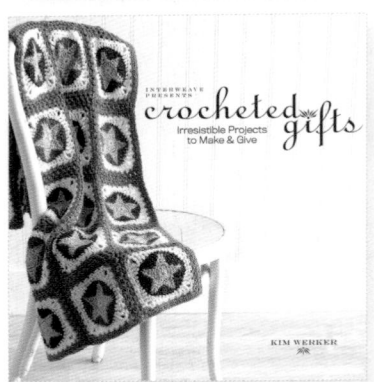